SPENSER'S *AMORETTI*

SPENSER'S
AMORETTI

Analogies of Love

William C. Johnson

Lewisburg
Bucknell University Press
London and Toronto: Associated University Presses

Associated University Presses
440 Forsgate Drive
Cranbury, NJ 08512

Associated University Presses
25 Sicilian Avenue
London WC1A 2QH, England

Associated University Presses
P.O. Box 488, Port Credit
Mississauga, Ontario
Canada L5G 4M2

The paper used in this publication meets the requirements
of the American National Standard for Permanence of Paper
for Printed Library Materials Z39.48-1984.

Library of Congress Cataloging-in-Publication Data

Johnson, William Clarence.
   Spenser's Amoretti : analogies of love / William C. Johnson.
      p.   cm.
   Bibliography: p.
   Includes index.
   ISBN 0-8387-5164-4 (alk. paper)
   1. Spenser, Edmund, 1552?–1599. Amoretti.   2. Love poetry.
English—History and criticism.   3. Sonnets, English—History and
criticism.   I. Title.
   PR2360.A53J64   1990
   821'.3—dc20   88-43409
                                                                          CIP

For Linda

For now your light doth more it selfe dilate,
and in my darknesse greater doth appeare.
Yet since your light hath once enlumind me,
with my reflex yours shall encreased be.
                                    —*Amor.* 66

Wonder it is to see, in diuerse minds,
How diuersly loue doth his pageants play,
And shewes his powre in variable kinds:
The baser wit, whose idle thoughts alway
Are wont to cleaue vnto the lowly clay,
It stirreth vp to sensuall desire,
And in lewd slouth to wast his carelesse day:
And in braue sprite it kindles goodly fire,
That to all high desert and honour doth aspire.
—FQ 3.5.1

CONTENTS

r

PREFACE

Thomas Browne wrote that as "all things [begin] in order, so shall they end, and so shall they begin again." That he was correct about the universe, no Elizabethan would deny; that his statement could be applied to academic endeavors, however, remains doubtful. One has but to consider the generally confused state of affairs during the beginning stages of a project, the uncertainties during the middle period of writing, and the uneasiness about order even at the end. And at that end, when returning to the early notes for assurance of progress, how often it is that one finds, as did Montaigne, that not only the essay but the essayer have changed.

So it is with this study. Although it began in darkness and moved toward light, its progressions have only made me more aware of vaster darknesses. It is with a profound sense of what yet should be examined in that vast corpus of Spenser's works that I both conclude the study and preface this book. And "so shall [I] end, and so . . . begin again."

A few preliminary comments about the presentation of the materials in this study might prevent misunderstanding of parts (or all) of the following interpretation, particularly because of the relatively unique approach taken here with Spenser's sonnet sequence. First, in preparing this study I have attempted always to read the sonnets first, and primarily, as works of poetic art, and only secondarily as they form a systematic presentation of Spenser's theological and philosophical analogies. Next, my observations concerning the sequence design are meant to be descriptive, not prescriptive, and while this study lays forth what I believe is Spenser's method, the study also leaves room, I trust, for other interpretations. Third, with each aspect of the study I have attempted to let the poetry lead the way and only then to let the cumulative evidence concerning the whole sequence direct my judgment about each of the parts. If at times I seem to have overstepped, to have directed too much, the fault may be attributed finally to one who, like Milton, finds Spenser a better teacher than Aquinas.

In compiling information for this work I have taken many persons as masters; studies by Alpers, Bennett, DeNeef, Dundas, Evans, Hamilton, Hardison, Hieatt, Lewis, MacCaffrey, Nelson, Nohrnberg, Parker, Prescott, Roche, Thompson, Tonkin, Welsford, and Williams—among others—have provided shape and inspiration. These scholars are cited, accordingly, in the various notes and in the text itself. But to have taken the same approaches as they, to have restated at length their work, would have produced but a mirror of their studies—and possibly a dark one at that. I am also cognizant of having drawn so deeply from their wells that I am not always sure what was originally theirs and what is finally mine. The good in this study I will attribute to them; that which is left I will accept as mine.

It is also to many others, some of whose names do, and some of whose names do not, appear in the notes, that I here offer special acknowledgment of, and gratitude for, assistance, direction, and encouragement of many sorts:

Rhodes Dunlap, Oliver Steele, and the late Rosalie L. Colie years ago influenced the kind of reading out of which this book developed; to them goes very particular gratitude for leading me to the cool wells of Spenser's works and inviting me to taste with deep drafts. To my students, especially those who refused to allow me to get away with easy interpretations or stock answers, I owe an ongoing debt that I hope this study, in some small way, can help repay. While many of my students are in that category, I especially acknowledge Eileen Casey, Thomas Dean, Joyce Dvorak, John Eaton, Janet Gilligan, Gann Hartley Herman, Thomas Kalackal, Denise Lamb, Steven Owley, Susan Smith, Susan Porterfield, Gwen Walker, Barbara Wilkinson, and Janet Youga.

Given the diversity of material touched on in this study, many individuals, in many areas, have aided my investigations and pursuits; to the following is due this small recognition for much help in sundry ways: Rose Marie Burwell, Ralph Choate, Howard Corry, Jack Ferstel, Carla Fisher, Elayne Haaker, Thomas Hanson, Carmen Johnson, Ceil Koleski, David Medow, Peggy Person, Velma Pikey, Denise Rode, Arlene and Robert Rowan, Father Steven St. Jules, Ulla and Peter Scharr, Wyatt Stahl, Gustaaf Van Cromphout, Kristin and Christopher Weber.

My colleague and friend, Jenefer Giannasi, indefatigably listened and questioned—and then listened again and questioned more. Her expertise is exceeded only by the generosity of her spirit. Sarah and Marty Brennan were of immeasurable help in preparing the manuscript, especially since they had to wend their way through the dark seas of Elizabethan orthography.

My greatest indebtedness—for understanding, patience, encouragement, and for immeasurable assistance through many stages of this book's, and my, development—is noted in the dedication; it is a debt I can acknowledge but never hope to repay. I truly could not have understood the real meanings of *amoretti* had it not been for her.

I also acknowledge, with thanks, the Johns Hopkins University Press for permission to quote from *The Works of Edmund Spenser: A Variorum Edition*, edited by Edwin Greenlaw, et al., Baltimore, 1932–1957. All citations to Spenser's poetry are from this edition.

INTRODUCTION

You would know our Lord's meaning in this thing? Know it
well. Love was his meaning. Who showed it you? Love. What
did he show you? Love. Why did he show it? Love. Hold on to
this and you will know and understand love more and more.
— Julian of Norwich

The event Spenser presumably celebrates in the *Amoretti* is his
courtship of Elizabeth Boyle. That is the last "simple" thing one
might say of the method by which that celebration is effected.
Building in sonnets, pretty rooms—and very little rooms, at
that—Spenser fits them with an amazing store of furnishings
gathered from numerous sources. Yet writing within the sonnet
sequence tradition, he stretches the limits of the genre in ways
unlike those of any other sonneteer. Like Dante, Petrarch, Bembo,
even Minturno, before him, he uses sonnets as a means of self-
realization. Like his contemporaries Sidney and Lope de Vega, he
treats the theme of love's progress concomitantly with the theme
of a poet's progress (although unlike Lope, Spenser never stoops
to the salacious or libelous). And like Donne, Huygens, and
William Drummond shortly after him, Spenser commingles the
sacred and profane, the divine and mundane. But, paradoxically,
in Spenser's hands that small sonnet form yields vast multitudes,
and that which is vast is microcosmically contained in the ordi-
nary.

It is easy, even for the inexperienced reader, to spot in the
Amoretti sonnets all the traditional devices: Spenser's fourteen-
line stanzas are as blown by lovers' sighs, as soaked with tears,
and as frozen by the lady's coldness as are the sonnets of other
writers in this genre. Certainly Spenser's Elizabethan readers
would have seen these and, in many cases, would have recalled
many of the sources. And today, even if a reader doesn't always
recognize the influences of Tasso, Petrarch, Du Bellay, Ovid,
Ariosto, Dèsportes, Serafino, Lucretius, Cazza, Tebaldeo—or, for

13

that matter, any of the classical, Italian, French, or English sources of Spenser's sonnets—readers know enough of the tradition to see how very much a part of it Spenser's sonnets are.

But Spenser's sonnets, unlike those of his contemporaries, bear a cargo that stretches the possibilities of their slender frame. As well stocked in the traditions as his sonnets are, it is in his untraditional use of the tradition that the evidence of Spenser's great genius lies. It is less easy for many readers to see and hear the subtle yet amazing variations Spenser plays on his themes, and even more difficult to catch the quiet mermaid calls to look beneath the sonnets' calm surfaces into their expansive depths— but the variations and depths are there. With the *Amoretti* one can grow rich with looking.

The sequence's limits are immeasurable in great part because they are so diffuse. To put it another way, there is *so* much in these poems that doesn't appear at first sight that one tends not to give them a second look at all. What is not found in the *Amoretti*, unfortunately, is what keeps most sonnet-readers from rereading these poems. There are few, if any, bold lines here; no quotables such as " 'Foole,' said my Muse to me, 'looke in thy heart and write' " or "Not marble nor the gilded monuments / of princes shall outlive this pow'rful rhyme." None of the *Amoretti* lines or sonnets has been afforded the close scrutiny given Petrarch's "Quando io movo i sospiri a chiamar voi," Ronsard's "Quand vous serez bien vielle," Drayton's "Since there's no help," Sidney's "With how sad steps, o Moone," or Shakespeare's "Th'expense of spirit." Even relatively rough translations, such as Surrey's "The soote season" and Wyatt's "The long love that in my thought I harber," have received more critical attention than the smoother lines of Spenser, and more has been written on Milton's "Avenge, O Lord, thy slaughtered saints," and in inquiries about his "late espoused saint," than on all eighty-nine *Amoretti*.

It is perhaps because we judge Spenser's sonnets by criteria not thoroughly applicable to them that they do not receive the kind of attention given other such works. Long ago we learned that sonnet "sequences" were sequential only in the most impressionistic sense, and that whatever "narrative development" one might find was probably more by critical accident than authorial intent. Petrarch, for example, may have given us a psychological, even epistemological, investigation of love and loving, with some literary criticism intermixed, but "narrative," as the term is usually used, is only vaguely present. We also learned to look at sonnets as limited in length (both real and suggested), and as

forms that share with other Elizabethan favorites (such as ax-
ioms, emblems, and adages) the quality of "smallness" (this,
despite Rosalie Colie's astute, and witty, observations on how
sonnets seem always to have "aspired" to be what they are not).[1]
We learned, as well, to look at them as examples of how much an
artist could do within a limited space. Hence our affection (and
that of Elizabethans, too) for the clever line, the metaphysical
conceit, the epigrammatic ending, the witty turn of phrase, the
attraction for the clever employment of "rhetorike" (Arcadian
and otherwise) and, even, for ornament (catachresis, metonymia,
antonomasia, metalepsis, ad nauseam). In short, we learned to
read sonnets as witty displays in little forms.

But "wit" in Spenser's works has greater affinity with the
works of Herbert and Marvell than with Shakespeare's or Don-
ne's. And we rarely remember Spenser's poems for notable one-
liners. Few persons, if any, ever think of Spenser as a writer of
small forms. It is as though Spenser's thought refused con-
finement in the procrustean bed of generic kinds and sought,
instead, some way to meet the needs of form while still tantaliz-
ing readers with the means he found of escaping the limitations
such form demands.

Orthographically, onomastically, rhetorically, Spenser dilates
meanings—"dilates" almost in Plotinus's sense, in the fifth *En-
nead*. There, "forms" expand to include matter, and then to
infuse that matter with their essence in such a way that every-
thing that *is* is infused with its own form. In like manner, in
Spenser, small becomes large, and large gets ever larger by ex-
panding its essential nature. The "plaine" of *FQ* 1.1. eventually
expands into the cosmic courtroom of Dame Nature, and even
that opens, as space melts into time, in the poet's desire for "that
Sabaoths sight." The "bachelor" and his "beloued" at the start of
the *Epithalamion* eventually are lost in their "large posterity,"
which, finally, increase the count of "blessed Saints." Even the
"simple laye" at the start of that same poem becomes "an end-
lesse moniment." Like Augustine, Spenser searches backward,
etymologically, for the true meaning implicit in words that, for
various reasons, have devolved; but like Lucretius, Varro, and
Ovid, he is also fascinated by the infinite variations and the
fecund possibilities of expanding words.[2] One often finds a mod-
ulated compression and expansion, a telescoping in and dilating
out, the motion of which, as it picks up words, phrases, and
echoes, builds in Spenser's poetry to something of great incons-
tancy, where little of anything is ever at rest.

Every reader of *The Faerie Queene* knows that although the journeys and quests are depicted in great detail, it is the journey itself, not its ending, the ontological search, not the teleological, which yields not only the great length of that poem but the real point of Spenser's interest. The famous line "Nel mezzo del cammin di nostra vita" may focus on Dante's age, but it is the *cammino* that eventually provides for Dante, as for Spenser, the real subject of attention. For Spenser in his great epic—as with Spenser in virtually all his poetry—stanzas, while of interest in themselves, serve even greater functions as blocks in the larger poetic constructs; and only rarely do individual stanzas, or individual sonnets, tempt the readers to linger in the hall of mirrors of admiring speculation. While it is known that Spenser revised his works, making changes to accommodate his expansive and expanding vision, the impression is given that his was a mind possessed of a unified apprehension of all that it wanted to say before composition; Spenser views the *whole*, which is comprised of but not contained in the smaller parts. The mistake with the *Amoretti* is in looking at the parts individually and neglecting their importance as parts of the process of dis-covering the larger picture.

In the *Amoretti* this poet-of-great forms can be seen at work again, accomplishing his limitless enlargement by providing a sequence that, more than any other amatory sequence of its type, truly represents a sequential narrative. While on one level the narrative does not progress straightforwardly, on another level its movement is regular—even calendric. Each sonnet has its place in the progress, and the effect of the single poems eventually yields to the effect of the larger poem. The sonnets *are* of interest individually. But, as I suggest in the following pages, the sonnets are also of interest as they form a much larger poetic construct.

A peculiarity of the *Amoretti*, which also suggests Spenser's thinking in larger forms, exists even in their printed format. One reason why the sonnets tend to be read more for the effect of single lines than for their larger patterns is that virtually all are printed with uppercase letters at the start of every line. Looking at first editions of virtually any English poet of the period, one finds only Spenser's sonnets unique in this respect. Uppercase letters in the *Amoretti* occur almost exclusively at the start of sentences—but not at the start of every line. One reads an *Amoretti* sentence through to the period, not line by line. Thus Spenser's images grow to clusters, the clusters to motifs, the motifs to themes that transcend individual works and eventually link the whole canon. Thus, too, lines give way to longer sentences, which provide larger blocks; these blocks, in turn, grow to sonnet length—and then expand further into groups of sonnets linked thematically, or by repeated words, or (in some cases) by forming parts of dialogue.

It is primarily by analogy—by what his structures, poems, lines, words *suggest*—that Spenser, like Shakespeare and Milton after him, opens immense vistas of further possibilities. It is well known that Saint Thomas speaks about analogy almost as often as he does about act and potency and participation, and the topic had been (and is) discussed at length among mathematicians, philosophers, and theologians for centuries. Spenser never even mentions the word. Yet it is by analogy, and through analogy, that he most often operates. Analogy itself expresses essential ambiguities, since its terms are simultaneously "like as" and "different from." For instance, God and creation are like one another, and yet even in this resemblance completely unalike. And in every similarity, no matter how great, the dissimilarity is greater.

The beauty of analogy in Spenser's poetry is that it holds a vast range of meanings in temporary unity, keeping them both balanced yet open to fresh interpretations. The analogies hover between images, both saying and unsaying what is and what is not, both reconciling paradoxes and creating new ones. Spenser uses the analogues as a means of expanding and extending our consciousness. Certainly one of the reasons we read his poetry is that he is careless of boundaries; *The Faerie Queene* is very like— and not at all like—other epics; the *Epithalamion* is so much the perfect example of its kind that it is quite unlike its kind. The analogies, then, help the reader to see and to see more fully. The analogies do not offer explanations; they invite reflection.

In his fine study of *The Faerie Queene* Nohrnberg considers Spenser's "analogies" at great length and suggests that the epic itself is "gradually shaped by an analogy of inner and outer government, between the legends of temperance and justice; an analogy of sexual and social love, between the legends of chastity and friendship; and an analogy of theological and human grace, between the legends of holiness and courtesy."[3] The sonnets may be explored analogically as well, and the exploration shows that the "analogies" Spenser suggests in the eighty-nine-sonnet sequence are not only vast but are in many ways the same as those found in the epic.

Slightly over two centuries before Spenser, Dame Julian, in concluding her "showings," commented of Christ that "Love was his meaning." In many ways these words hit the mark as one considers the *Amoretti*, where "love," in a multiplicity of ways, is the poet's meaning, and where the development of right love itself is presented as analogous to the development of right poetry. As the lover learns the correct means of expressing his heart, so the poet learns the correct means of expressing his art; inner "feelings" and their outer expression not only meet but intermingle. "Heart" and "art," auditorily close homophones in Spenser's pronunciation, thus become significant not only as wordplay in the sonnets but as suggestive of two major themes developed in the sequence.

The *Amoretti* "little loves" are both the various kinds of love the lover experiences before gaining the lady's hand and the various sonnets in which the poet attempts Petrarchan, *stil novistic*, neo-Platonic types of poetic wooing before the transformative experience that puts all these lesser, little loves in proper perspective, thus allowing for a different kind of poetic expression. These various attempts at Petrarchan courtship, for example, provide yet another level of analogy as the reader finds in them the similarities that both do and do not link Spenser with his predecessors and that both do and do not connect the sonnet narrator with previous sonnet narrators.

Further analogies shape the *Amoretti* sequence. As in several of his other works, Spenser clearly identifies himself, the empirical Elizabethan poet, with the narrator. The connection is suggested as early as *The Shepheardes Calender (S.C.)* and is overtly stated in "Colin Clout's Come Home Againe." Colin himself becomes an intermediary figure who is and is not Edmund Spenser. In *The Faerie Queene*, Spenser separates himself as narrator of the epic from himself as lover. However, in the *Amoretti* this is not the case. Though Colin is not mentioned, the narrator takes pains to identify himself with the empirical Spenser (who "also" loves a woman named Elizabeth, "also" has a mother and queen named Elizabeth and a friend named Lodowick, and "also" simultaneously is working on an epic poem about the queen of faery even as he is in the midst of courting the lady). The sonnet narrator thus shares much in common with Colin, the poet-lover "graced" by visions, concerned about his craft, and troubled by love—the same poet-lover frequently and self-consciously identified with Spenser himself.

These connections, suggesting a Spenser-Colin-narrator analogue, point to the metafictional nature of Spenser's canon, in which the same narrator speaks out at various times, sometimes commenting on other of "his" works, sometimes drawing in terminology, characters, even concerns, of one work into another, and always suggesting the interconnectiveness of the imaginative, poet-created world with the empirical, God-created one. In another sense, the "realistic" situation depicted in Spenser's sequence, whereby the empirical Spenser presumably relates his experiences in courtship, gives this sequence the kind of auto-biographical authority one finds analogous to Dante writing of Beatrice, to Petrarch and Laura, Ronsard and Hélène, Sidney and Stella, and to all those hosts of other sonnet lovers and their ladies. The process of creating such an auto-graph suggests another analogy—that of the empirical poet with his fictional self. T. R. Wright suggests that "to write an autobiography, to construct a coherent narrative out of the scattered events of one's life, is to interpret those events as part of a significant plot with an overall meaning. In this sense, autobiography has been seen to meet the religious needs of those 'looking for an order and meaning in life.' . . . Autobiography therefore becomes a good place to look for literary constructs of the self and of God."[4] As we shall see, this, with Spenser's variations, is precisely what lies at the heart of the *Amoretti*.

More specifically, in the *Amoretti* many of the same activities portrayed allegorically in *The Faerie Queene* are found enacted by a "real" lady and lover. By analogy the sonnet lady is at times like Una, Britomart, Belphoebe, and Amoret; likewise, by analogy the lover is at times like Red Cross, Scudamour, Artegall, and Calidore. Furthermore, just as one might find analogues between male/female allegorical figures (Arthur and Gloriana, for example) so in the *Amoretti* it is possible to see the contrasexual analogues of the grace-filled, rescuing Arthur-lady and the fancy-filled, petrified Amoret-lover.

The imagination that provides suggestions of the analogues, that hints that the sonnet lady is like Una—who is like Arthur, who is like God, who is like his Son, who is like Everyman, who is like us—is the same one that finds in ordinary life those things which make us extraordinary. Dante and Petrarch, in their sonnets, may take us to the lady, and then to heaven, and then to God; but in his paradoxical, analogical, epistemological and, ultimately, ontological process, Spenser's narrator points us to his lady as his "lower heauen," his heaven on earth.

The progress of the courtship is also depicted analogously. While the drama of human passion is played out between lover and lady, and between the lover as lover and the lover as poet, a simultaneous progression of Divine Passion, as recorded primarily in the liturgy of Lent-Easter, is portrayed. Furthermore, liturgy itself is another form of analogue in which, and through which, mundane ritual time and mundane formal rite suggest the timelessness of the always-already, not-yet reality of God's interactions with mankind. Human love, suffering, triumph, and joy are thus seen in light of, and, with all their human limitations, as analogous to divine love, suffering, triumph, and joy. Love/love is the analogous relationship the sonnets present, just as Logos/word suggests the analogy of the two creators—God and the poet.

The progress of the courtship also suggests analogy on yet another level. By linking human love with divine love, and human loving with divine loving, and especially by suggesting a lady-Christ analogue (in which the lady-Christ reforms the misdirected lover), Spenser suggests that education in loving is much like being educated in faith and for redemption. The lady-Christ is at the heart of the process. Her light analogically acts as the brightness of Christ, which, as Origen (*De Principiis* 1.2.7) writes, "falls softly and gently on the tender and weak eyes of mortal man and little by little trains and accustoms them, as it were, to bear the light of its clearness."

Implicit in any literature and any theology that explore the educative work of the Logos/word is the notion of process, whether from the latent to the explicit (as in Socrates), or from the less to the more complete (as in Paul). "Process" itself is an ambiguous word. It implies both that the sensible world is a world that already has happened (something already exists in a certain state or condition), and that it is a world that is simultaneously happening or becoming. It is the world of becoming as well as of being, the world of Heraclitus, Lucretius, and Ovid, as well as the world of Paul, Augustine, and Luther. It is Spenser's world in *The Faerie Queene*, to be sure, and it is the world as experienced in the *Amoretti*, where an education in "being" is both one's teleology and ontology. "Put in another perspective, education in an art or craft—including 'the art of loving'—involves a progressively deeper grasp of mystery and nuance, understanding the other, understanding the medium of a particular form of art. . . . There is an important connection between education and 'the pursuit of excellence,' which may be understood as a way of speaking of the possibilities of human self-transcendence."[5]

This is precisely what happens in the *Amoretti*, where "teaching," "learning," and "lessons" not only are words the narrator uses in reference to his and the lady's activities, but where those terms become major motifs as the lover's loving, and the poet's poetry, are transformed by proper relationship with the lady. Relationship is at the heart of all education; when it pertains to divine mystery, this yields a theology of presence. In the sonnets, it is relationship, not with the stylized *donna angelicata* or the *donna guerrera* or even with the perfect lady-as-Ideal, but relationship with the real woman, which results in self-correction and right-writing.

Analogically, the sonnets treat the Christ-lady presence as central to the poet-lover's growth. The deity *is* present in the lady, and when the poet attempts to describe her eyes, he finds he can do so only by suggesting what she is like—"the Maker selfe" (*Amor.* 9). In short, God is encountered in and through other human beings; and much of the "divine pedagogy" occurs through human-to-human relationships. Awareness of this interaction is the beginning of the *circulus fiduciae*, the circle of faith (also a pedagogical circle), which calls into being faith in the present, hope for the future, and a tradition based on the past. In the *Amoretti*, that tradition is found both in the liturgical calendar that structures the sequence and in the various poetic traditions the poet first tries, and only later effectively uses, once they, and he, have been transformed.

Now, what may appear to have been a Shandian digression on divine pedagogy may be worked back into the argument by pulling together some of the threads woven into the fabric above. I have noted that in the sonnets there is the analogy of the lady teaching the lover—as the Creator-God and Logos-Christ assist the creator-poet. In making my analogy I have written of the process, the progress, the development that occurs in these interactions. These terms return to the idea of the *Amoretti* as a narrative and to the observation that although the *Amoretti* is usually called a sequence, we are accustomed not to read it, or other sequences, as actually sequential. With the *Amoretti*, not reading the sonnets as a developing process, as a progression of related poems and developing themes, is a mistake. What Spenser presents here in verse form—especially when one considers the calendric and liturgical patterns that move the lovers and readers sequentially from one part of the sequence to another, and when one considers the changes both in the lover's art of loving and the poet's art of writing—is in many ways (although using the term loosely) a bildungsroman in verse—a portrait of the artist as a middle-aged man, a pilgrim's progress, a history of

Paul Morel one page after Lawrence has him turn from darkness toward the city's gold phosphorescence.

A reading such as the one that follows here in chapters 2, 3, and 4 acknowledges Spenser's accurate measurement of continuing empirical time and space. It also recognizes his allegiance to the mimetic reality of sensation and psychological apprehension. Underlying the reading is a belief that these sonnets must be read as parts of a larger whole, that in their present order they portray the developing character of the narrator whose two major attributes—he is a lover and a poet—are realized, confirmed, "salved," and redeemed as he proceeds through a pedagogical process that, in the course of time, parallels the slow, often painful, progress of human salvation, atonement, and redemption. The process of these various pedagogies is, on all levels, a "gracious" one. As Simone Weil asserts, "The intelligence can only be led by desire. For there to be desire there must be pleasure and joy in the work. The intelligence only grows and bears fruit in joy . . . [and] desire directed towards God is the only power capable of raising the soul."[6]

Although Coleridge applied the epithet "myriad-minded" to Shakespeare, the term fits Spenser equally well. I suggested above that Spenser's use of analogy serves not to explain but to invite reflection. For the individual who brings little to the sonnets, the reflection probably will not exceed by much the expectation. For the reader for whom literature is an opening, the sonnets can become a springboard, a Narnian wardrobe, a vista inviting exploration of that always-already, not-yet-reality of a grace-filled world.

In great part, through the analogies (only some of which have been suggested here) Spenser dilates the *Amoretti* into echoing words that now turn in, and then turn out, and then return one upon the other, not just filling the time and space of eighty-nine sonnets but far exceeding the limits the sequence seems temporally and spatially to suggest. The progress of the educative process is meaningful only when one engages in the *process* itself; for that purpose, Spenser provides his incredibly rich narrative structure. The subject of the process is self-realization— as a poet, as a lover, as a full person; for that purpose, Spenser provides his rich, often-witty, amazingly subtle individual sonnets. Form and content, then, inseparable and equally significant, share in the unfolding disclosure of Spenser's varied and various analogies of love.

SPENSER'S *AMORETTI*

AMOR AND THE CALENDAR: LOVE IN A TIMELY ROMANCE

In *Amoretti* 67, at the turning point both in the sequence and in the described courtship, Spenser's narrator laments "seeing the game from him escapt away." In saying this the poet reveals more on second view than on first. It is only after the phrase is isolated that various image clusters, motifs, and structural patterns in the entire sequence come into focus. And it is only after one examines what has been effected by, in, and through the "game" of Spenser's sequence that the narrative process of his sonnet series makes sense within the context of the Spenser canon.

At the time of structuring his sonnet sequence, the mature Spenser was at the height of his artistic ability; with three books of *The Faerie Queene* already in print, he prepared the next three (if we are to believe his sonnet narrator) while concurrently fashioning his *Amoretti*. What some critics consider a defective sequence with various inconsistencies of characterization, an "oddly indecisive" ending, even groups of sonnets that must be excised if the sequence is to make sense,[1] is actually one of the most sophisticated, most subtle, and wittiest examples of Spenser's art. To this sequence Spenser brought many years of the poet's craft. Not only did he reiterate themes used earlier (from *The Shepheardes Calender* through the works leading up to and including *The Faerie Queene*) but he textured the sonnets with dense image clusters from, and cross-references, analogies, and allusions to, his other works. In doing so he extended the sequence's "frame" far beyond the eighty-nine sonnets constituting its portion of Ponsonby's 1595 volume *Amoretti and Epithalamion: Written not long since by Edmunde Spenser.* His concerns with time, nature and art, poetry and, above all, love—notably human love as a reflection of divine love, love both as eminence and emanation, and proper courtship as that which culminates in a fruitful marriage—find expression in the various sonnets and experiences of his *Amoretti*.

Readers of Spenser's poetry know that myriads of roads lead to the temples and into the mazes informing the various allegories and narratives. Historical, biographical, linguistic, comparative, psychological, epistemological, hermetic, and theological approaches inevitably lead the critic to assumptions that, each in its own way, provide ways for coming to terms with the experience of the poetry. In treating the *Amoretti*, for example, critics describe it both as having a complexly designed structure and as being a flawed sequence, as being original in its approach to a Christian courtship leading to marriage and, conversely, as depicting a neo-Platonic progression up a vaguely defined *scala*. The sequence, depending on whose criticism one reads, presents either no definable time period, a multiyear progression, or a period of eighty-nine days in 1594. It should be read as an autobiographical account of Spenser's own courtship of Elizabeth Boyle, or perhaps as poems in honor of Lady Carey, or perhaps not as autobiographical at all. The narrator is the traditional Petrarchan lover or he is a bifurcated poet-lover in the throes of an intense epistemological, emotional, even ontological, agon. The lady is either the central focus of the narrator's attention or, narcissistically, he himself is his own focus. In brief, through the centuries the *Amoretti* sequence has proven an enigma.

Yet "enigmatic" is a description none would deny any of Spenser's writings, and most readers would affirm that one of the poet's greatest strengths and attractions lies in the allusive nature of his texts' "methods and meanings," all of which continue to puzzle and intrigue readers who pursue the author's game of hide-and-seek. It has been a game Spenser and his readers seemingly have played with equal enthusiasm and earnestness.[2] The interplay (the very word suggests "gaming") of the poet and his reader, in which the two act out a series of moves (as in a chess game), is complicated and enormously sophisticated. Spenser is steeped in a literary tradition rich with rhetorical theory (in itself a highly complex game of author-and-reader responses) and literary "playing," in which poets, as bricoleurs (in Levi-Strauss's sense of the term) have played with words, structures, names, and "secret meanings" suggested, but never fully revealed, to readers.[3]

The playing in Spenser's *Amoretti* is highly complex. It is not merely that he uses wordplay, ritual, rhetorical devices, games, contests, entertainments, masques, and tournaments. It is, as any reader of Spenser knows, that the playing has both a social and, quite often, a personal function. In most cases, especially in *The Faerie Queene* and the "major minor works," one of the functions is on one level moral and on another level profoundly "religious" (not in the sense suggesting Spenser's denominational leanings but pointing to his wider and deeper theological views). Spenser as poet, prophet, philosopher, rhetor, historian, priest, and mystagogue incants his poetry, from start to finish, with sounds rich in meaning on many levels.

The interplay of these meanings and their incantations fashions his art, and in the *Amoretti* it yields the fabric of a fine sequence of love sonnets and a striking example of artistic and ludic virtuosity—profoundly serious in purpose while delightfully nonserious in presentation. Spenser's success as a *ludimagister*, as an artist of supreme talent, was already established by the time William Ponsonby published the small *Amoretti* quarto; that the book appeared during the golden years of English sonneteering only further ensured the work's successful reception.

But the wedding hymn portion of that 1595 book drew more praise than the sonnet cycle, and to this day the *Epithalamion* has received far more critical attention. Laudatory statements about its "organ-like roll and majesty of numbers," "allusive and descriptive . . . picturesqueness," and its expression of "free delight in beauty and passion without taint of luxurious decadence" contributed to critics labeling it "the finest composition of its kind . . . in any language."[4] In spite of the poem's well-deserved popularity for four centuries, only relatively recently did A. Kent Hieatt uncover its complex symbolic and architectonic structure, revealing the great intricacy of Spenser's wedding poem and the surprising fact that much of its elaborate patterning went undetected for hundreds of years.

Hieatt's discovery of the symbolic relationship of the twenty-four stanzas to the twenty-four hours in the marriage day and the precise tracing of the poem through the hours, even minutes, of the exact day of Spenser's wedding (11 June 1594) are significant. They suggest that by paralleling the progress of the wedding day to the cyclical measure of the sun's time, Spenser acknowledges a special connection between the two. Furthermore, such junction makes it possible to make "short time" an "endlesse moniment," in which temporal existence can become "eterne in mutabilitie." By Spenser's method, "in spite of the subjection of life to change and death, and in spite of the subjection to mutability of the most important of the heavenly bodies . . . the individual, mortal life of man is renewed in generation, just as the insufficiency of the sun is recompensed in its annual journey, with all the recurring, time-given variety so created."[5]

These are lofty statements about the latter part of a book. But what of the *Amoretti*? Unlike the marriage hymn, the sonnets (which constitute the first portion of the book) have not enjoyed a lasting popularity, nor have they attracted an enthusiastic following. In fact, neither singly nor in sequence have they been regarded as exceptional, and by comparison with Sidney's or Shakespeare's sequences, Spenser's series often has been considered undistinguished both in quality and ingenuity of argument. The poetic heights reached by the encomiastic *Epithalamion* far surpass the quiet plateaus and generally moderate fluctuations of the *Amoretti* sonnets. Those who prefer the colorful action and epic scope of *The Faerie Queene*, the overt philosophy of the *Fowre Hymnes*, or the rustic charm of *The Shepheardes Calender* find little in the sonnets to remind them of those same qualities in Spenser's more widely read works.

Yet the sonnets do contain narrative "action," and metaphorically there is scope as extensive as the epic's, philosophical profundity as deep as the *Hymnes*, and charm as pleasant and warm as that in the *Calender*. As a sequence, the sonnets join the *Epithalamion* to form Spenser's two "anniversary" poems, the one celebrating his courtship, the other his marriage. Between them are the puzzling little poems generally labeled "anacreontics," whose presence has only recently been explained structurally in such a way that they now appear to provide both an intentional numerical and thematic link between the courtship sonnets and the marriage hymn, making of all "three" works (sonnets, anacreontics, hymn) one work.[6]

Nevertheless, there remains something lacking in the general estimation of the sonnets, something Hieatt's original study only suggests, and something only proportionately small numbers of studies address.[7] Accomplished so subtly and covertly, even with all the perusal and scrutiny of the accompanying wedding song, various elements of the sequence have remained Spenser's secret these ensuing four centuries. His game of authorial hide-and-seek, well exercised in *The Faerie Queene* and in the enigmatic *Hymnes* and now revealed as having been elaborately played in the *Epithalamion*, spills over into the playing field of the sonnets, with all its masking, playing, and gaming whereby love becomes both an art and, as the sonnet narrator says, an "entertaynment" (*Amor.* 4).

The wedding hymn celebrates Spenser's marriage to Elizabeth Boyle on 11 June 1594; the *Amoretti* provides the record of the courtship and betrothal leading to that marriage. But the sonnets also contain an extended, complex, and sustained framework of metaphors and analogues presenting the experience of the poet's love for his lady in the much larger context of Christian belief and cosmic time. When viewed as an entire cycle, the sonnets constitute a remarkably (though not thoroughly) consistent working out of a bilevel pattern in which one reads both horizontally and vertically. Earthly love provides the material for the horizontal, or *surface level;* this level of the narrative is made up of the episodes in the eighty-nine sonnets (individually and in their groups, as they may be approached grammatically and syntactically). This is the level of interaction between poet and lady, and the level in which the poet struggles with his own artistry, refining his poetry as he refines his methods of loving.

Divine love supplies the matter for the vertical, or *analogic level.* This subsurface yet concomitant level of narrative unfolds its meaning as the developing patterns of metaphor (found in individual poems and in the sequence structure) reveal themselves to the reader's close scrutiny. This is the level in which, by analogy, the poet assumes the role of the Christian making a pilgrimage of faith to attain the Christ-lady. By further analogy this is the movement of animus and anima in a drama of Self-discovery, in which God's great patterns of love, sacrifice, and transformation are reflected in space and time, both of which are eternally sacralized on earth through God's presence.

The love story on the sequence's surface level is not complex. A man about forty years old is in love with a younger woman and is amazed that he, at his age, is so deeply in love. As a poet he is well aware of the conventions used in winning a lady's love; he draws on those conventions repeatedly in his courtship. Slow to be won, the lady at times protests his wooing and occasionally makes light of the whole situation. Yet underneath her denials, jokes, and chidings, she both permits and encourages the lover's attempts. Even his friends advise him to dismiss plans of winning her, yet the lover continues. Such "events" as his preparations for the coming spring (*Amor.* 19), his sickness (50), and his leaving the woman's house during a storm (46) provide the early action. After numerous unsuccessful attempts to win her he eventually forgoes the pursuit; immediately she surrenders herself in an act attesting to her acceptance all along (67). Together the happy lovers visit the beach (75). Later, some gossip upsets the lady (86). Finally, for some unexplained reason, the two are separated and the lover longs to be reunited with the lady (89).

The love story on the analogic level is also not complex. In its most general sense it portrays the penitent Christian seeking by various means to "woo" Christ and be "married in the faith." Relying on many past accomplishments, and unaware at first of his own human frailties, he "courts" religion, thinking he is "courting" Christ. But the old means of courtship, the half-hearted lip service, the Old Covenant, will not suffice and must be put away before a right relationship can develop. The season of Lent demands certain trials and tests, which cannot be met except by total, unaffected devotion. Nothing the penitent actually says or does brings about the desired "betrothal." Though he seeks Christ by all the means he knows, Christ really is the one who seeks him, who refuses to let the seeking cease, and who, only when the sinner realizes his own inadequacy and inability to win, wins the sinner.

Easter (68) marks the celebration of Christ's commitment, his New Covenant. In the ontological, teleological, and eschatological implications of Easter the Christian finds the promise of his own salvation. Joy follows, yet the world must be faced; the Christian must live this life in community with others, presumably living in the world but not as part of it. Old things assume new meanings because of the Christian's new awareness and new perspectives; he finds joy not only in Christ but in all creation. Finally, though the world still afflicts, the Holy Spirit remains to give hope of the Beloved's return, at which time will occur the mystic marriage.

By such counterpoint patterning of his sequence, Spenser plays with the very nature of the sonnet, superimposing two playfields, one upon the other. He puts aside the old views of courtly love as well as the metaphors of neo-Platonic aspiration and Petrarchan adoration, placing in their stead an outlook reflecting Christian love. The great analogy of the sonnets is precisely the same as Nohrnberg finds in *The Faerie Queene*—that Spenser connects in these works the Word of God with the words of men, thus creating an analogy of Logos and the poem. Poetry thus becomes the nearest thing to a direct revelation of divine truth that human language affords. He surprises readers by shifting the focus from the "I" (found both in Petrarch and in almost all English sonneteers as well) to a focus that keeps the woman in the foreground of almost all the poems. Using the rhetoric of the humanists and the diction of the Petrarchists, Spenser develops a type of poem virtually unused in English poetry—the analogical sonnet set in an analogical framework.

This is not to say that both sequence levels, surface and analogic, were any more obvious to Elizabethans than they are to modern readers, or that earlier readers recognized the extent of the puzzle presented them. Such was also the case with the *Epithalamion*. But the double-reading puzzle is, as Charlotte Thompson observes, "clearly addressed to the cognescenti who need little of eros but must be conversant in a spectrum of topics: cosmology, history, political theory, theology, biblical exegesis, and number lore, along with the usual complement of the classics and poetic theory. . . . For a generation to whom the created world was one intricate hieroglyph, its parts linked by hidden analogies, a faithful imitation might logically produce something of an enigmatical composition."[8] Spenser's versatile and informed reader (like Lewis's "ordinary, educated and Christian audience" of Milton's time), would have heard and seen in the sonnets much to which we are unattuned or for which we are unprepared.

The lack of any contemporary critical commentary on just what that reader might have seen suggests that most informed readers today are not that much more ahead of the game than Spenser's fellow Elizabethans. However, once apprised of the general correspondence of the sequence's larger structures, its interplay of sacred and profane time, space, and characterization, its serious and nonserious levels of rhetorical and psychological playing, and its various interactions between the rituals of Christ's passion and the rituals of human courtship, the reader can understand how skillfully Spenser integrates two significant "stories" in a remarkably distinguished frame. By means of such contrapuntal sequentiality, the love of a poet and his beloved and the stirrings of all persons for love's ultimate goal, God, are synthesized and syncretized. Through Spenser's methodologies, earthly love is "eternalized" by means of the divine, and divine love humanized by means of the earthly.

What Spenser accomplishes concerning the double-reading of a multilevel sequence is not unprecedented. Biblical[9] and medieval allegories, iconography, architectural and musical symbolism, the "riddling" technique employed by Quintilian and

Virgil, in fact all the arts of double-meaning earlier ages found so fascinating may be called predecessors. Spenser's chief accomplishment is not that, but how, he engaged his readers in an elaborate game of reader-response and writer-play. Unless another example of such complexity is uncovered, a part of Spenser's acclaim must rest on his being the only poet to have carried through so well, so long, with such a method.

It is unnecessary to argue the difficulties of sustained double reading; others, such as Tuve, Lewis, Honig, Hardison, and Hieatt, have done so, and well, already. And it is undeniable that reading a literary work with a double focus on its sustained horizontal and vertical, surface and analogic levels alters the experience of any poetry or prose. Yet Spenser has drawn his readers into just such a game of serious nonseriousness, one that all poets and their readers play—but rarely as extensively as here. He plays that game not only within the individual sonnets but among the sonnets in the whole sequence, eventually breaking the fictive boundaries of the sequence and carrying his game over into his other works. In doing these things, Spenser demands of his informed reader a good ear for echoes of sounds, words, even whole lines, used in his other poetry. He further expects his reader *not* to see through the surface level to the analogic; if this were not so, the latter would not have remained hidden so long.

It appears relatively easy to arrive at the *Amoretti*'s surface-level meaning. Spenser plays the sonneteer's game well, presenting a "typical" Petrarchan lover, a distant lady, unfulfilled love, extravagant conceits, and so forth. Through a lexical, syntactical, and grammatical reading of the eighty-nine sonnets, and by means of tracing the plot through its fictional representation of a verse autobiography, one follows the course taken by most readers of these poems for the last four hundred years. Such a reading assumes an illustrative connection between the imaginative world in the sonnets (where art only suggests or illustrates a reality) and Spenser's own apprehensible "real" world. But such a reading fails to account for those sonnets in which Spenser unmistakably identifies himself, the empirical writer, as part of his imaginative world. When the author's "real" world conjoins with the narrator's imaginative world an additional reality is added. What readers originally view as illustrative fiction is now seen as representational fiction as well. That is to say, the narrative not only attempts to suggest or illustrate one kind of reality, but it also attempts to duplicate or represent yet another reality. As the first-person empirical narrator (in himself a fictionalized "real" Spenser) blends with the first-person fictional speaker (the poet-lover), the new reality is formed by the development of a clear distinction between the narrator-author and the Spenser of historical fact.

Clearly none of this is readily apparent, and the usual "open" course of reading the surface level generally leads to glossing such matters. Yet the game of narrator intervention raises suspicions; readers begin looking for other clues, other instances, where the "real" Spenser plays with making his illustrative fictions representational ones. Furthermore, illustrative fiction by definition suggests multiple aspects of reality. If the *Amoretti* is both representational and illustrative, of what is it illustrative?

The answer to this question is found in the "reality" of the sequence's analogical level. Whereas the open method is easily accessible and yields a reading of the surface level, the allusive course needed for reaching the analogical level is greatly more complicated and far more difficult to discern. Yet the course is "allusive," not closed; were it closed it could not be reached at all. It *is* attainable, although the method for doing so is allusive. The sequence's two levels share corresponding or parallel elements throughout the narrative, partly in terms of bifunctional imagery and particularly in terms of their presentations of (1) love, (2) time, and (3) the church calendar. Examining these we find the closed sequence opening to us.

(1) Love, the *amor* of the *Amoretti*, is simultaneously simple and complex, as love always is in the Spenser canon. In the sequence's eighty-nine sonnets the word "love," in one form or another, appears eighty-one times. Love is the lady herself, it is that which "cruelly tormenteth," it is sometimes "meane" or "proud," and is that which inspires the soul to life. At times Petrarchan, neo-Platonic, *stilnovsitic*, or erotic, it is at other times playful, even silly, or mature and tender. The nature of true love is both the narrator's and Spenser's focus in this extended "analogy of love" played out by the characters, the author, and the reader.

A quick reading of the *Amoretti* yields an incomplete account of Spenser's views on love.[10] Though for Spenser "love" contains elements of neo-Platonism, the *Amoretti* love (as with that in *The Faerie Queene* and the *Hymnes*) is more than a theoretical philosophy. Although the narrator employs traditional Petrarchan conceits, his "love" becomes more than a fixed decorum of expressions for winning a lady. Although for the most part he refrains from overt sensuality in his sonnet sequence, Spenser's heavy reliance on the lush imagery of the *Canticles* affirms that he does not reject physical love for a purely spiritual love; even in the Garden of Adonis a part of the "goodly meriment" and "gay felicitie" found there exists because "franckly each paramour his leman knowes." The complex love depicted in the *Amoretti* changes from the early to the later sonnets and plays out its pageant through the narrator and his poetry.

Like his allegory in *The Faerie Queene*, Spenser's *Amoretti* treatment of love demonstrates the darkness in which fallen beings live as well as the light to which they might attain. Tho sequence's "artificial" loves form part of the "dark conceit," with the darkness imitating everyday, ill-informed experience. Yet for Spenser there is always a light, always a hope, and always the accessibility of truth, whether it appears in the form of Una, Arthur, or Elizabeth Boyle. As Isabel MacCaffrey writes of *The Faerie Queene*, Spenser's "demonstration proceeds by introducing us to a fictive world whose enigmatic surface darkly reflects the everyday darkness in which we grope. It also provides us with clues, simple, complex, obvious, subtle, and above all diverse, for penetrating that surface. The result is a model for us in learning to fathom our own lives."[11] In the *Amoretti* those diverse clues are verbal, contextual, dramatic, and structural; all lead to the recognition of the lover's initially incorrect, yet finally right, ways of loving.

Like Book 5 of *The Faerie Queene*, the *Amoretti* stresses the difference between existence in Faerieland (with its accompanying dreamworld) and existence in the actual world. But Books 3 and 4, which move from self to society, from the virtues of the individual to those of the collective, do the opposite, while stressing the similarity and potentially dangerous proximity of fancy and reality.[12] Like the "Book of Chastity," the *Amoretti* is largely concerned with the purging of fantastic, imaginary types of "bad" love and the glorification of love leading to wholesome generation. In both the *Amoretti* and *The Faerie Queene* Spenser distinguishes between false and true love—and the expressions of each. These differences are of major importance in understanding Spenser's poetic canon.

Those who make illusions in love (such as Malecasta, Paridell, and Busyrane) pander to the death wish; those who live in those illusions do so at the risk of losing life. Spenser almost always associates the illusory life with inaction. Just as the pastoral world pulls away from the heroic quest, so romantic love strives toward a condition of stasis that daily experience attempts to deny. Among other things, the Bad Genius of Acrasia's garden embodies the imagination's impulse to ply us with illusion and play us into stasis. Illusory passion ruins both heroic and generative endeavor, as the entire Garden makes amply clear; such illusion is the great enemy of dignity and order and the great untuner of degree, so powerful it can turn even gods into beasts.

The *Amoretti* lover is much like Artegall, who falls victim to idolatry in his relationship with Radigund (5.5.12):

> But when as he discouered had her face,
>   He saw his senses straunge astonishment,
>   A miracle of Natures goodly grace,
>   In her faire visage voide of ornament. . . .

His "straunge astonishment" at the "miracle of Natures goodly grace" is the same kind of "falsed fancy" that afflicts Malecasta and the same kind that causes Red Cross to fall in love with Duessa (1.1.47–54). These are inversions of right order, perversions of right love. The manly force of the romantic hero (by extension, the poetic ability of the *Amoretti* poet) is useless if incorrectly directed. The very tradition that insists that every knight and every sonneteer have a lady is that which forces loyalties that sometimes are misdirected. Spenser apprises the reader in *The Faerie Queene* and in the *Amoretti* that a good knight's love for a woman, like a good poet's love for his lady, leads as easily to error as to virtue. Britomart's true beauty (chastity) paralyzes Artegall; Radigund's false beauty (sensuality) disarms him. The problem is always to distinguish between the two. But the real choice, as is seen in the *Amoretti*, is very often the woman's.

Furthermore, Spenser shows that once anatomized, "love" is not the same as right-love-in-action, and it is right action, even in the sense of right motivation, that the sonnet lover must learn during the courtship. The danger always is for love to become stylized, formalized, methodic, an end in itself instead of a state of becoming. The courtly rules of the Provençal poets and the advocates of *fin amours*, like the psychological apprehensions of the *stilnovisti*, can become false love, in which the lady is an object, not a person. Petrarch's amorous rhetorical philosophy, with its psychological analysis of love's effects, its rudimentary neo-Platonic references to the "Idea" of Laura's beauty, and its reflections upon the folly and vanity of life, can be systematized into a theory, and then a practice, of love. It is not that Spenser condemns wholesale any of these; what he shows through the character of the lover is that each of these can lead toward false love, a falling in love with love or with a system, a code, or a philosophy. Such static, idolatrous, false love must be destroyed before right, active love can develop.

Like Artegall and Red Cross, the *Amoretti* lover must reject such idolatrous worship of the lady before he can be set on a productive, life-asserting course. Like the young lover of the *Vita Nuova*, he must realize he has sought a false goal. As a lover he must love the lady, distinguishing between the real lady and the ego-centered projection of the lady depicted in his "preconversion" sonnets. Just as the ladies scoff at the *Vita Nuova* lover for his efforts at poetic loving, forcing him to begin his approach anew during the midst of that courtship (chapter 18), so the *Amoretti* lady laughs at the lover, causing him to question the object of his love and the vehicle in and by which he expresses it. Yet only by such examinations and alterations can he grow and develop.

The many demonstrations of the lover's failure must finally register as just these, failures, so that he can determine his own sense of what is right love. His busy acts of writing are just so much stage business, so much artificiality, so much false love that the lady is unmoved by them. His busy poetic demonstrations remind one of Busyrane who, as Berger suggests, is simply "Busy-reign, the male imagination trying busily (because unsuccessfully) to dominate and possess woman's will by art, by magic, by sensory illusions and threats—by all the instruments of culture except the normal means of persuasion."[13] Like Amoret and Scudamour, the lover is a victim of his own prescribed *ars amores*, compelled to enact roles enshrined in the codes of *amor courtois*.

The lover repeatedly thinks in images of treason, capture, and bondage in order to express the warlike situation of love he experiences. The negative, death-directed focus is clear, yet the lover in the early part of the sequence fails to recognize his own need to free his mind from the tyranny of so narrow a concern, so narrow a vision, before it can open to the fulfillment of true love and generation. The pains he experiences and expresses are not the result of the lady's rejection of him, but of her refusal to accept false, idolatrous love. Because his love is turned toward the external world and away from the lady, the lover is subject to abrupt changes and to mutability. The nets, webs, and bonds he uses so often as images describing the lady's motivations are merely examples of his own captivity in an unfruitful image-worshiping of a lady he himself has conceived and whose roles he has defined.

The lover's use of images of bondage are part of his Petrarchan heritage. But those images change during the courtship; those same items which in the first stages are used negatively later become images of free consent and play. The lover's bondage to his own egocentric views, Petrarchan language, and other forms of self-enclosure give way to a free binding of himself to higher will and to a concomitant taking-captive of those internal and external forces threatening man's moral and spiritual well-being.[14] As the lover discovers in *Amor*. 67, love can liberate as well as bind, and being bound to divine and human "good" love, as various Faerieland characters find, delivers one into the freedom of human fulfillment.

The only effective weapon against the whole system of false love, against Busyrane, is reason. Because reason perceives reality and truth it can overcome the unreal. Amoret's prison disappears. Britomart overcomes the wall of fire because she is undaunted by the "idle shewes" and "false charmes," not because she has a magic lance. Like Una, the *Amoretti* lady serves a reality-testing function for the lover; she refuses to listen to or be moved by the "pageants" the lover plays and the passions the Busyrane in him displays. Passion, like the deceiver Busyrane, is both an enchanter and an enslaver. The great danger for Amoret, as it is for the *Amoretti* lover, is to literalize the fantasy, to become content with the enchanted world and to relish passion for its own sake. Busyrane's desire that Amoret fall in love with him, like the lover's hope that the lady will fit the image he has portrayed of her, is the same—a romanticization of love in which one falls in love with love.

True love, on the other hand, is embodied in a few characters, among them Britomart, Amoret, Sir Scudamour, and Sir Calidore. It is usually linked with generation. The tension between generation, which is life-giving and dynamic, and fantasy, which perverts love and is sterile and static, is the central issue in Book 3, just as it is one of the matrices of the *Amoretti*. Spenser shows this "right love" in the Garden of Adonis and in Belphoebe's bower, both images of "good" love, which provide the corrective elements to the Bower of Bliss and Phaedra's island. Those who would reject love, as Marinell does, just as those who would turn it to lustful ends, as the Foresters do, are equally guilty. The

Amoretti lover's ego-generated "pourtraict" of the lady early in the sequence is a perversion of the outer-directed generative nature of right love. It is a portrait that, as a reflection of his own conception of her, must change before right love can come to fruition and yield generation.

The link whereby Spenser conjoins his religious and philosophical beliefs appears in his interpretation of that "right love." For Spenser, this is Christian love in its widest sense. Such love objectifies and makes practical the neo-Platonic theories, reinvests time-worn and artificial Petrarchan conceits with their own *vita nuova*, and makes "amore e'l cor gentil" really "una cosa." In the *Amoretti*, however, the *cor gentil* is not a matter of birth but of an inner worth created by a loving God as well as by loving God. To carnality Christian love adds marriage, in which the physical nature of man can find its perfection. It is this Christian concept of love fulfilled in marriage that distinguishes the *Amoretti* from other such sequences of the time and that provides a most-significant element in the "pageant" played before the lady and the reader.

Spenser anatomizes this Christian love in *The Faerie Queene* and develops it as an applied poetic progression (and as an application of poetry's progress) in the *Amoretti*; he fulfills it in the *Epithalamion* and professes it as a cosmic, universal philosophy in the *Hymnes*. It emanates from God and makes itself manifest in law, both cosmic and earthly, universal and individual. Not merely a human passion, it forms a living force that acts on the human level in ways analogous to those in which it operates on the cosmic. For the theologian as for the mystic, "the cosmos is an amatory poem. God, who is Love, created the universe through love, and all His creation is moved by love of Him and aspires to ultimate union with Him. Thus a tide of love circulates unceasingly through the universe."[15]

We have heard this elsewhere in other words. From the earliest times poets adopted the language of religion, and, vice versa, psalmists addressed songs of love to God in unmistakably physical terms: "My soul thirsteth for thee: my flesh longeth greatly after thee." Theologians interpreted the passionate language of the *Song of Songs* as a reflection of Christ and the Church, and Christ himself spoke of the Church as his bride, he as its bridegroom. The *Deus ludens* plays gracefully with the universe, which, by reflection, plays gracefully as *homo ludens* and *homo religiosus*.

The poetic union of divine and mortal love, accomplished

partly through Spenser's use of language common to both, is
familiar both in medieval and Renaissance thought. But we mis-
interpret Spenser if we view such "union" as a purely mystic
device for describing man's ascending to meet with God at a
point where mortality no longer seems meaningful. Arthur de-
scends to Red Cross's dungeon before Red Cross can ascend the
Mount of Contemplation. True, Spenser describes highly spir-
itualized aspects of the *Amoretti* poet's love for his lady, as in
Amor. 24:

> When I behold that beauties wonderment,
> and rare perfection of each goodly part:
> of natures skill the onely complement,
> I honor and admire the makers art.

But Spenser's interest lies not in a mystic union with God in
heaven but with the fulfillment of divine love in a perfected
creation on earth.[16] Though "diuinely wrought," the sonnet lady
also constitutes the poet's "lower heauen," in whom he sees a
"most goodly temperature" (*Amor.* 21). As his "lower heauen,"
his heaven's bliss on earth, the lady stands between earthly love
and divine love as a new human ideal combining both. She is not
a door leading away from earthly love to a union of reality with
the ideal. Instead, she is the embodiment of that union herself,
the perfection resulting from the wedding of heavenly and
earthly qualities as presented in the sequence's combined analo-
gic and surface levels.

This, then, is the *amor* of the *Amoretti*. Love, the single, all-
encompassing Christian concept of it, of which the lady not only
forms a representative part but of which she, like Christ, con-
stitutes an embodiment, is the underlying as well as the overlay-
ing theme of Spenser's love story. It is a theme involving and
necessitating human action and self-realization, whereby the al-
legorical figures of *The Faerie Queene* are vivified by being pre-
sented in the "real life" personages of the sonnets' lady and lover.
And it is a theme expressed in the individual sonnets, through
the sequence structure, and by the unequivocal Johannine asser-
tion echoed in *Amor.* 68, that *Deus caritas est.*

(2) Through the illustrative action of characters and their
"loves" on the surface level, corresponding actions emerge on the
analogical level; the secular space of the narrator's world finds
analogues in the sacred space clarified by and observable

through a vertical reading of the sequence. Even more important are the various conceptions of time with which Spenser plays out the love stories of both levels. It becomes evident throughout the *Amoretti,* as it does in the *Epithalamion,* that time is one of the narrator's prime concerns (as it is in virtually every one of Spenser's poems). By exploring the sequence's temporal patterns, the "allusive" approach to the *Amoretti* unfolds further. These interconnected and long-neglected structures exhibit the most remarkable sonnet-sequence architecture yet uncovered. Furthermore, the thematic analogues to the sequence patterns suggest radically new dimensions of interpreting Spenser's sonnet cycle. The double frame both figuratively and literally defines the sacred space of the sequence game, bringing into focus the various levels of time and love Spenser incorporates in the sonnets.

In the widest sense the structural technique Spenser employs involves calendar references alluded to several times in the *Amoretti.* Through these references Spenser provides his clues to the game's secrets, teasing readers' ingenuity, gamesmanship, and skill. In a more particular sense, that framework technique corresponds to the church calendar, which, when examined, suggests some remarkable features of the sequence. In their most direct thematic relationship, these calendar references suggest that Spenser intends informed readers to observe the empirical movement into, through, and out of Lent as paralleling the narrator's fictional movement from early hopes through frustration and eventually on to victory in courtship. The pursuit of acceptance is alluded to on both secular and religious levels; the similarity in the passion/Passion times indicates Spenser's attempt to reconcile human with divine love, the "self" of romantic fiction with the Self of historical fact.

Critics working with these interplays, and particularly with the sequence structure, generally agree that the individual poems, when arranged as they are, form some kind of pattern, either thematic, tonal, or psychological; most agree as well that the *Amoretti* achieves such patterning better than most other cycles of the period.[17] Yet for centuries it was accepted that Spenser had little or no superstructure in mind beyond small groups of sonnets representing units among the eighty-nine poems. Critics such as J. W. Lever explained away what they considered disorder in the sequence frame "by setting apart those sonnets which evidently belong to an earlier phase and [which] run counter to the general stream of thought and feeling," and then by dealing only with the "remaining seventy-one

sonnets [which] make up the solid core of the *Amoretti* se-
quence."[18] Others, such as Casady, Winstanley and Bhat-
tacherje,[19] describe the montage of poems as fluctuations of the
human mind on the neo-Platonic scala. Still others, such as
Ellrodt and Welsford, counter this idea by attempting to show
that Spenser's sonnets present no such scale. Nobuyuki Yuasa
suggests psychological divisions corresponding to the stages of
courtship as the structural device used by Spenser. Dunlop and
Nohrnberg, in turn, present the "Lenten sequence" as the foun-
dation on which Spenser builds the entire sonnet series. Hardi-
son, working with the calendars, adds that the Lenten section is
part of a tripartite sequence developed along the lines of Pe-
trarchan "cruel fair" and *donna angelicata* motifs.[20]

Many of these studies provide valuable suggestions for reading
the *Amoretti*. Nonetheless, while making good inroads into the
Amoretti—calendar structuring, psychological divisions, Pe-
trarchan motival fluctuations, neo-Platonic movements up and
down the ladder—these earlier studies, either by nature of in-
completeness or misdirection, give only partial views of the
sequence. None applies its methodologies in sufficient detail to
reveal the magnitude of Spenser's accomplishment, and none has
entered the sequence's labyrinths in such a manner to suggest
more than a single way of penetrating the *Amoretti* core.

Those sonnets constituting the Lenten sequence *do* represent
the structural key to the *Amoretti*. Encompassing sonnets 22–68,
they form a sub-sequence analogically referring to the liturgical
period of Lent, where the penitent, by analogy, experiences the
agon and the Passion of Christ. Furthermore, Spenser indicates
the ordered and controlled world of his game field by setting this
play of Self, time, and eternity in a balanced symmetrical setting,
with the forty-six sonnets making up the Lenten sequence pre-
ceded by twenty-one (1–21) and followed by twenty-one (69–89)
non-Lenten poems.

Yet there is more, much more, to the bifold drama. Not only do
twenty-one sonnets precede and twenty-one follow the Lent-
Easter core, but both groups of twenty-one may be divided into
balanced, contrasting groups with the three introductory sonnets
(1–3) paralleling the three "concluding" sonnets (87–89). Both 4
and 86 are transitional poems, with seventeen sonnets separating
them from the sequence's two key "holy days"—Ash Wednesday
(*Amor.* 22) and Easter (*Amor.* 68).

Two of the three *Amoretti* full blazons appear in both numer-
ically and thematically balanced positions in the sequence, 26

coming twenty-six sonnets after the beginning of the sequence (and four sonnets after Ash Wednesday), and 64 appearing twenty-six sonnets from the end of the sequence (and four poems before the Easter sonnet). Spenser positions the first spring poem nineteen sonnets after the sequence starts; after the second spring sonnet there follow nineteen poems until the sequence conclusion. Two of the three poems employing ship images appear in balanced positions as well, the first being thirty-four from the start (34) and the other thirty-four from the end (63). Twenty-three sonnets from the start (23), immediately following the commencement of Lent, appears the complicated poem comparing the poet to a spider weaving webs to capture the lady; twenty-three sonnets from the end (67), immediately preceding the Easter sonnet, the poet as hunter again tries to "capture" the lady.

Many readers have ignored these significant balances, these significant clues to the complex frame, in the sequence design.[21] In their efforts either to prove or disprove the structural sequentiality and calendric analogues of the *Amoretti*, still other critics encounter even greater difficulty in just those areas where the sequence makes its own divisions—the temporal references. By eliminating eighteen of the sonnets, Lever utilizes what he considers the "two new year's sonnets" (4 and 60) as part of what he sees as the *Amoretti*'s flawed structure, yet he omits other time referents. Dunlop makes the two church calendar references (22 and 68) the basis of his theory but neglects other elements that would strengthen and extend his fine argument. Yuasa, who employs the "new year's" sonnets as well as the Lent-Easter ones, overlooks the significant Spring sonnets (19 and 70).

An approach that includes these referents and that acknowledges that differing temporal patterns (i.e., various calendars for measuring time, particularly the historical, ritual, psychological, and generative time schemes) may exist and function synchronistically is clearly appropriate for reading through the sequence, which must be viewed as "occurring" both horizontally/teleologically and vertically/ontologically at the same time. This multitemporal system is exactly what Spenser presents in the allusions and analogues that suggest the various days, weeks, seasons, and even the specific year of the courtship.

One particular element of the calendar pattern that has led many readers astray comes from taking *Amor.* 4 and 60 (the poems often considered the beginning and ending of the sequence "year") as the major time referents. Generally called the New Year sonnet, *Amor.* 4 provides the sequence's first time referent. Yet when counting to the next "new year" poem, one actually discovers two sonnets, 60 and 62, which appear to conclude one year and mark the beginning of another. Both do complete "years"; the problem many readers encounter is in confusing the kinds of years the two sonnets conclude.[22]

A year does terminate in 60; however, it is not a calendar year but the period of time elapsed since the start of the poet's love for the lady. The distinction is clear when one considers the differences between psychological time and historical time. Spenser, like Donne, is writing an anniversary poem; like Petrarch he celebrates the anniversary of his love, and like Dante he commemorates his *vita nuova*, which in this case he describes as a "new year" of the soul.

Spenser's reference in 60 to Mars is noteworthy. As a point of comparison for the planet of the "winged God" who moved the poet for one psychological year, the narrator mentions that Cupid's sphere keeps an appointed time during which it completes its circle, just as "Mars in three score yeares doth run his spheare." The sixty-year period is not without significance.[23] The number of Mars's year matches the number of the sonnet; furthermore, no additional mention of the love-warfare theme appears in the sequence. The only other martial imagery occurs in 69, where the poet remembers "my loues conquest." However, no actual "warring" occurs in *Amor.* 69, and the allusion is to a past event, the metaphoric battle of Mars's year having ended. The simile Spenser uses applies to more than astrological years, for as the war-god Mars completes his year in sixty "yeares," so the poet completes his Petrarchan "war" in sixty sonnets. Additionally, Spenser includes here the reference to "the spheare of Cupid [which] fourty yeares containes." *Amor.* 62 is forty sonnets from the Ash Wednesday poem (22). Then, beginning with 63, we move to the last few sonnet days preceding Easter. In these poems Spenser presents sonnets suggesting more successful courtship than that found earlier in the sequence, leading directly to the lady's acceptance of the lover.

Unlike *Amor.* 60, *Amor.* 62, the second of the two "new year's" sonnets, actually refers to the end of an old year and the beginning of a new one. More significantly, however, 62 refers to a specific historical day during Spenser's lifetime, thereby suggesting the possibility of other corresponding dates for other sonnets in the sequence. This is precisely how Spenser set an elaborate stage for the sequence activity. Internal evidence indicates Spenser organized his poems into a sequence representing the spring of 1594, the period of his own courtship.[24] Whether the "real" courtship occurred at this time is unimportant to the sequence; the fictionalized narrative courtship coincides with the span of days in 1594 preceding Spenser's wedding on 11 June. Furthermore, it was 19 November 1594 when Ponsonby entered *Amoretti and Epithalamion* into the Stationers' Register, eventually publishing it the following year.

The title pages of the 1595 *Amoretti* relate that Spenser's sonnets were "written not long since." There is no reason to suppose the poet would have assembled his sequence more than a year or two prior to that date and then not published it until the middle of the decade. Though some phrases, some lines, even whole parts of the sonnets, appear to have been created earlier and then used (or reused) in their new form in this sequence, it is their use in this sequence, as published in 1595, with which we are concerned. These sonnets reveal that *Amor.* 62 corresponds to the first day of the new calendar year, which in the Old Style, or Julian calendar, makes *Amor.* 62 analogous to 25 March, Lady Day (the Feast of the Annunciation). It was on this day that the civil year began, a situation which existed in England until 1753, when "new year" was changed to 1 January.[25]

There are those who insist the Elizabethans did not actually use this date as the start of the year even though the date existed as "new year's day" for another century and a half.[26] However, such an assertion denies Spenser the license to do what he wishes in the play of his own sequence. As a poet, Spenser exhibits vast integrative capabilities; he draws freely and widely from whatever sources he chooses, selecting portions of information he needs for his own purposes. He overlays several calendars even in so early a work as *The Shepheardes Calender.* The point is that Lady Day existed as a new year's day whether or not it was celebrated as such, and there is no reason to suppose Spenser would have felt obligated to ignore it if he wanted to use it in the sonnets for the elaborate play he presents as "a pageant," "a game," and "an entertaynement."

Easter "occurs" in *Amor.* 68, six sonnet days after the announcement of a new year's beginning. The only year close to the publication date in which Easter falls six days after the change of the year number (making it 31 March) was 1594, the wedding year. During Spenser's lifetime this situation occurred in only one other year, 1583, an impossible date for a sequence that refers specifically to "Elizabeth" (his queen, his mother, and his betrothed) and to the progress toward completing the halfway mark in *The Faerie Queene.*

The six sonnet days between the two ascertainable, historical dates of 25 March (*Amor.* 62) and 31 March (68) need to be considered strong evidence for the 1594 calendar parallel, as does the reference to Mars's taking sixty years to end his war, the reference to which appears near the end of March (Mars's month in the mimetic zodiacal calendar). Both astronomically (zodiacally) and calendrically (historically), these sonnet days serve as referents to actual days in spring 1594.

How then does the sequence's Lenten period begin in *Amor.* 22? And what gives the Lent-Easter section (22–68) such import in the overall sequence? With Easter "falling" on *Amor.* 68, we need but to count backward, not by forty sonnets but by forty "fast" days and six interpolated "feast" days, to arrive at *Amor.* 22, in which the poet marks "this holy season fit to fast and pray." By labeling *Amor.* 22 Ash Wednesday, all the other sonnets may also be labelled as Thursdays, Fridays, Saturdays, Sundays, and so forth. *Amor.* 68 thus represents Sunday, 67 Holy Saturday (the Great Easter Vigil), 66 Good Friday, and so forth. The sacred time of Lent becomes the sacred space of the sequence's synchronistic passion story, clearly a passion of a different form but one that forces the narrator to see that love, real love (not a stylized Petrarchan form or an ascetic and otherworldly neo-Platonic type), is "the lesson which the Lord vs taught" (*Amor.* 68). Christ's self-giving, yielding, and dying to an old life before a new and better life could begin provides the pattern for the narrator's own transformed, sacralized life, love, and poetry.

Just as Spenser distinguishes certain sonnets by internal calendar or sequence structural references, so he demarcates those sonnets identifiable as falling on Sundays. Ash Wednesday 1594 fell on 13 February; the first Sunday in Lent, corresponding to 17 February, appears then in *Amor.* 26. The second Sunday in Lent, 33, relates to 24 February and the third Sunday, 40, corresponds to 3 March. *Amor.* 47 represents the fourth Sunday in Lent, 10 March; and 17 March, the fifth Sunday, is paralleled by *Amor.* 47. *The Book of Common Prayer* (hereafter *BCP*) calls Palm Sunday the "Sunday Next Before Easter"; it is represented by *Amor.* 61, 24 March. All lead to Easter, 31 March 1594, celebrated in *Amor.* 68.[27]

Spenser's great familiarity with the *BCP*, the Bible, and various missals is undeniable. He would have heard the Bible read con-

secutively at Morning and Evening Prayer and would have heard
it discussed topically in the homilies. At school he would have
learned the catechism, the Psalter and the Articles of Faith; under
Mulcaster he would have had his instruction in Old Testament
Hebrew, and at Cambridge, where prolusions, exercises, and dis-
putations were conducted in Latin, the *Latin Vulgate* had to be
known—well known—and used. In Spenser's poetry one may
find traces of services from various prayer books, from the *Great
Bible, Geneva*, the *Bishops' Bible*, the *Latin Vulgate*, Sternhold
and Hopkins—even *Sarum*. The variety of borrowings testifies
both to his wide familiarity with a large number of sources and to
his recasting and remolding of such sources to fit the eclectic
needs of his particular poems.[28]

What Spenser creates here is both subtle and extraordinary.
First, he plays with simple narrative time by providing a se-
quence that may be (and has often been) viewed as similar to that
displayed in other sonnet sequences. Second, for more attuned
readers he provides another level in which one enters the com-
plex epistemology of empirical, and fictional, time. Third, for
those willing and able to delve yet deeper, he provides another
calendar, that of the church year, superimposed on the civil
calendar of 1594. Fourth, the temporal systems with which he
works are coincident with the space he creates in the narrative
drama. And fifth, the characters with which he peoples his
fiction—the narrator, the lady, the fictional "Spenser," those
whom the narrator addresses ("venemous tongues"), and the
Lodowick addressed by the character "Spenser"—are admon-
ished and taught to see their own time and space in the two
levels of the sequence, the earthly (surface) and the divine (anal-
ogic).

The Sunday sonnets are significant. Some are easily recogniz-
able as being thematically dissimilar to those sonnets surround-
ing them. But without knowing the sequence's church calendar
structure, we probably would not find these Sunday poems es-
pecially marked by distinguishing features. When considered in
the total structure, however, their importance as markers indicat-
ing both the narrator's progress through his courtship and the
calendar progression through Lent becomes clearer.

The first Sunday in Lent, for example, breaks the sequence
narrative, doing so with a catalog of favorable and unfavorable
aspects of plants (*Amor.* 26). The sequence resumes after that
botanical interlude, and the narrative progresses until 33, the

Second Sunday poem, when the address to Spenser's friend
Lodowick Bryskett arrests the narrative's forward movement.
Having little relationship with anything around it in the se-
quence, the poem's significance rests in part on its introducing
the fictional character "Spenser" into his own series of poems,
thus adding to the fiction an autobiographical element. Follow-
ing this sonnet, the narrative again resumes; the poet once more
complains of his despair, his woe, and the lady's guile, until the
arrival at a weekend celebration of the lady's smile (39 is a
Saturday, preceding 40, the third Sunday in Lent). After *Amor.* 40
the tone shifts again to the lady's cruelty, the lover's pleading,
and the poet's problems with writing.

Sunday Sonnet 47 introduces the fourth week of Lent. Were it
not that the poem appears in its peculiar position, its signifi-
cance, as with 40, would be difficult to determine; its rela-
tionships with the *BCP*, however, are subtle and will be discussed
later. Sonnet 47 ushers in a whole week of emotional conflicts
and pleas for mercy as the passion story intensifies and as the
lover gets closer to the sequence's emotional climax. *Amor.* 47
also ties to the liturgy—but not overtly; to note its connections
necessitates an awareness of the poem's and the pericopes' over-
lying and interpenetrable themes. *Amor.* 54, marking the fifth
Sunday in Lent, presents a different case. It is one of the se-
quence's key sonnets—"Of this world's theatre in which we stay, /
my loue lyke the Spectator ydly sits." Representing Passion Sun-
day, *Amor.* 54 appears in the middle of the sequence's emotional
crisis; here, for the first time, the narrator sees and comes close to
understanding his true relationship with the lady. Here, too, is
the important *theatrum mundi* image, significant because of its
Renaissance representation of the world as a stage on which the
Self is created by the playing of parts, and significant because the
narrator recognizes his own game-playing in his relationship
with his lady.

Represented by the poem positioned between the old year's
ending (60) and the new calendar year's beginning (62) is the
sixth Sunday in Lent, Palm Sunday. The lover's jubilant praise of
the lady constitutes the focus of the entire sonnet; knowing that
the poem parallels Palm Sunday adds a meaningful dimension to
the poem's interpretation. The poet's praise of his lady easily
transposes to an analogical encomium on Christ's entry into a
joyful Jerusalem—an entry marking the beginning of the end of
his Passion. For the narrator the sonnet likewise marks the start

of a week of sonnets culminating in the death of his self-directed love of the lady, followed by the resurrection of a love that transfigures both him and his poetry.

As the keystone of the entire sequence, the Easter sonnet, *Amor.* 68, focuses on Christ's resurrection, the critical event in Christianity and the crucial center of Christian worship. The Church's whole liturgical direction is always connected to this day, and the entire action of the sonnet sequence, both on the analogical as well as on the surface levels, would change meaning were it not for the significance of this sonnet. The poem is neither numerically nor structurally the sequence's center, but it is the one sonnet that serves to shift the focus from a fruitless to a fruitful love, from an "I" to a "you" and then "we" perspective. As the old love ends at the pivot point of the narrator's relinquishing "the game" in 67, so the message of Easter introduces and commences a new love and a new life in which all the old rules are transformed. In *Amor.* 68 the "real" Easter comes crashing through the sequence's surface level by conjoining, as nowhere else in the sequence, the analogy with its own analogue. In 68 Christ's love unmistakably joins with human love; love becomes the "lesson" that the lovers, and all the world's people, are taught.

In general, the Sunday sonnets in the Lenten sequence provide respites from the troubles the poet encounters during the weekday poems. There are exceptions, as noted with 47, but they are few.[29] Yet even with the inconsistencies, the Sunday sonnets reflect the Church calendar more closely than most other sonnet days of the sequence. To understand this we must look to the *BCP* lectionary. Comparing the propers for the various Sundays in Lent with the respective Sunday sonnets provides interesting parallels. These indicate that in addition to presenting a series of sonnets about his courtship, Spenser underscores the whole *Amoretti*, in calendric design and *BCP* echoes, with a depiction of the Christian's search for salvation by becoming atoned to and with Christ. These *BCP* analogies, and the love by which the courtship is distinguished, suggest that the love of the lady and the love of Christ, as elements of and foci for pure human love, are also aspects of divine love; both of the "loves" sanctify the narrator's loving in terms consonant with his Christianity and with Christian ethics. Likewise the Lenten agon of the eager penitent has similarities with the struggles of the sonnet lover, both (agon and struggles) being aspects of the same greater love and both preparing them, and us, to assume a new life.

The seasonal references grounding the action in historical time add a concreteness, a factuality, to the sequence. Yet with the vague suggestions of "new year" and "spring," Spenser keeps these same references ambiguous, shifting the temporal back-drop against which the drama is played. By doing so he moves the sequence on the analogic level out of historical time and into ritual time. Such movement helps establish the external and internal worldviews, indicates parallels between those two views, and permits the action to occur in any time, at any place, with any persons. The narrative may be repeated again and again; each change of characters changes the game plan somewhat, but for each pair of lovers the same rules, the same lessons, give direction on how to play and indicate for what ultimate reason one plays the love game in the first place. The structural move-ments provide patterns, balances and pivots, interplays and in-teractions, all within a bilevel structure of interpenetrating (sacred and profane) themes. The movements are seen as just that—movements—as Spenser develops and analyzes his sub-jects in motion, displaying the changes and turns of mind and heart, and the agonies and ecstasies of lovers (human and divine) in a timeless drama that is both a love story and The Love Story.

(3) Many details of these "two" love stories may be traced to the *BCP*. In some instances Spenser liberally fills entire sonnets with verbal, stylistic, or thematic echoes of biblical texts, extend-ing the meanings of those texts and enlarging the scope of the sonnets. At other times the shared material is only an echo of a few shared words, a particular joint focus, or mutual imagery. Cumulatively these words and echoes form a complex network of correspondences; in the church services as well as in the son-nets, these portray the Lenten season during which penitents prepare through fasting, repentance, confession, and contrition for their acceptance of and by Christ. This occurs in baptism at the Easter Vigil and at the subsequent Easter celebration.

The paralleling of the sonnet actions with the liturgical inter-actions asserts and reinforces the community of reader and characters, of characters and author, of author and Church, of Church and Christ. In this nonserious seriousness Spenser sug-gests that "a reality is glimpsed through the datum of experience or expressed in it, which is completely beyond and beneath it and imperceptible to sense per se. The experience is not for its own sake described and made more vivid through the use of comparison drawn from other data of sense, as is the case with

descriptive symbols, but it is given importance only as a gateway
into something beyond. Such usage would make the symbol in
some wise a semblance of a reality greater and truer than the
symbol in all its aspects, a sort of initiation in which thought
may be led through meaning to deeper meaning."[30]

That "deeper meaning" is an integral part of the *Amoretti*; and
to reach it the fabric of the sequence must be examined more
deeply for the specific allusions Spenser makes and the par-
ticular analogies he draws, remembering that, as in his other
writings, Spenser's allusions are just that—allusions—not one-
to-one parallels. Una, we recall, appears as a woman and as
Truth, sometimes more one than the other and at other times
equally both; Arthur exists as a lover, man, prince, Everyman,
and Christ. The sonnets' allusions suggest that the love of the
lady is similar, though not equivalent to, the Christian's love of
Christ. In much the same way, the poet narrator, at times the
concerned lover and at times the concerned poet, is similar to the
earnest and penitent Christian seeking redemption and grace.

What often appear to be "inconsistencies" in Spenser's method
of characterization actually maintain or assert the expanded
analogic reading of the sequence in a way that clear-cut, defini-
tive, and rigidly maintained parallels never artistically could.[31]
Spenser learned early that structural or rhetorical parallels,
tightly controlled and consistently exact, "divert attention from
the accidentals which give character to the specific object of
interpretation."[32] His outstanding achievement in the *Amoretti*
is his ability to present a proliferation of accidentals that make
the lady (on the surface level) one of the most lifelike and attrac-
tive sonnet ladies in our literature, while concurrently suggesting
connections (on the analogic level) between man's love for a
woman and humanity's love of Christ.[33]

Such an interpretation does not make the lady Christ; it would
be unfair to Spenser and his lady to make of the analogy a symbol
or an allegory. The lover is not asked to worship the lady literally
as one worships Christ, but to be mindful of Christ's self-sacrific-
ing, loving example, and to become himself Christ-like. In doing
so the lover, like the lady, joins a whole troop of Christ analogues
spanning the centuries—right up to Faulkner's Dilsey and Joe
Christmas, Greene's Whiskey Priest, and Mann's Herr
Peeperkorn. And the lady as a Christ analogue is preceded by
examples in countless poems prior to the *Amoretti*. The actions
that appear analogous both in the scriptures and the sonnets may

even be viewed as part of a rather set pattern of such correspondences:

> This more than human, angelic or divine power always had that relation to the human mind which the beloved has to her lover in the courtly experience—to be above him, to shed her light upon him, thereby actualizing his innate potential virtue, to raise him towards herself and thereby to perfect him, granting him a share, as far as she is capable of it, in her immortal and blessed state, to allow him to apprehend the divine through her—this is the paradigm, whether the language is metaphysics or love.[34]

By means of the sequence's calendar structure, by means of the biblical echoes and *BCP* parallels, Spenser suggests not that the human story related here is merely a substitute for the penitent in love with (and in pursuit of) Christ, but that the process of earthly love is integrally related to and infused with the divine love from which it essentially springs. All human love stories ritually reenact aspects of a more mythic and fundamental Love Story, which puts all other courtships, loves, and marriages in proper perspective.

Just as on the surface level the central action of the romantic courtship appears between sonnets 22 and 68, so this same group of sonnets, from Ash Wednesday through Easter Sunday, forms the central metaphoric and mimetic description of the Christian's vain attempts to "attain" Christ. The biblical references for the sonnet marking Ash Wednesday (22) are among the most obvious ones Spenser employs. The *BCP* lists Joel 2 as the epistle for the day: "Turne you vnto me with all your heart, and with fasting, and with weping, and with mourning, and rend your heart, and not your clothes: and turne vnto the Lord your god. . . . Gather the people: sanctifie the congregacion, gather the Elders." The gospel lesson is from Matthew 6: "But when thou fastest, annoint thine head, and wash thy face, that thou seme not vnto men to fast, but vnto thy Father which is in secret: and thy Father which seeth in secret, wil rewarde thee openly." The psalm for this *dies cincerum* (Ps. 6) provides a series of laments over past deeds as well as pleas for mercy against God's anger (transformed to "ire" in *Amor.* 22). The Collect further prays that God will forgive past sins and "creat and make in us newe and contrite heartes"; in the sonnet this is echoed in the poet's sacrificing his heart, now burning in "pure and chast desyre."

Sonnet 22 draws upon several images found here. The poet

identifies the time as the holy season "fit to fast and pray." The epistle injunction to "turne" is transposed to the poem's observation that men "ought to be inclynd" to devotion. Just as Matthew directs readers to fast and pray in secret, so the lover performs services within his mind, where he sacrifices his heart.

Amor. 26 parallels the first Sunday in Lent. The Collect for this day records two things: first, it commemorates Christ's fast of forty days, and, second, it contains a prayer for grace to use abstinence: "O Lord, whiche for oure sake dyddeste faste fortye dayes and fourtie nightes; Geue us grace to use suche abstinence, that, oure fleshe beying subdued to the spirite, wee maye euer obeye thy Godlye mocions in righteousnesse." The epistle, 2 Corinthians 6, describes the trials Paul endured: "So we therefore as workers together besche you, that ye receiue not the grace of God in vayne. . . . But in all things we approue our selues as the ministers of God, in muche patience, in afflictions, in necessities, in distresses, in stripes, in prisons, in tumultes, in labours . . . in loue unfained . . . by honoure, and dishonour, by euil reporte and good reporte, as deceiuers, and yet true, . . . as sorowing, and yet alway reioycing: as poore, and yet make manie riche: as hauing nothing, and yet possessing all things." The Matthew 4 gospel lesson records Christ's fasting and subduing of the flesh to the spirit.

The parallels between the readings and the sonnet are subtle. The sonnet interrupts the narrative progress and thus is important as marking a certain position in the overall narrative. Yet Quadragesima Sunday, originally marking the beginning of Lent, is traditionally tied with the Easter Vigil and is more associated with redemption than with a preoccupation with penance. The Collect refers to Lent, but the tone is confident. The negative values of Lenten abstinence balance the positive ones of good actions. Like the Ash Wednesday readings from Joel, this day's readings from 2 Corinthians refer to tribulation, but in a larger context than the "fasting, weeping, and mourning." Paul mentions "stripes, imprisonments, tumults, and labors," difficulties that are overcome by the "word of truth [and] by the power of God." He also uses "loue unfained" as one of his examples; this is precisely what the Amoretti lover must learn during his progress through the sequence courtship.

Christ's agon is depicted in Matthew's gospel account, a reminder that the emphasis in Lent is on Christ's life and that his forty-day fast in the desert provides the analogical source of the believer's own forty-day fast through this holy season. For the

Amoretti lover the message is also to be a positive one. Christ's fast ends in fullness, his Passion and death in resurrection and life. Implicit in the lessons is that "little paine" yields "endlesse pleasure" (*Amor.* 26).

Marked by *Amor.* 33 and paralleling 24 February 1594, the second Sunday in Lent at first appears to present a problem of inconsistency. Neither the epistle (1 Thess. 4) nor the gospel (Matt. 15) contains anything similar to that found in the corresponding sonnet. We must look elsewhere to distinguish Spenser's method. The twenty-fourth of February functions as one of the immovable feast days, the Feast of Saint Matthias. As such, the church follows the service for Saint Matthias's Day, not the regularly appointed one for the second Sunday in Lent. But Spenser does not draw directly from either the epistle (Act 1) or the gospel (Matt. 11) for this feast day. What he appears to have done is more complex.

First, the temperament of the day, as well as its being a saint's day, must be considered more closely. Saint Matthias's Day marks the only festival day in which both sorrow and joy commingle— sorrow that the Church reflects both on Judas, who committed the most impious of acts, and joy that the Church commemorates Matthias as the "faythful and true pastor" chosen to replace Judas among the Apostles. In *Amor.* 33, it is a troubled mind that finds expression, yet the trouble comes from the poet's love for his lady. But even when he complains, the poet simultaneously praises the woman he loves. While it is certainly not the same sorrow and joy expressed in the saint's day service, the double nature of such feelings in the sonnet provides a link.

Second, this is the only sonnet in which Spenser specifically identifies the person addressed, thus penetrating the sequence frame with an "autobiographical" element added to his "biography of a lover." That he would direct his prayer to a named figure (other than a muse) would be appropriate for a saint's day. Instead of a prayer naming Matthias, the poet requests: "lodwick, this of grace to me aread" (the "grace" possibly carrying double meaning here, too). Although the Roman Catholic practice commemorates saints by prayers addressed to them, the Church of England traditionally celebrates the saints more for the benefit of the living than for the saints themselves. Without much difficulty this redirection may be applied to *Amor.* 33, which structurally (as with 26) breaks the narrative and marks another step in the calendric progress through Lent and the courtship.

Sonnet 40 represents Lent Three. The suggested analogues

appear mostly in imagery. The psalm for this day, *Judica me, Deus* (Ps. 43), with the *judica* possibly reminiscent of the imperative "mark" with which the sonnet begins, includes: "Send thy light and thy trueth: let them lead me: and let them bring me vnto thine holy Mountaine and to thy Tabernacles." Containing an exhortation to "walke in love, even as Christ loved us," the epistle for this day (Eph. 5) concludes with: "Ye were once darknes, but are nowe light in the Lorde: walke as children of light, . . . approuing that which is pleasing to the Lord. . . . But all thinges when they are reproued of the light are manifest: for it is light that maketh all things manifest. Wherefore he sayith, Awake, thou that slepest, and stand vp from the dead; and Christ shal give thee light." The light pervading the psalm and this epistle correspond to the sunshine and light suffusing *Amor.* 40. The epistle's contrast between heathen and Christian (in terms of light imagery and as a contrast between darkness and light) itself suggests the transformation that will occur in the penitent's forthcoming baptism (Easter Even) and the lover's "conversion" (*Amor.* 67).

In *Amor.* 40 the lady smiles "with amiable cheere"; the poet compares the cheerfulness "vnto the fayre sunshine in somers day" after a dreadful storm. The sun's goodly rays, the poet writes, spread throughout the world, and all creatures "lift vp theyre drouping hed" when the light reaches them. Furthermore, while the epistle encourages penitents to become "children of light," the gospel (Luke 11) relates Christ's exorcism of a devil. The narrative repeats the imagery of conflict, reminding hearers (and readers) that spiritual warfare is not over, either during Lent or in the sequence. The warfare imagery is precisely that which is picked up immediately again in *Amor.* 41, when the lady is once more depicted as a cruel warrior.

Sonnet 47, "Trust not the treason of those smyling lookes," appears in the position of the fourth Sunday in Lent. In this case Spenser appears not to have used a correspondent *BCP* reference. The psalm, 46, *Deus noster refugium*, expresses quite the opposite feeling of what the poet describes in the sonnet, and the Collect consists of a prayer for merciful relief. The epistle (Gal. 4) and the gospel (John 6) contain nothing corresponding to what Spenser inserts in the sonnet, the former lesson concerning the covenants of grace and law, the latter the parable of feeding the five thousand. Furthermore, although sometimes referred to as Dominica Refectionis (Refreshment Sunday), nothing in the sonnet in any way indicates "refreshment." That Spenser includes some distinctive features for the other Sunday sonnets, either in the special handling of a theme, the echo of allusion, or even in providing a break in the narrative, suggests there is a parallel here, too. As will be discussed later, the tie comes not so much in what is contained in the sonnet but what the sonnet does in the narrative, providing for the transitus of Easter, which links the old with the new, the past with the future.

Lent Five is represented by *Amor*. 54. Known as Passion Sunday, this day corresponds to the time when Christ began remarking openly about his forthcoming sufferings and tribulations. The day's Collect begins: "We beseche thee, almyghtie God, mercifulle to *looke* upon thy people" (italics mine); the sonnet begins in "this worlds Theatre" where the lady sits "beholding" the poet. Recorded in John 8, the gospel for the day relates Christ's conversation with the Jews judging him; the sonnet records the lady's judgments of the various roles the poet has been playing. John presents the conflict as a gigantic trial, with Christ and the Church on one side, the world and the devil on the other. Christ appears in various roles—as judge, witness, advocate, accused, and accuser. The gospel lesson concludes with "then tooke they up stones to caste at hym"; the sonnet ends with the only appearance of the word "stone" in the sequence: "What then can moue her? if not merth nor mone, / she is no woman, but a sencelesse stone." Although no thematic correspondences appear between the two, the psalm for the day represented by 54 is 54. This, of course, might be a mere coincidence—until we consider that the psalm for the sixth Sunday in Lent, *Amor*. 61, is Psalm 61.

With the exception of the Ash Wednesday and Easter sonnets, *Amor*. 61, the sixth Sunday, contains the most overt liturgical analogues in Spenser's sequence. The first lines of the sonnet, "The glorious image of the makers beautie, / my souerayne saynt, the Idoll of my thought," and almost every line that follows contain some suggestion of Christ, who on Palm Sunday made his triumphal entry into Jerusalem.

The Collect for this day reads, in part: "Almightie and euerlastynge God, whiche of thy tender loue towarde man, haste sente our sauior Jesus Christ, to take upon him oure fleshe and to suffre death upon the crosse, that all mankynde shoulde folowe the example of his greate humilitie. . . ." A comparison with the sonnet shows that in tone and in theme, the parallels are clear. Likewise, the epistle from Philippians 2 is a reminder that Christ, "being . . . diuinely wrought, / and . . . heuenly borne" (to use the sonnet's words), when he was in the shape of God "thoght it no robbery to be equal with God: But he made him self of no reputation, and toke on him the forme of a seruaunt, and was made like vnto men, and was founde in shape as a man. He humbled him self, and became obedient vnto the death." And because he, like other "such heauenly formes ought rather worshipt be, / then dare be lou'd by men of meane degree" (*Amor*. 61), so God "hathe also highly exalted him, and giuen him a Name aboue eurie name, that in the Name of Jesus shulde euery knee bowe, bothe of things in heauen, and things in earth, and things vnder the earth." In the sonnet the poet refers to the lady as the "bud of ioy" and "blossome of the morne"; while not suggested by the rubrics, these terms possibly refer to the old custom of calling this day not only Palm Sunday but "flowering Sunday" and "Blossom Sunday."

Holy Week officially commences with Palm Sunday. With the exception of the lessons for Maundy Thursday, which recount the Lord's Supper, the epistles for this week all describe Christ's suffering. The gospels, in turn, list the incidents of Christ's Passion and crucifixion. Also called Passion Week and the Great Week, Holy Week is "holy" in the sonnets because of the sequence's analogic level. As the superimposed record of Christ's Passion and the fulfillment of the lover's own purified passion and poetry, the week is "great" because of those things Christ enacted during this period; it is also the great week of the sonnets because here the most important events of the sequence's surface level occur.[35]

During this week, time changes; the sonnets and the liturgy move ahead through linear time, progressing day by day as the week is marked off. Whereas events can be viewed as "occurring" within psychological, absolute, or cyclical time, in Holy Week each of the days moves the story forward toward a specific future date (Easter, *Amor*. 68). The week's unity is marked by a definite beginning (Psalm Sunday, *Amor*. 61, as well as *Amor*. 62, denoting Lady Day, 25 March, and the sonnet's call for new year's changes and renewal). The week has an internal progression toward Easter and the culmination of courting; the sonnets and the various liturgical services share a tonal continuity, all moving toward the great "turning" of Easter.

Monday of this week, *Amor*. 62, notes the new calendar year's beginning; Tuesday, *Amor*. 63, records the lover's finally seeing "the happy shore." *Amor*. 64, Wednesday, marks the couple's first kiss, and 65, Thursday, presents the account of the lover's allegorized proposal. Good Friday, *Amor.* 66, commemorates the lover's exaltation at receiving the lady's "light"; Spenser's analogous emphasis here is not on Christ's death but on what that death implies. Through Christ's suffering and death his own light is "dilated" (to use the *Amoretti* term). So, too, is the "light" of the Christian, whose "enlumined" self will now "reflect" Christ's redemptive act through his own life or, as in the poet's case, through his poetry. The sonnet is one of the few in which the whole poem may be read as referring to Christ as well as the lady. It ends on a positive note—that "since your light hath once enlumind me / With my reflex yours shall encreased be." Its ending makes even more dramatic the transition to the quiet, solemn start of *Amor.* 67, Holy Saturday, where Church and lover proceed towards their respective peripeteias.

In the sonnets, Easter Even has its own peculiar "connections" to the liturgy. No parallels between the propers for the day and the content of the sonnet are immediately evident. However, the scriptural reference to the familiar *Sicut Cervus,* Psalm 42 ("As the hart braieth for the riuers of water, so panteth my soule after thee, O God"), is a key to the poem's meaning. The sonnet, a record of the lady's yielding and accepting the lover's proposal, remains in tone one of the quietest of *Amoretti* poems, yet it marks the turning point, the pivot, in the sequence events. All sonnets preceding it lead to this particular acceptance and all sonnets after it are marked by what transpires here. In the ritual time of the Church calendar this day is universally observed as a day of fasting and quiet preparation; it commemorates Christ's descent into hell. In the ecclesiastical year it denotes a time for baptism, to which the day's epistle (1 Pet. 3) refers. Baptism, the death and rebirth of the individual, fittingly coincides here with Christ's own death and resurrection. The return of the "gentle deare . . . thinking to quench her thirst at the next brooke" supplies the reference to water and then to baptism. Yet the analogue is greater than this.

During the Holy Week of sonnets, Spenser suggests references to Christ's last words as variously recorded in the Gospels. We find, for example, the first few words are alluded to early in the week, none, in the middle, and the remainder, close together at the end. The first words concern forgiveness: "Father, forgiue them" (Luke 23:34). *Amor.* 62, Monday, elucidates its own type of forgiveness, presenting the lover's hope that the new year's change of weather will indicate a change in the temper(ature) of his and his lady's minds and that they will thus amend their lives and "old yeares sinnes forepast . . . eschew." Then, in 63, the lover sees the "happy shore" to which he hopes "ere long for to arryue":

> fayre soyle it seemes from far and fraught with store
> of all that deare and daynty is alyue.
> Most happy he that can at last atchyue
> the ioyous safety of so sweet a rest.

The paradisal "fayre soyle" noted here reflects Spenser's integration of Christ's mention of paradise (Luke 23:43) in the "second words": "To day shalt thou be with me in Paradise."

After these two allusions Spenser does not refer again to the "words" until the last day of the sonnet Holy Week, when the rest are used or suggested. For the most part the allusions exist as single words serving as subtle suggestions of Christ's words; that they appear in one sonnet helps take us to the analogical level of the sequence, setting the lover's actions within a framework of divine interaction. The words are as follows: John 19:26 records the third "word" on the cross: "Woman, beholde thy sonne." The sonnet echoes this by "There she beholding me. . . ." The fourth "word," "My God, my God, why has thou forsaken me?" (Matt. 27:46) parallels "When I all weary had the chace forsooke." The fifth word, "I thirst" (John 19:28) recalls the gentle deer who came "thinking to quench her thirst at the next brooke." Spenser suggests the meaning of Christ's sixth statement, that "it is finished," not by a word but by the whole surrender of the lady to the lover. Furthermore, the poet relates that the lady "sought not to fly, but fearlesse still did bide," thus finishing the pursuit of the previous sixty-six sonnets. Luke 23:46 contains Christ's last words on the cross: "And Jesus cryed with a loude voyce, and said, Father, into thine hands I commend my spirit." The last action of the sonnet provides the echo: "till I in hand her yet halfe trembling tooke." Quietly, seriously, the Lenten sequence in the Church calendar, and in the sonnets, ends.

The moderate and solemn tone of *Amor.* 67 helps by contrast to make the following lines such a jubilant, joyous apostrophe: "Most glorious Lord of lyfe that on this day, / Didst make thy triumph ouer death and sin." Thus begins 68, and with the great "Gloria" ("glorious" in the poem) begins the Easter sonnet celebrating Christ's resurrection and the new life of the now-betrothed lovers. The calmness of the previous poem, still part of the Lenten section, yields to the rejoicing displayed throughout this sonnet as the triumph of human love is paralleled to Christ's triumph over death. The poem is filled with and consists of overt praise for Christ and prayers that "we for whom thou [Christ] diddest dye . . . may liue for euer in felicity." It is by far the most overtly scriptural poem in the sequence, so much so that the surface level is almost buried as Spenser brings to the foreground its analogues from the metaphoric level. Spenser draws the sonnet's materials from scattered passages throughout the Easter narration, echoing scripture and liturgy in his own hymn of joy. The Christ-Christian love stories are presented in their proper perspective, where Christ's love provides the model, the "lesson," for the sequence's human love. (Discussion of 68 will be reserved until later, when its significance in and for the sequence will be clear.)

After Easter various weekdays follow for which the BCP lists special orders; this is true as well of some days immediately preceding Easter. However, Spenser does not appear to have used the pericopes for those days in the Amoretti, and, with only a few exceptions (primarily in Holy Week), it is the Sunday sonnets that provide the real analogues to the Church calendar. One of those exceptions occurs in Amor. 3, corresponding to 25 January, the fixed feast day commemorating the conversion of Paul. Here Spenser takes one of the chief effects of Paul's conversion experience and transposes it to the lover's experience when looking at the lady. Briefly, Amor. 3 praises "the sourerayne beauty" whom the poet "admires" (wonders at); her light "kindled heauenly fyre" in his frail spirit to the point "that being now with her huge brightenesse dazed," he can "no more endure to view" base things. Standing amazed at the "wondrous sight of so celestiall hew," he is unable to speak or write.

The fixed epistle for this same day records Paul's description of his experiences on the Damascus road: "Suddenly there shined round about him a light from heaven. And he fel to the earth, and heard a voyce, saying to him, Saul, Saul, why persecutest thou me? . . . He then both trembling and astonied, said; Lorde, what wilt thou that I do? . . . And Saul arose from the ground, and opened his eyes, but sawe no man" (Acts 9:3–8). The blindness, astonishment, and Paul's later preaching of the gospel provide parallels between the sonnet and the lesson. While assimilating (but not necessarily eliminating) a possible neo-Platonic explanation of the imagery, the Christian (biblical) context of the sequence predominates.

For one particularly key sonnet, however, the parallels and

structural significance admittedly remain troublesome—*Amor.* 4. The sonnet day's liturgical and calendric-date analogues are consistent and plentiful enough to leave little question as to their actual existence. But within the sequence architecture as it has been described, three Sunday sonnets precede the Ash Wednesday poem, balanced by three Sunday sonnets following Easter. These establish the ritual time in its structural calendric sense.

The earliest Sunday sonnet appears in *Amor.* 5: "Rudely thou wrongest my deare harts desire"; in the 1594 calendar the corresponding day is Sunday, 27 January. *Amor.* 3 has just briefly been looked at, in which the poem's allusions to the suggested calendar readings for 25 January (the Feast of the Conversion of Saint Paul) make the correspondence between the poem and the scripture fairly obvious. *Amor.* 5, however, necessitates reading *Amor.* 4 as representing 26 January, even though various indicators point to its denoting 1 January, the start of a new year and the commemoration of the Circumcision. The difficulties with the sonnet's liturgical connections are complex.

Amor. 4 begins:

> New yeare forth looking out of Ianus gate,
>   Doth seeme to promise hope of new delight:
>   and bidding th'old Adieu, his passed date
>   bids all old thoughts to die in dumpish spright.

The sonnet introduces the first time scheme (seemingly in the historical time mode) in the sequence. Abruptly the sighs and sorrows of the courtly lover-poet of *Amor.* 1–3 are replaced by the plain speaking of the lover, suddenly drawn from his ecstatic praise and made aware of the coming spring:

> And calling forth out of sad Winters night,
>   fresh loue, that long hath slept in cheerlesse bower:
>   wils him awake, and soone about him dight
>   his wanton wings and darts of deadly power.
> For lusty spring now in his timely howre,
>   Is ready to come forth him to receiue:
>   and warnes the Earth with diuers colord flowre,
>   to decke hir selfe, and her faire mantle weaue.

Seizing the opportunity to project himself fictionally into the description of empirical spring, the poet-lover nevertheless cannot dismiss the season's underlying sexuality and his own romantic reaction to it (though both become sublimated within the imagery of spring and fresh love). He calls love to prepare "wanton wings and darts of deadly power" so that love may join spring (the poet-lover) in entertaining "new loue" to the earth-lady. The allegory appears easy. The reference to Janus seems a direct allusion to January as well as to the passing of the old and the beginning of the new year. Likewise the call to renew and prepare for the coming spring also appears to lead the way to the now-beginning fresh year.

In one sense the corresponding date for this sonnet *is* 1 January; an initial reading of the sequence would have it so, and the intentional ambiguity of Spenser's language, in addition to his frequently throwing out false clues, directs the reader to a Janus/January parallel. For the sequence's "uninformed" readers the date is probably of no significance, anyway. It is only when looking retrospectively at the sequence and at its calendar (and *BCP*) parallels and structuring that one finds the 26 January connections. Janus does not necessarily refer only to 1 January; he is a god of all beginnings, not exclusively the god of the new year. Considered by some ancients a sky-god, even a cosmic god (Ovid *Fasti* 1.101ff.), he is frequently named in classical prayers at the beginning of lists of gods (as in Livy *Epitomae* 8.9:6). As a "beginner," Janus leads us into the liturgical period of Lent, which begins on Septuagesima Sunday, represented by *Amor.* 5 (immediately after this sonnet). There Janus prepares us for the "new yeare" in the church calendar and the *vita nuova* in a Christian sense.

It is also noted that the new year is now at his "passed date," possibly suggesting that although right at hand for a new season (a "new yeare" of the church) the lover may have passed the date for the change in the new calendar year. In such a case his subjective psychological time would have taken precedent over objective, historical time. In *Amor.* 70, where spring appears on 2 April, there is a similar reference to "passed time," possibly alluding to the season (empirical time) beginning a few days later than expected (fictional time). Contextually, the immediacy of *Amor.* 4 to *Amor.* 5's beginning of the pre-Lenten "countdown" argues for *Amor.* 4 as 26 January. The sonnet's reference to "new loue" is to the new type of love that will be exhibited, modeled, and unfolded during Lent. It is a new love for the poet, who will find the tired "loves" of Petrarchanism and neo-Platonism ineffective and who must realize love as a "mode of self-transcendence by means of which the self perfects its identity."[36] And it is a new love asserting Christ's love for humanity more than the believer's love for him. It is this love for which the Lenten season prepares the penitent. Furthermore, the sonnet contains fairly obvious echoes of the Song of Songs 2:7–16, where the bridegroom and bride parallel Christ and the church (all Christians) as the latter prepares for the former.

Though not all passages are as expressly lovely as the one from the Song of Songs, both the Old and New Testaments contain numerous admonitions to "prepare" oneself for the Savior's appearance. The church summons its members to awaken, to overcome (in the sonnets's words) "old thoughts" by having them "die in dumpish spright," and to prepare for fresh manifestations of God's love. Lent, the season both of repentance and of the celebration and recognition of Christ's humanity, is most singularly that time during the Church year when one may "entertaine" (L. *inter-tenere*, "hold among") this "new loue." Likewise, Lent is most appropriately the period to consider the manifestations of this love (Christ's divinity) and to prepare oneself for acceptance at Easter.

One might also argue for the 26 January date on quite different grounds. *Amor.* 3, with its rather clear parallels to Paul's conversion (celebrated on 25 January) was already briefly examined. If *Amor.* 4 is read as corresponding to 1 January, and if each sonnet represents one day in a consecutive series, then *Amor.* 3 would parallel 31 December. Although the pericopes for 25 January apply to *Amor.* 3, those for 31 December do not. Unfortunately, neither the readings for 24 January nor those for 30 December have analogues in 3. But for *Amor.* 1, although there are no parallels between it and 29 December, the following correspondences to the propers are noted for 23 January: (Gen. 42) food, eyes ("long lacked foode"; "lamping eyes"); (Gen. 43) tears, weeping ("written with teares"); (Matt. 21) leaves ("happy ye leaues"). In the Table for the Order of the Psalms, the following parallels may be noted: (Ps. 110), brook ("sacred brooke"); (Ps. 115), hands, handle ("those lilly hands . . . , shall handle you"). Considering the number of thematic and verbal echoes for the 23 January reading and their absence for a 29 December reading, it appears that Spenser is using the former date (23 January) for the day corresponding to the sequence start.

Yet the problem of a "new yeare" reference in *Amor.* 4 remains. If the sonnet refers to 1 January (as some assume it does) then the poem refers liturgically to the Circumcision. Among the attendant associations of that day is the idea that at the Circumcision Christ fulfilled the old law of justice in order to initiate the new law of love, or charity. An obscure reference to this association appears in Joseph Beaumont's poem "Newyear Day," which, in order to contrast the Roman new year with the Circumcision, begins with a reference to "Faind Janus." Both the Beaumont poem and the notion of the old law might seem to support arguments for the 1 January date, the date which the variorum commentators generally agree upon as the one Spenser intended. However, the editor observes that the commentators "mean to say . . . the sonnet from line 5 describes New Year old style in traditional Spring terms, but that the first line actually labels the sonnet January 1."[37] This observation helps show the sonnet as possibly a cleverly disguised play upon the start of a new liturgical season—from the Christmas Pasch to the Easter Pasch, from Epiphany to the new pre-Lent preparation. If the first lines refer to the movement from old to new liturgical periods, then the references to "fresh loue" become clearer. "Lusty spring" is ready to come forth and greet "fresh loue." Here, in simple terms describing earth's preparation for Christ, the allegory of Lent (the season and the word that refer to "spring") is contained.

The difficulties with 4, indeed the problems with these first four sonnets, remain thorny. The arguments for both possibilities rest mainly on *Amor.* 4, which enigmatically eludes definite placement. If one considers the analogic level of the whole work it appears that Spenser intends 4 to represent 25 January, not 1 January. If *Amor.* 4 is read as a symbolic preface to the extended Christian analogy following it, it does not seem amiss (whichever date we assign it) to read it as a metaphoric prelude to Lent. The parallels between the sonnet and the liturgy, the simple allegory within the poem (later expanded in the Lent-Easter section of the sequence), its position immediately before the sonnet representing Septuagesima Sunday, all suggest more strongly than the single reference to Janus that the sonnet represents 26 January and is thus part of an unbroken sequence of sonnet days stretching from 23 January to 21 April 1594. Likewise, the calendric structure of the full sequence

> has not only a temporal correspondence but also a causal relationship to the central theme. Clearly, Spenser saw the religious and the amatory elements not as two levels of meaning but as inseparable aspects of the same story. Spenser's story of love is based on the proposition that Christ is in man. Christ is Beauty, which causes and sustains desire. And Christ is love.[38]

Just as Spenser superimposes the analogic movement on the surface movement, so he sets the narrative of both against a backdrop of seasons and a panorama of narrator-generated time. Likewise, Spenser takes the old macro-microcosm conventions and integrates them with his newer approach, not only to the earth-cosmic force of love moving all things, but to his own dramatic search for that which "seemes on earth most heauenly." He accomplishes all this subtly, artfully, and with gentle wit in a narrative considerably more unified in its developing patterns than any similar sequence of this type.

I turn now to that unfolding narrative, watching and listening carefully to those visual and aural indicators that show the movements into and through Spenser's intricate analogies of love. The movements are subtle—more subtle than ever before noted. And the indicators are incredibly rich, yielding patterns of words and images, lines and allusions, that together affirm a textural and textual artistry rarely, if ever, paralleled.

AMORETTI 1–21

"There with Love's daughter Pleasure they do play /
Their hurtless sports . . ."

Within the tripartite *Amoretti* pattern Spenser deftly inter-weaves numerous other, smaller patterns, some involving the poet's struggles with writing, some the lover's reappraisal of the proper form of love and loving, some the narrator's quest for self-awareness and enlightenment. Spenser textures the sequence by means of repeated words, images, motifs; at times he groups thematically similar sonnets to convey the narrator's special attention to one detail of the courtship, while at other times he extends a form of wordplay for three, four, even five sonnets.

The first twenty-one sonnets prepare the reader and the narrator for the struggles to be endured during the Lenten season, the forty-six sonnets of which form the central panel of the triptych. Spenser then rounds the shape of the larger sequence by balancing the first twenty-one sonnets with the last twenty-one. Generally the patterns are not observable as the sequence unfolds, and an unfolding sequence is what the narrator presents. Only by following the development from start to finish of the sequence can it be received as the poet discovers it to his fictive audience. Only by means of such a sequential reading can the development of the courtship be followed as the narrator himself presumably experiences it. These unfoldings and these developments imply what for Spenser is a major concept—that love, as part of life, is a process, not so much (as with Socrates) from the latent to the explicit, but (as with Paul) from the less to the more complete. Lovers must learn love, just as poets learn poetry. The *Amoretti* lover will be put through many educative processes in the course of the sequence in order that he might realize both love and himself, that he may be more fulfilled (and therefore more creative), and that he might (as Buber suggests) became an I through a Thou.

The importance of *Amor.* 1, both as the initial poem and as part of a trio of poems with which the sequence commences, cannot be overstated. It introduces the poet, his first comments about the lady, and his plan for courting. Additionally, this sonnet presents the poet's concerns for his craft and sets forth a significant part of the game plan that will be followed through the first two sections (*Amor.* 1–21; *Amor.* 22–68) of the sequence. The poem is highly balanced, carefully and cleverly framed—and conventional.

> Happy ye leaues when as those lilly hands,
> > which hold my life in their dead doing might
> > shall handle you and hold in loues soft bands,
> > lyke captiues trembling at the victors sight.
> And happy lines, on which with starry light,
> > those lamping eyes will deigne sometimes to look
> > and reade the sorrowes of my dying spright,
> > written with teares in harts close bleeding book.
> And happy rymes bath'd in the sacred brooke,
> > of Helicon whence she deriued is,
> > when ye behold that Angels blessed looke,
> > my soules long lacked foode, my heauens blis.
> Leaues, lines, and rymes, seeke her to please alone,
> > whom if ye please, I care for other none.

There is no questioning here of the traditions; the poet accepts and uses them. Like Astrophil, the poet is already in love when the sequence begins; both pursue their ladies by means of Petrarchan ploys, assuming that poetry, as rhetoric, is intended to move and persuade. His "leaves, lines, and rymes" seek only to please her, and, being pleased, she will be moved.

The sonnet also has its ambiguities, and it introduces elements of the courtship and poetic processes that will reappear frequently in the poems. The poet depicts his beloved as a combination of goddess and saint, with an emphasis on the latter. Her "lilly hands" have "dead doing might"; paradoxically they are also "loues soft bands." "Bands" will become a major motif in the sequence, eventually extending to bondage, ties, traps, webs, and a variety of other terms. By rhyme, the bands are associated with "hands," a word that also will appear later at the sequence's pivot (*Amor.* 67), when the lover takes the lady by the hand and ties her with her own "goodwill."

The lady's lamping eyes (line 6), reminiscent of Belphoebe and other Faerieland women, provide an ethereal quality that both is and is not a valid attribute; as a hierophanic participator in

divinity-made-human, she certainly does have "lamping eyes."
As a common Petrarchan hyperbole the phrase merely petrifies the
lady in frozen conceits. Yet she is called an angel, derived from
the "sacred brooke"; she is his inspiration and, in truth, as the
inspiration of the sonnets she is also its object, his muse as well
as his musings.

Thus far the poet has addressed his poetry, not the lady. The
poet may claim that his interest is the lady, but he clearly is also
concerned with his art. His "thrice happy" poem provides an
invocation as well as an indication of the directions he will take
as he prepares to have the lady "reade the sorrowes of [his] dying
spright, / written with teares in harts close bleeding book." Even
the couplet concludes the poem ambiguously: "Leaves, lines,
rymes, seeke her to please alone, / whom if ye please, I care for
other none." The line raises several possibilities. Is the poem
being directed to "seeke her to please alone," or is the phrase
intended to clarify the poem's intent? Further, is the last line to
be understood as "whom, if ye please, I [will] care for other
none" (in which case the courtship depends on the efficacy of
the poetry)? Or, also possible, is the line to be read as "her [she]
. . . whom, if ye please, I care for none other?"

Amor. 2 continues the poet's rhetorical pose as well as the idea
of the poet's "love pined hart" fed with "sighes and sorrowes."
Yet the voice is also that of the lover. One might see *Amor.* 1 as
providing the form of his poem and 2 as yielding the content. In 1
the narrator spoke of his "harts close bleeding book"; by 2 this
has become his "love pined hart," which feels sorrows (as does
the "dying spright" of 1) and produces the unquiet thought to
which the poem is addressed.

> Vnquiet thought, whom at the first I bred,
>   Of th'inward bale of my loue pined hart:
>   and sithens haue with sighes and sorrowes fed,
>   till greater then my wombe thou woxen art.
> Breake forth at length out of the inner part,
>   in which thou lurkest lyke to vipers brood:
>   and seeke some succour both to ease my smart
>   and also to sustayne thy selfe with food.
> But if in presence of that fayrest proud
>   thou chance to come, fall lowly at her feet:
>   and with meeke humblesse and afflicted mood,
>   pardon for thee, and grace for me intreat.
> Which if she graunt, then liue and my loue cherish,
>   if not, die soone, and I with thee will perish.

Again, the sonnet is not addressed to the lady; were it so directed there would be no "chance" involved in its reaching her or not. The leaves, lines, and rhymes sent to her in *Amor.* 1 are now only by chance to come before her. And love itself has already taken a dark shape; whereas in *Amor.* 1 it apparently gave rise to the happy lines, here it is equated with restlessness, bale, and isolation. Both the poet's poetry and the lover's love should provide "succour" and an easing of the "smart." But neither the poetry nor the love appears up to the challenge. Whereas the lady's appearance had been his "soules long lacked foode" (1), now he is fed on sorrows and sighs. Spenser transforms Sidney's "pregnant with wit" conceit both into the unquiet thought growing "greater than my wombe" and into being called upon to "breake forth at length out of the inner part, / in which thou lurkest lyke to vipers brood."

Love here is disquieting, as it will be for a good part of the courtship. His "unquiet thought" may be the subject of his poetry, but it is also the source of great discomfort. It is the same "vnquiet Care" Amoret sees in Cupid's Masque (3.12.25), the same "vnquiet strife" that moves Canacee's lovers to battles (4.2.37), and the same "vnquiet fit" that has Britomart "close afflicted long in vaine" (5.6.15). Love is also compared to a wound, a "smart," that will afflict (both "distress" and "conquer") him for a long time; it becomes his "payneful smart" in *Amor.* 18, his "bitter balefull smart" in 24, a "continuall smart" in 42. It is finally a "dying smart" in 48, and merely a "smart" in 54. It does not appear at all after the betrothal, and his "wound" (noted in 6, 8, 50, and 57) is only finally healed when "simple Truth and mutuall Good Will / seekes with sweet peace to salve each others wound" (65).

Until that "salvation" the lover must endure the anxieties, discomforts, and hunger, which Spenser describes again in his *Hymne in Honour of Love,* where the lover "feeds his hungrie fantasy" and yet is "neuer satisfyde with it" (198–99). Yet the lover in the *Hymne,* like the poem described in *Amor.* 1, is "thrise happy" in the hope of possession of, and being possessed by, the lady. Both the lover in the *Hymne* and the lover in the sonnets experience the same "progress" in their loving:

> Then forth he casts in his vnquiet thought,
> That he may do, her fauour to obtaine;
> What braue exploit, what perill hardly wrought,

What puissant conquest, what aduenturous paine,
May please her best, and grace vnto him gaine.

(*HL*, 218–22)

Both are disquieted by a "troubled mynd" (*HL*, 218; "vnquiet thought"), which "to his fayning fansie represent[s] / sights neuer seene, and thousand shadowes vaine" (*HL*, 254–55), all of which (including "gnawing enuie," "hart-fretting feare," "vaine sur-mizes," "distrustfull showes," "false reports," "doubts," "daungers," "delayes," "woes," "fayned friends," and "vnassured foes") make "a louers life a wretches hell" (*HL*, 259–65).

Yet the sonnet remains another highly rhetorical complex of images, intricately wrought parallels, and verbal interplays. Love may disquiet the lover but it does not stop the poet; as a Pe-trarchan lover he suffers deeply, but as a poet his "unquiet thought" can be externalized in the form of poems that "break forth out of the inner part." In such a way the autobiographical mode (represented by the lover-narrator) combines with, yet is viewed as a distinct function of, the "romantic" poet-narrator. Psychologically, by expressing his sorrows he can diminish them, thus succoring himself and easing his inner pain.

But again it is through poetry, not direct expression of the situation to the lady, that the narrator seeks to ease the smart. Seeking security in staid Petrarchan conceits, the poet finds the surety he needs in the only role he knows, that of the poet-lover (in that order), not just the lover or just the poet. Spenser thus provides at the outset a "divided" narrator, one who is a poet and who is a lover. The real integration of the two, their own unifica-tion, does not come until their atonement in *Amor.* 67–68.

Having given *Amor.* 1 to the poet and 2 to the lover, Spenser completes his triadic prologue by introducing the lady. Throughout these first poems the poet enthusiastically develops the description of his beloved: her "lilly hands" appear "soft bands," her "lamping eyes" give forth "starry light"; derived from that "sacred brooke of Helicon" she is an angel whose "blessed looke" is his "heauens blis." Worshiped both as an angel and as a saint she grants grace and pardon but must be entreated to do so with "afflicted mood" and "meeke humblesse." In 3 he writes:

The souerayne beauty which I doo admyre,
witnesse the world how worthy to be prayzed;

the light whereof hath kindled heauenly fyre
in my fraile spirit by her from basenesse raysed.

Amor. 1 and 2 addressed themselves to "things"—the "leaves,
lines, rymes" and the "unquiet thought." Amor. 3 begins with a
statement. Through the octave, the lover moves from describing
the lady to noting her effect on him; he moves in the sestet to the
problem of her effect on the writing of his poetry. Again, the lover
and the poet may be viewed as distinct. The poet's "dying
spright" (1) and the lover's "love pined hart" (2) are drawn
together in the "fraile spirit" and "hart" of Amor. 3.

That being now with her huge brightnesse dazed,
    base thing I can no more endure to view:
but looking still on her I stand amazed,
    at wondrous sight of so celestiall hew.

Various elements of theological machinery are worked into the
poem: circumlocuting the name of the divinity, an epiphany and
its manifestations in those present, and the "huge brightnesse" of
incomprehensible light. Like God's light, the lady's stuns and
cannot be described. On the sequence's analogical level Amor. 3
parallels 25 February, the Feast of Paul's conversion; what might
otherwise be viewed as neo-Platonic imagery or Petrarchan hy-
perbole here becomes God's own light as well as the lady's, both
of them dazzling the respective beholders to blindness. God's
light, his "heavenly fyre," lifts Paul out of baseness just as the
lady does the same for and to the lover, who, "being now with
her huge brightnesse dazed," can no more endure viewing "base
thing[s]."

Importantly, the word "souerayne" describes two significant
aspects of the lady. First, the word implies her supreme nature:
she is the most important woman, the one highest in the hier-
archy of earthly beings. Her beauty surpasses human reason. But
the lover also perceives her as divine, one who approaches what
the fourth Hymne refers to as "that souerayne light." She causes
amazement and the freezing of the senses: "but looking still on
her I stand amazed, / at wondrous sight of so celestiall hew." So
stunned that "his wit cannot endite," the poet claims the lady's
"huge brightnesse" and "celestiall hew" have "kindled heauenly
fyre" in his frail spirit. It is no surprise that such admiration
manifests itself in worship; the poet's noting that he "admyre[s]"
the lady needs to be read (as it would in the Renaissance) as
"worships," thus carrying the strength of the Latin admiratio,

picked up later in the sonnet by "amazed," "astonishment," and "wonderment."

The lady also appears "souerayne" in the courtly sense of her being an all-powerful ruler. The "leaues" the poet sends will be "lyke captiues trembling in the victors sight"; her eyes will "deigne sometimes to look" on the lines; she may or may not grant pardon to him. Here are the roots of the cruel-fair image so often applied to the lady of the first two sections of the *Amoretti*.

In addition, the weakness of the poet's spirit, a theme to be treated at considerable length, is already well-established in the sequence. In *Amor.* 1 it was "dying"; by *Amor.* 3 it is "fraile." But something has happened to it as the lady raises it from baseness while kindling in it a "heavenly fyre." The fire may be ardor, or it can be the heavenly fire, fervor, which causes the penitent to burn for a spiritual refinement or consummation. In the *Hymne* in *Honour of Love* (186–92) it is a "flaming light of . . . celestiall fyre, / Which kindleth loue in generous desyre." In the *Hymne* and the sonnet, Spenser adapts neo-Platonic concepts to his own purposes. The lustful (base) man is concerned only with the lady's outward appearance because he dare not expose himself to the lady's spiritual beauty; true love refines the lover's mind so that it becomes more conformable to the lady's spiritual beauty. He can "no more endure" to view base things. The sonnet's analogical positioning on the Feast of Paul's conversion, however, helps us see the transformation of the neo-Platonic images into their Christian counterparts. The lover may be on the second rung of the Platonic scala, but Spenser's real interest is more with depicting the effects both of God's "light" in the human spirit and the differences between false love and true love than with describing the lover's progress away from the earthly and toward the divine.

The sonnet's sestet deserves special attention. It artfully describes the difficulty of artful description. The poet's work, announced in *Amor.* 1 as his writing "with teares in harts close bleeding book," and shown in 2 as the lover's painful labor, now becomes the expression of inexpressibility. The sestet turns from the lady and from the lover to the poet's concerns with poetry; the lines reveal why the narrator, who attempts the empirical retelling of the situation as a lover, must move to the fictional mode and use the voice of the poet:

> So when my toung would speak her praises dew,
>   it stopped is with thoughts astonishment;

and when my pen would write her titles true,
    it rauisht is with fancies wonderment:
Yet in my hart I then both speake and write
    the wonder that my wit cannot endite.

Just as the lover by saying he cannot speak *has* spoken in the first part of the poem, so the poet does write. By feigning inadequacy he actually magnifies the subject matter. He writes concerning those things about which he says he cannot write, and in this way he has already given her titles—she is "the souerayne beauty" of "celestiall hew" who kindles "heauenly fyre." As Dante in *La Vita Nuova* divides his praise of Beatrice into sections of prose and sections of poetry, so too does the narrator divide his praises here, with the lover "speaking" his thoughts while the poet writes his fancies.

Though the narrator cannot speak aloud or write "her titles true" (suggesting both her "actual" titles or an "accurate" description of her titles), he is at least able to write of the wonder it is that he cannot endite (*indico*, "to make known, to proclaim"). The process of transforming oral presentation into a revised literary mode is clearly part of the fiction, as is the narrator's final act: speaking and writing in his heart. Astrophil's "look in thy heart and write" assumes another meaning when the *Amoretti* lover's statement is examined; instead of examining the heart and then writing the poetry, both the poetry as well as the verbal expression here are actually "endited" within the lover's heart ("the harts close bleeding book" of *Amor.* 1). The narrator's looking within himself is important; within him the lady is framed in his thoughts (8), and there he finds the "goodly ymage" (22) of "that goodly idoll" (27). Until he can move outside his "inner part" (2) there is no chance for any interchange with the real lady and no opportunity to resolve the conflicts he himself produces. Inside him she embodies his concept of the ideal; part literary and part archetypal, she is as much his own creation as is his poetry. Like his poetry, the interior lady can be fashioned and made conformable with all the requisites of the Petrarchan cruel fair—but not with the real lady. His poeticized concept of the lady distorts both the lover's thoughts and the poet's fancies, and his clouded vision will not clear until much later in the courtship.

Thus far, little narrative action has occurred, and Spenser has provided no referents to indicate any time awareness. Because of

the poet's amazement and the lover's astonishment, no move-
ment occurs in the three prefatory poems. Still in a state of
confusion due to the lady's overwhelming power, the narrator
uses these poems to organize his thoughts about the situation
and, in his own way, to create his interior game. The reader is
drawn quickly and subtly into the poet's ludic exercise; without
realizing it, by the end of *Amor.* 3 the first-time *Amoretti* reader
has already been introduced to many of the sequence's major
motifs, has distinguished between the lover and the poet, and has
had the first brush with what later is found to be the sequence's
analogic level.

On the analogic level the "action" has been minimal. There are
a few liturgical analogues for the days these first three sonnets
represent, and the surface level predominates. Nonetheless, the
allusions to the suggested *BCP* readings for January 23 (the day
paralleled by *Amor.* 1) includes cross-references to food, eyes,
tears, weeping, brook, hands, handle, and leaves. That similar
words appear in the sonnet and in the *BCP* would not be evident
to the reader on an initial reading of the text. Yet it is not
important that the analogies be recognized at this point in the
sequence. What is important here, as it is in the "hidden" aspects
of all allegories and other closed texts, is that the analogues are
there, can be found, and can be integrated into an expanded
reading of the surface text. The liturgical and theological signifi-
cance is that these analogues provide a reminder that the life of
Christ serves as a sacralizing pattern of our lives and a pattern,
especially, for love. The surfacing of the liturgical calendar at
various times in the sequence reminds us of the ongoing and
constant human/divine correspondence, even when we neglect
to recollect it.

Not until *Amor.* 3, where the lady, like Christ, "astounds" the
lover (just as the bright appearance of Christ astounded Saul) are
there any liturgical references of any import. Then in *Amor.* 4 the
allusions to the Song of Songs concerning preparations for the
coming of the bridegroom suggest the actual start for the "new
yeare," the "new life," of the penitent seeking union with Christ.
Just as the gospels again and again "awaken" members of the
Church from sluggishness, calling them to awareness of fresh
manifestations of Christ's love, so on the surface level *Amor.* 4
prepares the lover and his lady to new relationships and
awarenesses.

In *Amor.* 4 Spenser introduces action and time. Having now

presented the poet, lover, and lady—the actors in this masque of various loves—Spenser proceeds in 4 to mount the stage and begin the drama:

> New yeare forth looking out of Ianus gate,
>> Doth seeme to promise hope of new delight:
>> and bidding th'old adieu, his passed date
>> bids all old thoughts to die in dumpish spright.
> And calling forth out of sad Winters night,
>> fresh loue, that long hath slept in cheerlesse bower:
>> wils him awake, and soone about him dight
>> his wanton wings and darts of deadly power.
> For lusty spring now in his timely howre,
>> is ready to come forth him to receiue:
>> and warnes the Earth with diuers colord flowre,
>> to decke hir selfe, and her faire mantle weaue.
> Then you faire flowre, in whom fresh youth doth raine,
>> prepare your selfe new loue to entertaine.

Abruptly this sonnet introduces the sequence's first time scheme. As the sequence thus begins, "the lover, in a pagan setting, is troubled on the one hand by the 'inward bale' of a baser desire that gives rise to 'vnquiet thoughts' . . . and on the other by his recognition that the lady, as an embodiment of angelic qualities . . . deserves worship rather than passion."[1] Love is called to prepare his "wanton wings and darts of deadly power" so that he may join with spring (the poet-lover) in entertaining "new loue" for the Earth/lady. Just as the empirical lady is addressed as a fictional "faire flowre," the fair flower with which the earth decks herself, so the Earth is told in turn to prepare herself "with diuers colord flowre." The lady, flower, and Earth are to be greeted by the lover, spring, and love; all will participate in the "fresh" love, renewal, the *sacre du printemps*— "*sacre*" as springtime rites and as the holiness of spring. By analogy the lady and lover become part of the cosmic force bringing new life to the earth; love accompanies the lover and spring. "Fresh love," like the lady, must prepare. As Earth, the lady receives; as love, she also participates. As the lady, "fresh youth" reigns in her; as the Earth, "fresh youth" (i.e., spring) rains (engenders) in her.

The reference to Janus is important. As noted earlier, many critics have assumed this reference is to the start of the year in January. Yet the abundance of other calendric references in the sequence indicates that the suggestion of January is part of

Spenser's game, a red herring to distract and, perhaps, to downplay the calendars he employs. More important than the date to which Janus corresponds is his function.[2] Perhaps it was for etymological reasons (because the word "initiation" suggests a new beginning, hence a doorway to a new life) that neophytes were passed through doors, metaphoric and real, in being admitted to secret mysteries. Janus, Ovid's celestial "janitor" (*Fasti* 1.63.288: "Ianitor immensus superis et manibus imis"), associated with doors, has the power to open *and* close. Shortly after Spenser, George Wither (*Emblems*, 1635) was to categorize Janus as the god of mysteries in general; both Erasmus *(Praise of Folly)* and Burton *(The Anatomy of Melancholy)* capture the sense of Janus's "mysterious" qualities in references associating him with double images, double pictures, double vision. Janus's "mystery" here concerns "ambiguity," and in the *Amoretti* the ambiguity often concerns appearance and reality, a theme picked up by the narrator's confusing the fictional with the empirical woman, by the lover's needing to distinguish the patterns of love, and by the reader's misreading the sequence's various levels.

Janus's two faces fit the sequence's quest theme well; one face moves from the old toward the new, eventually leaving the past as the future becomes the present. Yet the old is necessary for marking progress, whether linear (teleological) or vertical (ontological). Janus reminds the narrator, the lady, and the reader of newness as well as oldness. The threshold of his open gate is a mixture of anticipation and trepidation, and the gate itself can become either a closed door or a bridge, both of these terms serving as metaphors for the psychological "crisis" on the path towards enlightenment. Spenser shows this elsewhere in the double face of Doubt (4.10.12):

> Th'one forward looking, th'other backeward bent,
> Therein resembling Ianus auncient,
> Which hath in charge the ingate of the yeare:
> And euermore his eyes about him went,
> As if some proued perill he did feare,
> Or did misdoubt some ill, whose cause did not appeare.

It is significant that this description is of Doubt as the warder of the Temple of Venus, thus associating him with the very situation in which the sonnet narrator finds himself. The sonnet's second line ("doth seeme to promise hope of new delight") is, at best, tenuously hopeful, with "seems" always a watchword in

Spenser's poetry and a good reminder of the "perill" accompany-
ing the "new." Yet the promise of spring is a strong one, par-
ticularly in the sonnet's octave, and the temporal change
encourages the lover to anticipate a season of clear weather and
reciprocated love.

The poem moves from a simple statement of historical time to a
play of personified seasonal figures, progressing then to a gentle
admonition to the lady to prepare herself for love, the lover, and
spring. But while this is being presented we (and the poet) are
also subtly taken out of the abstract idealized world of sonnets 1–
3. As the poet makes his spring/lover, Earth/lady analogies, the
lover finds himself forced to recognize and acknowledge the lady
as a lady, not as an angel or a saint; the courtship is put in motion
because of the sense of time created here and because the first
steps are taken in moving out of the "inner part" into an objective
external world. The poet-lover and the reader gradually realize
that what is about to happen concerns not only the lover and his
lady but forms part of a complex cosmologic system in which
years, seasons, and humanity commingle, moving together in
synchronistic correspondence.

The poem, with its "forth looking," "forth out," "come forth"
refrain, is rich in images reminiscent of Lucretius's invocation to
Venus, various short lyrics by Tasso, Du Bellay's "Du 1er jour de
l'an," the *Georgics*, and numerous medieval and Renaissance
lyrical depictions of springtime. Nor can the carpe diem theme
be overlooked, the introduction of which adds an element of
gentle humor—an element of the sequence that cannot be ne-
glected. The poet who wrote so purely of souls, unquiet thoughts,
sovereign beauties, and writing, now turns to "lusty spring," fresh
love, and wanton wings. The concern with inarticulation is re-
placed by confident depiction; meek humbleness and an afflicted
mood are transformed by an eager wit.

The sonnet also introduces various motifs important later in
the sequence. As the poet plays with language, using the rhetori-
cal game of expressing the inexpressible, and while he assumes
various poses, here in 4 is the first reference to the whole
courtship as an "entertainment." The lady is called on to "enter-
taine" (receive, admit) new love, and is also called on to "enter-
taine" (cherish) a new love—the poet-lover. The two lovers, in
turn, will entertain each other through the sequence, he with his
poetry, complaints, and pleas, she with her smiles, laughter, and
her "stage directions" (*Amor.* 54) for the entertainment. Addi-
tionally, she is to entertain (*inter-tenere*) a new love, both mortal

and divine, which on both levels of the sequence asserts the necessity of proper Christian courtship leading to marriage.

The Earth/lady is also called upon to "decke hir selfe" with "divers colord flowre," and in doing so to weave "her faire mantle." The metaphor of weaving is associated in the sequence both with the lady and the poet; as with so many items in Spenser's poetry, the weaving can be positive as well as negative. Here the "mantle" is both a diversely colored floral garment as well as a covering, something that hides. The weaving thus serves a dual purpose, as it does later in *Amor.* 22, where the lady, like Penelope, weaves a web and then unweaves her work (just as the poet weaves his own verbal web, which the lady unweaves with a look). Thus in *Amor.* 4 weaving has subtle metaphoric connections with cloaking and with webs, connections, in turn, that expand later in the sequence to include nets, baits, hooks, and a host of other constructs, verbal and otherwise.

Sonnets 1–3, then, introduce the persons in the sequence, categorize and create the events. *Amor.* 4 provides the temporal setting. None of these provides any action. Sonnets 5–8, however, display the characters in action, preparing them, as the penitent prepares himself, for that other period of preparation, Lent. The lover's rapturous elevation and the poet's exalted praises now yield to the conflicts of early courtship. In the lady's eyes the lover finds encouragement, spiritual renewal, and a sustaining of the relationship, yet her pride retards his advances. Throughout this approach-avoidance conflict the poet describes the situation in true Petrarchan fashion—as a strong battle fought between two forces, one wishing victory for autonomy, the other seeking it for love and union.

First mentioned in *Amor.* 2 when the poet described the lady as "that fayrest proud," the lady's pride is portrayed in *Amor.* 5 not as an affectation but as an expression of her ideals:

> Rudely thou wrongest my deare harts desire,
>> in finding fault with her too portly pride:
>> the thing which I doo most in her admire,
>> is of the world vnworthy most enuide.
> For in those lofty lookes is close implide,
>> scorn of base things, and sdeigne of foule dishonor:
>> thretning rash eies which gaze on her so wide,
>> that loosely they ne dare to looke vpon her.
> Such pride is praise, such portlinesse is honor,
>> that boldned innocence beares in hir eies:

and her faire countenance like a goodly banner,
spreds in defiaunce of all enemies.
Was neuer in this world ought worthy tride,
without some spark of such self-pleasing pride.

While describing the lady's peculiar "pride," Spenser carefully introduces something new into the sequence; here for the first time we find the "real" world of other people. The "thou" of the first line breaks the inner circle of poet-lady-poem created in the first sonnets. "The world's estimate is based upon the treatment the lady accords it, and she is sometimes censured for what is thought to be arrogance."[3] As a result of the world's castigation the lover immediately finds himself ready to come to the lady's rescue and defense, his argument resting on what he feels is due the lady: praise and honor.

The lady's "portly pride" is worth noting. The poet uses the term and then analyzes it by separating it into its parts, turning the conventional meanings around to suggest it is praiseworthy to have such pride (which will scorn base things). Furthermore, dignity (portliness) in combination with such pride is an honorable quality. By extension, honor is then defined as precisely this kind of stately bearing, and praise itself becomes such pride. Praise and honor come from without; others attribute them to the lady. Pride and portliness come from within; she projects them in her appearance. Their effect is important; implied by her "lofty lookes" is "sdeigne of foule dishonour." The pride and portliness "thret[en] rash eies which gaze on her so wide," a minor motif in which rash men's frail eyes, which look on base things and wander in darkness, must be lifted by being "enlumind" (*Amor.* 66).

The couplet "Was never in this world ought worthy tride, / without some spark of such self-pleasing pride" is not only the poet's defense but his recognition that the lady's pride is a necessary element of the angelic qualities earlier attributed to her (in *Amor.* 1 and 3). It also provides a humorous statement on his own condition. Nothing worthwhile was ever "tride" ("attempted," but also "proved," as well as "refined")—even the poetry as well as the forthcoming agon of the bilevel "courtship"—without an element of self-regard. That "spark," in turn, is ambiguously either "a small amount" or a reference to a "spark" of the same "light whereof hath kindled heavenly fyre / in my fraile breast" (3). In either case the lover takes a stand against the intrusive, uncomprehending world.

Yet when the tables are turned, when the lady's "portly pride" affects the lover as it affected the world in 5, the poet is ready to pen a different remonstrance. Like Mirabella's pride (6.8.19), the pride here causes a "direfull smart"; in the sonnets, though, it is the lover, not the lady, who feels the pain. In *Amor.* 6 that same pride (which he called "praise" in 5) becomes "rebellious pride" and the cause of his self-comforting monologue:

> Be nought dismayd that her vnmoued mind
>   doth still persist in her rebellious pride:
>   such loue, not lyke to lusts of baser kynd,
>   the harder wonne, the firmer will abide.

Rebellious because it will not yield to him, this pride is worshiped (*Amor.* 2) and admired (*Amor.* 5). But the lover quickly qualifies his love, and in doing so gives the poet the opportunity for another analogy among the lady, love, and nature: "Such loue not lyke to lusts of baser kynd, / the harder wonne, the firmer will abide." The poet then presents what might be viewed as the exemplum of this sermonic sonnet:

> The durefull Oake, whose sap is not yet dride,
>   is long ere it conceiue the kindling fyre:
>   but when it once doth burne, it doth diuide
>   great heat, and makes his flames to heauen aspire.
> So hard it is to kindle new desire,
>   in gentle brest that shall endure for euer:
>   deepe is the wound, that dints the parts entire
>   with chast affects, that naught but death can seuer.

The lesson the lover supposedly will learn from the poet is this: "Then thinke not long in taking little paine, / to knit the knot, that euer shall remaine." Here, in the early stages of the sequence, is the preparation for the great turning of *Amor.* 67, when the lady is "fyrmely tyde." And here also is a reminder of Red Cross who, with "his owne two hands the holy knots did knit, / that none but death for euer can deuide" (1.12.37).

Although readers may note the poem's submerged sexuality, the lover assures himself his love is pure; the "new desire" is not, he states, like to baser lusts. Its rebellious pride compared to sap, the lady's oaklike, unmoved mind must be purified of that same pride so that the oak can burn with a pure ardor. Yet the solution appears easier in theory than in actual practice; the little pains the lover intends to take do not remain little very long. The lady's "proud heart" does not turn to him, and in *Amor.* 10 he complains of her lording "in [the] licentious blisse / of her freewill" and scorning love. She refuses to be "moov'd with reason or with rewth" (11) and the confidence with which the poet sermonized on the eventual drying of her pride is short-lived. By 18 he will complain that he cannot "with many a dropping teare, / and long intreaty soften her hard hart." Her "hard hart" and her pride, he forgets, are aspects of that "boldned innocence" he so recently praised as an admirable quality. Being part of his rhetorical pose, the poet's "long intreaties" and dropping tears are ineffective with the lady, who demands complete sincerity, not affected and planned strategy.

The poet, however, protests too much. For all the poem's emphasis on the heavenly aspirations of the flames, the new desires kindled in gentle breasts, and the chaste effects of this love, there remain the baser lusts, the conception of kindling fires, burning heat, and deep wounds. Even the "knot" of line 12 has its sexual connotations, as Donne was later to depict in "The Ecstasy," where the lover seeks "to knit / that subtle knot, which makes us man."

The sonnet contains an admirable balance of images concerning the lady and the poet; those associated with her, testify to her "unmoved mind," which the poet only later comprehends as constancy. That unmoved mind is supported by words such as "still," "hard," "firm," "durefull," and "endure." Those images associated with him, derive from his own fire: "kynd," "kindling," "kindle," "burn," "great heat," "flames." Spenser is a master of positioning key words in rhyming situations; not only do the words have aural connections, but they often provide etymological and semantic connectives that enforce and support one another. The lady's "pride" (line 2) is partly that which will "abide" (line 4). But the "dride" oak (line 5) will eventually "divide" (line 7) its great heat. The heat is generated by its "fyre" (line 6), which will "aspire" (line 8); this rising motion is countered by the "new desire" (line 9), which will burn inside, in the "parts entire" (line 10).

With quiet humor, then, the poet plays on how his heat eventually will spark desire in the lady, who until then remains hard (L. *durus*, hence "durefull" and "enduring") as oak. All will be changed in the conflagratory dividing of great heat, that consummation (literally) devoutly to be wished. Even the "be nought" of the first line is changed into the verbal pun on "knit the knot" of the last line, and aurally the poem comes full circle in such sound.

At this point in the sequence the witty poet is clearly in control of his Petrarchan pose; he writes well, knows the correct images and proceeds with balance, antithesis, and clever word-play. He plays his part exactly as it should be played and assumes that the lady, both in her own "role" as *donna angelicata* and as cruel fair, is playing those roles, too. Hence she can be angelic as well as proud; hence, too, she should remain unwon by this first volley. In this game, he is to play the ardent suitor, she the cool, reserved Ideal. She is to rebuff and he is to complain of the pain such rejection causes, but he is to accept the pain with dignity— and then move on to further courting. In the game there will be some "little paine" involved before her acceptance—assuming the game goes as it should.

Nevertheless, the poet is concerned with more than just la-menting the lady's hardness, and his laments are quieted by his fascination with the lady's eyes. Over one half the sonnets in this first section (1–21) concern themselves either completely or par-tially with this aspect of the beloved. In Spenser, as in Dante and Petrarch, eyes almost always have ennobling powers. Addressed in *Amor.* 7 as "fayre eyes, the myrrour of my mazed heart," the eyes send forth darts of life and death. The lover worships their bright beams while the eyes "kindle liuing fire" within his breast.

Her eyes are noted in one way or another in *Amor.* 1, 5, 7, 8, 9, 10, 12, 13, 15, 16, 17, 21, 24, 35, 36, 37, 40, 44, 45, 47, 49, 54, 57, 61, 64, 73, 78, 81, 83, and 88, making those eyes one of the major and most complex motifs in the sequence. In various ways the motif has connections with the lady's light, her soul, her beauty; with inspiration, the courtly tradition, fashioning and reforming, beatitude and blessing; with mirror motifs, lusts (of various sorts), war images, rejection and acceptance. In other ways the extensive use of eye images, particularly before the betrothal, suggests that the poet has become caught in a semantic trap in which he exhibits his inability to express more than a simplistic, reiterated Petrarchan convention in which a life-death dichot-omy is reductively literalized.[4] In still other ways the eye images are connected with seeing, with vision, with looks and percep-tion; not "seeing" correctly is precisely the problem the poet and the lover experience when looking for and at the wrong lady while ignoring the empirical lady, who is visible to them only in the latter part of the sequence.

In *Amor.* 7, where the eyes are "fayre" (the most frequently used adjective in the *Amoretti*), they are the "myrrour of [the lover's] mazed hart," "mazed" suggesting both "amazed" and "confused."

> Fayre eyes, the myrrour of my mazed hart,
>   what wondrous vertue is contaynd in you,
>   the which both lyfe and death forth from you dart
>   into the obiect of your mighty view?

Spenser fills the sonnet with a "maze" of his own. On one level the sonnet appears to consist of a traditional extended Petrarchan conceit; on another it is a complex of images that do and do not "work" in traditional ways. For example, the lover's amazement is due to the eyes' power to send out beams of life and death (one of the great Petrarchan paradoxes) and the poet's bewilderment resulting from that situation. In *Amor.* 2 he had attributed life- and death-giving abilities to the lady; in 3 he was "dazed" by her brightness. Here he focuses on her eyes as that part of her that is responsible both for such power and for the light. While the lady's eyes function as a mirror, this lady is simultaneously giving light (the "lamping eyes" of *Amor.* 1) and mirroring the light she sheds on the lover. In many medieval and Renaissance "mirror" poems, the lady reflects the lover, who in turn reflects the lady; here, this is not the case.

Although the lover is the receiver of the lady's light, having taken the light into himself and fashioned an image with it, his own "light" (in the form of that image in his heart) can get only as far as her eyes, where it is mirrored back to him. Her heart is not reached by his light, although his heart is reached by her light. While she is the beloved object of his love, he is, at this point, only the object of her "mighty view." To put it more simply, the seeds are here of the important Narcissus image used later in *Amor.* 35 and 83; the lover looks upon the lady, sees in her the image of his own interior lady (anima), and is in love with, and awed by, that image. His problem with her reflection of his reflection (ad infinitum) will not be resolved until *Amor.* 66 (the Good Friday sonnet), in which the lady's and the lover's respective "lights" are distinguished from each other:

> For now your light doth more it selfe dilate,
>   and in my darknesse greater doth appeare.
>   Yet since your light hath once enlumind me,
>   with my reflex yours shall encreased be.

For the time, the poet contents himself in *Amor.* 7 with the life-death images:

> For when ye mildly looke with louely hew,
>   then is my soule with life and loue inspired:
>   but when ye lowre, or looke on me askew,
>   then doe I die, as one with lightning fyred.
> But since that lyfe is more then death desyred,
>   looke ever louely, as becomes you best,
>   that your bright beames of my weake eies admyred,
>   may kindle liuing fire within my brest.

There are various connections here with the previous sonnet; the words "inspired," "fyred" and "desyred" echo the earlier "fyre," "aspire," and "desyre." And the "kynd," "kindling," "kindle" image of *Amor.* 6, where "fyre" and "new desire" were bred, now is condensed and focused on the kindling of "living fire" within the lover's breast. Living fire is better than the "inward bale" that filled his "love pined hart" in *Amor.* 2, but he still has far to go.

The sharpness of "little paine" (6) is intensified in *Amor.* 7 in the lightning image of line 8, where the lightning not only becomes the physical actuality of the death that "darts" from the lady's eyes (line 3) but is in itself a dart; furthermore, in one of Spenser's semantically significant rhymes, the "dart" of line 3 is directed at the "hart" of line 1. A subtle ambiguity reminds us of the poet's craftiness: the lady's "louring" causes him to die "as one with lightning" consumed ("fyred"). The little flames that grew to great heat in *Amor.* 6 now become intensified and concentrated in the fire of the lightning bolt. But "lightning fyred" also refers to the darts the lady fires from her eyes, reminding him again of the power of those "bright beams." His own projected death in *Amor.* 7 is the hyperbolic result of the lady's look, just as in *Amor.* 25 it will be the "last ensample" of her pride.

In a series of parallels and juxtapositions the couplet conjoins the scattered images of the first twelve lines:

> Such life should be the honor of your light,
> such death the sad ensample of your might,

where "honor" and "ensample" serve as reminders of two major functions of the sequence, honoring the lady and providing (through the "lesson" of 68) an "ensample" of right loving.

In *Amor.* 8 (the only *Amoretti* sonnet written in a Shakespearean stanzaic form), the "fayre eyes" of 7 become

More then most faire, full of the liuing fire,
  Kindled aboue vnto the maker neare:
  no eies but ioyes, in which al powers conspire,
  that to the world naught else be counted deare.
Thrugh your bright beams doth not the blinded guest
  shoot out his darts to base affections wound?
  but Angels come to lead fraile mindes to rest
  in chast desires on heauenly beauty bound.
You frame my thoughts and fashion me within,
  you stop my toung, and teach my hart to speake,
  you calme the storme that passion did begin,
  strong thrugh your cause, but by your vertue weak.
Dark is the world, where your light shined neuer;
  well is he borne, that may behold you euer.

The "fyre" of *Amor.* 6, and the "living fire" kindled in the poet's breast in 7, now become the "living fire / Kindled aboue vnto the maker neare." The initial quatrain provides an apostrophe in which the descriptions provide a "second-thought" version of ideas begun earlier in 1–6, more closely formulated in 7, and now expanded into the superlatives of 8. The "fair eyes" are now "more than most faire." "Living fire" just kindled in the breast now fills the "most faire" (either the lady or the lady's eyes, or both). The fire first applied to both the lady and the lover in 6, then compartmentalized into the fire within him in 7, now is balanced by the fire within her in 8.

Various transformations also appear in this sonnet. The eyes, which had "wondrous virtue" in *Amor.* 7, now become "ioyes, in which all powers conspire." The "virtue" itself, in the sense of power, is further clarified in *Amor.* 8 when "al powers" appear, ambiguously, as the lady's power and as the lover's faculties (represented by his tongue, thoughts, heart, base affections and his chaste desires), and as the powers of angels (line 7), the powers of Cupid (line 6), and the power of authority that comes from association with "the Maker" (line 2). The "aspire" of *Amor.* 6, changed to the "inspired" of *Amor.* 7, now becomes "conspire," as all the powers "breath together" for mutual effect. Her "bright beams" appear again, but whereas in *Amor.* 7 they were associated with eyes that darted forth death and life, in 8 they "shoot out . . . darts to base affections wound." In lines 5–6 the eye beams are used as vehicles for "the blinded guest," Cupid. In another ambiguous phrase Spenser allows Cupid to "shoot out his darts to base affections wound," either meaning the wounding of base affections or the providing of the base for affection's wound. Both work. Cupid may shoot but angels lead (line 7); the former action creates distance, the latter draws the mind closer. In writing thus, the poet finds in the lady's eyes not "base affection" but "heavenly beauty."

The third quatrain is especially important. Its verbs, "frame," "fashion," "stop," "teach," "calm," provide a miniature version of the lady's actions throughout a larger part of the sequence. Like Temperance itself in 2.12.1, the lady becomes the architect of the poet's soul, providing for it a "goodly frame." In the sequence the framing occurs, from start to finish, in the poems themselves; for the poet the "frame" is a necessity, and without it he could not be a poet. Throughout the sequence, the lady is both his inspiration as well as the *techne*, the framing craft through which the poet gives shape to his work.[5] For the lover, the "framing" provides the image of the lady (albeit a distorted one at first). The poet already has spoken of such framing and fashioning in his comments in *Amor.* 1–3 on the poetic process; he also observed in 3 how she stops his tongue and pen with "thoughts astonishment" and "fancies wonderment." She fashions him in various ways: the empirical lady forces him to alter his perspective, to see more correctly, to become a new person with a revision of reality. And she fashions him by providing a model of right behavior.

Furthermore, she provides the poet with ample criticism, "stopping his tongue" but leading him to more "natural" poetry. This is all part of the lover's educative redemption, through which process the lady eventually will lead him, both directly and indirectly, to his own self-realization. This, in turn, provides on the surface level his poetic salvation, redemption, and atonement. On the analogic level the same applies, but there the context is his soul's healing and at-one-ment. The poet's stilted Petrarchanisms, his well-crafted but opaque poetry, the lover's astounded comments, are "stopped," cut off, thwarted by the lady who then attempts to teach his heart, and his art, to speak correctly. Both he and his art are to have life—and more abundantly. This is dramatized throughout the sequence's Lenten section until finally "all these stormes . . . turne to caulmes" at the start of Holy Week (*Amor.* 62) and soon thereafter, when the lover is "taught" the Lord's lesson in 68.

Once again Spenser uses the couplet for a witty comment on the poem's action. In contrast to the great fire and the bright beams is the dark world when the lady's eyes do not shine; to make the condition even more emphatic, line 13 ends with "never." In contrast with this is the "ever" of the last line, not only the positive antonym of the negative previous rhyme word but a link with the "endure for ever" of *Amor.* 6 and the "looke ever lovely" of *Amor.* 7. "Well is he borne" also has several meanings with which the poet plays: "borne," in its most obvious sense, is born. But it is also (1) "held" (in the sense of borne up, and thus an extended pun leading to "that may behold you ever"), (2) "carried" (as with the angels leading "fraile mindes to rest"), and (3) "limited" (tying it to "beauty bound").

Finally, one cannot overlook the rather overt religious overtones of *Amor.* 8. Even without knowing the sequence's bilevel significance, it would be difficult not to hear echoes of traditional religious language and references. And while one-to-one parallels between the lady and Christ cannot be applied, much of the sonnet can be read as addressed not just to the lady but also to Christ, "more then most faire, full of the living fire," and so forth. The lady, like God, frames and fashions the lover; she, like Christ, calms his storms and teaches him. Such a reading adds meaningful dimensions to the poem's interpretation, and especially to the last lines, as the *homo amorosus* conjoins with the *homo religiosus.*

While on the surface level there appears a movement away from Petrarchan love to a neo-Platonized Christian love, the lover still views the lady as an idealized projection depicted in "poetical" language. Her presence is clearly an ennobling experience, but the action of the sonnet is internal, inside the poet, not external and not between the empirical lover and empirical lady, who does nothing in these sonnets. Her eyes emit and reflect, she "frames" and "fashions" and "stops," and so forth, but all these actions have no observable outer expression.

Outer expression is a significant problem for the lover as well as for the poet. For the lover it means the lady will have little way of knowing what he is thinking; for the poet it means being confined to writing as much about his problems with writing as to writing about the lady. Such is the case in *Amor.* 9, where his search for suitable expression constitutes virtually the entire conceit. In his sonnet-long highly rhetorical *aporia,* he writes:

> Long-while I sought to what I might compare
>   those powrefull eies, which lighten my dark spright,
>   yet find I nought on earth to which I dare
>   resemble th'ymage of their goodly light.

In *Amor.* 8 the poet again expressed his inexpressibility; his tongue was stopped and the "speaking" was in his heart. But the search for expression now becomes explicit; not only is the lover/ poet heard but he is seen searching for the right ways to "compare" the lady's eyes. Echoes of "noughts" immediately sound through what he has sought: "nought" and "knot" of *Amor.* 6 and "naught" of 7. And his concern with eyes reverberates not only through the "eies" but that word's sound repetitions in "I," "lighten," "spright," and "light." "I" blends into "eye" and vice versa, and the aural reception, combined with syntactical ambiguity, confuses the two. In line 3, for example, "find I nought on earth to which I dare . . ." may be comprehended as either "I find nothing on earth to which I dare" or "there is 'nought' eye on earth to which an eye dare. . . ." This impacts on the fourth line; if line 3 is heard as "I dare," then the meaning is simply "resemble, that is, compare, the image." But little in Spenser is simple, except Truth. If line 4 is heard as "eye dare" then there is a reference to the eye reassembling the image of the particularized "goodly light."

Capturing in words the "ymage" of the powerful eyes is part of the poet's problem. In one sense he strives to fashion, to reassemble, his various already-painted pictures of eyes that are lamping, have a blessed look, possess lofty looks, and dart forth death and life. Yet in another sense he, as a poet, is seeking the literary images in which to continue his already-vague description. And so his fixation with her "eyes" and their goodly light continues:

> Not to the Sun: for they doo shine by night;
>   nor to the Moone: for they are changed neuer;
>   nor to the Starres: for they haue purer sight;
>   not to the fire: for they consume not euer;
> Nor to the lightning: for they still perseuer;
>   nor to the Diamond: for they are more tender;
>   nor vnto Christall: for nought may them seuer;
>   nor vnto glasse: such basenesse mought offend her.

The items to which he might compare her eyes are, for the most part, concrete objects—sun, moon, stars, diamond, crystal, glass. But he is attempting to compare them with something nonsubstantive, the "goodly light." He generates conceit after conceit, metaphor after metaphor, never recognizing that each is a conceit for another conceit, each a metaphor for another metaphor. Thus, although expanding his list, he reduces his options. He lists eight items, each of which has a flaw. The ninth item in this ninth sonnet has all the qualities the others possess, as well as some they do not. If *Amor.* 8 implied an analogue between the lady and Christ, *Amor.* 9 makes the comparison directly. Since the other items he listed cannot be compared to the "goodly light,"

> Then to the Maker selfe they likest be,
>   whose light doth lighten all that here we see.

In *Amor.* 8 the lady and her eyes were full of living fire "kindled aboue vnto the maker neere"; here the closeness and identification are extended by noting that her eyes' goodly light is actually comparable to the "Maker selfe." Just as the lady's light lightens the world in *Amor.* 8 and in 9, and as the poet's dark spirit is lightened (line 2) by her brightness (lightened both in the sense of "illuminated" and also as "relieved of a burden"), so the Maker's light "lightens" all.

Having reached such a conclusion he can go no further; like Dante he must return from the vision of the Rose, and like Red Cross leave his Mount of Contemplation. Just as spring's intervention disrupts the amazement, astonishment, and wonderment of *Amor.* 3, so a Petrarchan love-as-war conceit shows the direction the narrator's poetry takes once he reaches an impasse. The three sonnets (7, 8, and 9) depicting the lady as a *donna angelicata* are contrasted with three (10, 11, and 12) showing her in quite a different role. Petrarch's "dolce guerrera," Baif's "belle ennemie," and Desportes' "douce adversaire" are here less *dolce, belle,* or *douce* than most readers would like:

> Vnrighteous Lord of loue what law is this,
>   that me thou makest thus tormented be?
>   the whiles she lordeth in licentious blisse
>   of her freewill, scorning both thee and me.
> See how the Tyrannesse doth ioy to see
>   the huge massacres which her eyes do make:
>   and humbled harts brings captiues vnto thee,
>   that thou of them mayst mightie vengeance take.

Martz notes that the tone of this poem is hard to describe, and that it is touched with "humor, parody, or comedy."[6] On one level he is certainly correct. The same eyes just lauded as godlike now cause "huge massacres" and will soon attempt to ambush the lover (*Amor.* 11). Her proud heart needs shaking; her high look needs humility.

The poet begins with a universal: Love is responsible for problems. He moves to the particular: Love has somewhat lost control of this situation. The expansive movement of the lady's free will is reversed in lines 7–8, when the lady returns her captives to Love, who, therefore, must still be in control. The third quatrain suggests some punishments:

> But her proud hart doe thou a little shake
>   and that high look, with which she doth comptroll
>   all this worlds pride bow to a baser make,
>   and al her faults in thy black booke enroll.

The couplet, which refers to the poet for the first time since line 4, gives perhaps the first clue as to what really is happening: "That I may laugh at her in equall sort, / as she doth laugh at me and makes my pain her sport."[7]

Outside the frame of the sequence the empirical lady has apparently been laughing at the poet-lover's efforts. Her reality is beginning to enter the interior world and his own "hart" is being "humbled" in a way he finds disconcerting. His love play apparently is proving ineffective; his poetry, ineffectual. The "litle paine" (6) has proven greater than he anticipated and the lady simply is not playing the game the way he feels she should. His depiction of the situation, humorous to readers (Tuve calls this tone "delicate mockery") and even witty to him as poet, nevertheless reflects exactly the kind of "loving" of which the lady disapproves.

The Court of Love language is far too familiar, both for the lady and for the reader. The poet's witty employment of the legal machinery in "unrighteous," "law," "licentious," "freewill," is supplanted in the second quatrain by military images in "tyrannesse," "massacres," "captive," and "vengeance." "Tormented" serves well to describe his condition; in addition to its usual meaning there is its Latin root, *tormentum*, referring, in general, not only to an engine of war but, in particular, to a torture device concerning twisting or pressing, a condition evident in the poems and the thinking they reflect.

A set of interior words further helps illuminate the situation. When the lady is said to bring the humbled "harts" to the Lord of Love, the poet is playing upon "hearts" and "harts," the deer image that functions so prominently in 67. Both hearts and harts are humbled, meaning humble in the usual sense of the word, but also a play on "umbles," the innards of a deer (Greene uses this term in *Friar Bacon*, where Margaret has "butter and cheese, and humbles of a Deere" for breakfast). The dear/deer image is picked up in the third quatrain where love is called on to "her proud hart doe thou a little shake," both in the sense of shaking her pride and of "shaking an animal" by worrying or scaring it out into the open. On the one hand the lady is the hunter in control of the situation; on the other hand she is viewed as the hunted. In yet another sense the lover himself is both hunter and hunted, terms that direct the reader to the last line, in which the poet's pains are the lady's "sport." He is one of the "humbled harts" of which she makes sport. Only much later, in *Amor.* 80, will the word "sport" appear again, at which time it will be the lover who will "sport his muse"/lady.

Amor. 11 continues in the same vein, with the poet complaining and pleading the same case he began in *Amor.* 10. The metaphor of captivity, begun in *Amor.* 1 when "those lilly hands" held the poetry "in loues soft bands, / lyke captiues trembling at the victors sight," had been recast in a Petrarchan setting in 10; in 11 and 12 the poet expands the literal implications of the tyranny and vengeance.

> Dayly when I do seeke and sew for peace,
>   And hostages doe offer for my truth:
>   she cruell warriour doth her selfe addresse
>   to battell, and the weary war renew'th.
> Ne wilbe moou'd with reason or with rewth,
>   to graunt small respit to my restlesse toile:
>   but greedily her fell intent poursewth,
>   Of my poore life to make vnpittied spoile.

The wit with which he entered his own game of love has drawn him into a world of metaphor in which he, like Amoret, finds himself captive. The "little paine" in *Amor.* 6, which became "my pain" in 10, here becomes "my restlesse toile," "torment and turmoyle." The lighthearted descriptions of a lady who could be sparked to burn, who could become an "ensample," and who could be compared only to "the Maker selfe," now "ne wilbe moov'd with reason or with rewth, / to graunt small respit to my restlesse toile." The inexpressibility motif of *Amor.* 2, 3, and 9 now takes a serious turn as he realizes his word-ability really is ineffective, thus threatening the poet's very existence as a poet.

The imagery from *Amor.* 10 carries into 11. In the former poem the lady took "humbled harts" (brought captive) to the Lord of

Love. Here it is the lover who brings the hostages (as he did with his poems in *Amor.* 1) to the lady, who now has assumed Love's position. The lover takes them daily as he "seeke[s] and sew[s] for peace." His seeking refers both to his search and to his requests, the legal connotations of which tie them both to *Amor.* 10 and to his "suing," which is his (legal) petitioning, his attendance on her, and his wooing. He is in the same position Mirabella's lovers experienced, she who "was belou'd of many a gentle Knight, / and sude and sought with all the seruice dew" (6.8.20). The "speaking" and "writing" to which he earlier referred have now become "restlesse toile," referring to his writing, his wooing, and his warfare (Middle English *toile*, "battle").

Once again the poet provides some personal reassurance. Earlier he had reminded himself with certainty to "thinke not long in taking litle paine / to knit the knot that ever shall remaine." Here the tone is more serious and the message a bit equivocal: "All paine hath end, and every war hath peace; / But mine no price nor prayer may surcease." His initial "seeking" and "suing" now connected with the "prayer" and "price," the poet admits the inefficacy of his poetry to accomplish that of which earlier he was so assured.

The most significant portion of this poem is its third quatrain:

> Yet my poore life, all sorrowes to assoyle,
> I would her yield, her wrath to pacify:
> but then she seekes with torment and turmoyle,
> to force me liue and will not let me dy.
> All paine hath end and euery war hath peace,
> but mine no price nor prayer may surcease.

What is learned from the extrasonnet relationship is that (1) he daily "seeke[s] and sew[s]," and (2) he and she are both willingly engaged in this continuing relationship. The alternative of abandoning the quest, accepting defeat, discontinuing the courtship, is never presented. If the lady were merely attempting to rebuff his advances, there most likely would not be daily suits, nor would she "force" him to live. As it is, and as we (and the lover) discover in *Amor.* 67, the steadfast lady is indeed forcing him to live, forcing him into life, so that a real, not a fictional, relationship may develop.

The warfare images continue for yet another sonnet. The "daily" seeking of *Amor.* 11 narrows to "one day" at the start of *Amor.* 12:

> One day I sought with her hart-thrilling eies,
>> to make a truce and termes to entertaine:
>> all fearelesse then of so false enimies,
>> which sought me to entrap in treasons traine.

The fresh compound-epithet "hart-thrilling" returns to his fixation with the lady's eyes, which in the usual sense of the word actually do "thrill" the heart; they also "thrill" in the old sense of "pierce." By rhyme and slant spelling the "eies" connect with "enimies." The legal imagery reappears in "truce" and "terms," and the military images in "truce," "enimies," "entrap" and "traine."

Once more the "eyes" have it throughout the poem, with verbal play, direct and indirect, asserting the eyes' importance:

> So as I then disarmed did remaine,
>> a wicked ambush which lay hidden long
>> in the close couert of her guilefull eyen,
>> thence breaking forth did thick about me throng.
> Too feeble I t'abide the brunt so strong,
>> was forst to yeeld my selfe into their hands:
>> who me captiuing streight with rigorous wrong,
>> haue euer since me kept in cruell bands.
> So Ladie now to you I doo complaine,
>> against your eies that iustice I may gaine.

"I," "eies," "enemies," "eyen," "t'abide," and "eies" are aural and visual connectives of the eyes. The "hart-thrilling" eyes become "guilefull eyen" in line 7 as the poet moves from his efforts to strike a truce toward the eyes' deception in thwarting his strategy. In Amor. 10 he sought to have her proud heart shaken and her high look lowered; that effort not working, he seeks "termes." A witty play on words is a reminder of the gentle humor behind what appears to be another very serious sonnet. Since Amor. 1 the poems, with their terms (leaves, lines, rhymes), have been sent to "please," that is, "entertaine" her. And the "truce" itself has etymological connections with fidelity (as when Artegall's friends are drawn "to termes of gentle truce," 3.2.24), a reminder that behind the wit, behind the complaints, is the love story that ends in betrothal and eventually in marriage.

The captivity motif is central in this sonnet; the lady's eyes are "false enimies" (either "not really enemies" or "deceptive enemies") that seek (as he "seeke[s]" in 11) to "entrap in treasons traine." Hidden ambushes, close coverts, "guilefull eyen," and captivity lead to the "cruell bands" in which the lover is kept. But noted above is that the painful Petrarchan captivity images are transformed into "sweet . . . bands" (65) in Christian betrothal and a "louely band" in Christian marriage (*Epith.* 396). Importantly, the poet prepares for this transformation by the connections here and elsewhere of "bands" and "hands," the pairing that already occurred as early as *Amor.* 1.

The couplet presents an important turn in the sequence. On the sequence's analogical level is the movement into a new phase of the calendar; *Amor.* 12 is in the position of 3 February, Sexagesima Sunday. Likewise, the courtship moves to a new phase as a result of the lover's action at the end of this poem. For the first time in the sequence, the poet-lover directly addresses the lady. In *Amor.* 1 he addressed his own poetry; in 2, his "unquiet thought." In the meditative 3 he wrote/spoke to himself; in 4 his focus was "you, faire flowre"; in 5, an external audience ("thou"); in 6, himself; in 7 and 8, her eyes; in 9, himself; in 10, the "unrighteous Lord of Love"; and in 11, himself. Here he finally turns to her: "So Ladie now to you I doo complaine, / against your eies that iustice I may gaine."

As subtle as it is, this is actually the first real step the lover has taken in moving from his internal projection of the idealized lady to recognition of the external, empirical woman with whom he is in love. Having complained to her eyes, having complained to the Lord of Love, he now presents his complaint (his lament, his charge, his poem) to her. The reference to "iustice" in the final line brings full circle the references to eyes in these three *dolce guerera* sonnets, thus returning to the "unrighteous" reference in *Amor.* 10.

The war metaphors, the Court of Love scene, the Petrarchan conceits, all serve as part of the lover's psychological defense mechanism against what he perceives as the lady's rebuttals and her laughing at his efforts. When approaching her as the *donna angelicata* does not prove effective, the poet's reflexive action is to move into the tropology of viewing her as the *dolce guerera*. Readers, removed and detached from the lover's actions, witness not only the involved poet but some of the actions behind the scenes. Yet the difficulties encountered at this phase of the sequence are precisely those the lady encounters at this stage of the courtship: the reader and the lady are not only involved with a man deeply in love, but with a man who believes he best expresses himself in the conventions of Petrarchan poetry. When he is sincere, when he is projecting, when he is suppressing, is not always clear to the reader or to the lady. The poet's "game" is one in which the poet at times loses himself; the lady's corrective game, at least at this time, occasionally intensifies the lover's misdirection. In reading the poems it is easily forgotten that the poet-lover willingly engages in the action and at any point could end the conflicts. The same holds true for the empirical lady, who has but to shut her door, return his letters, refuse to see him. Her own refusal to let the wooing/suing/battle cease and her "daily" hearing/reading of his "termes" are important in the ontological and spiritual development both of the lover and the poet. Like the spiritual goal on the analogic level, the lady remains stationary from the start of the sequence—so stationary, so steadfast, that she clearly *is* attainable. The major problem observed, then, is how to overcome the antagonistic and base nature in man (and his self-expressions—in this case, the poetry) so that one may conjoin the real with the ideal.

At one point in the early part of the sequence the lover comes very close to the view eventually taken much later when he discerns the lady not as a saint but as a woman. (By analogy this is much the same way the Christian contemplates that which the liturgical season of Lent actually celebrates—Christ's divinity *and* his humanity.)

> In that proud port, which her so goodly graceth,
>   whiles her faire face she reares vp to the skie:
> and to the ground her eie lids low embaseth,
>   most goodly temperature ye may descry,
> Myld humblesse mixt with awfull maiesty.

In these first lines of *Amor.* 13 the poet writes himself out of the constricting metaphors of the previous several sonnets; the opaque and obtrusive Petrarchan imagery yields to the lover's clearer explanation of those elements that have so distressed him:

> For looking on the earth whence she was borne,
>   her minde remembreth her mortalitie,
>   what so is fayrest shall to earth returne.
> But that same lofty countenance seems to scorne
>   base thing, and thinke how she to heauen may clime:
>   treading downe earth as lothsome and forlorne,
>   that hinders heauenly thoughts with drossy slime.
> Yet lowly still vouchsafe to looke on me,
>   such lowlinesse shall make you lofty be.

As in the previous sonnet, the lover first apprehends and then addresses the lady directly. Additionally, he is becoming more discerning as he analyzes her "goodly temperature," setting in juxtaposition her seemingly extreme qualities and then showing how the lady reconciles them. Her "proud port," for example, contains both "myld humblesse" and "awfull maiesty," just as earlier he discerned her pride as innocence and her "portlinesse" as honor. Heaven and earth are likewise juxtaposed, as are neo-Platonic and Christian interpretations of both. The couplet contains the Christian paradox that counters the neo-Platonic presentation of the lady's pride, and the psalmist's words are clearly echoed: "he who is humbled shall be exalted." Just as the lady will reconcile mental and physical beauty in *Amor.* 15 ("but that which fairest is, but few behold, / her mind adornd with vertues manifold"), and nature and art in *Amor.* 21, so here she becomes the perfect tempering of pride and humility.

The lady's "embasing" (lowering) of her eyes is love's answer to the lover's prayer (*Amor.* 10) that her "high look" might bow to a "baser make." Lowering of her eyes while holding high her "faire face" suggests a view of temperance depicted as "humblesse mixt with . . . majesty." The poet then proceeds with his more detailed analysis by giving the rest of the second quatrain to the "humblesse" and the third quatrain to her "lofty countenance."

The poet's wit and gentle humor are also evident, and he craftily directs attention up and down during the progress of his description. The first quatrain has the lady facing up, although her eyes look down. Line 5 begins with the "down"-viewed humility and moves "up" to the majesty. Lines 6–8 view the earth, while 9–12 show the lady's thoughts climbing heavenward. These actions are compacted in the couplet where the poet pulls the lady's attention back by asking her to look at him. "Yet lowly" can refer to her or to him; her looking will be an act of "lowlinesse," just as he himself represents the "lowlinesse" on which she is to look. The last direction is up, in the paradox of humbling for exaltation. Yet beyond the humor is Spenser's concern for the role of women, some of whom (like Radigund and Mirabella) are proud and lacking in the requisite and complementary humility.

The sonnet becomes a witty yet serious reminder to the lady, to whom it is addressed, that pride is acceptable if and when mixed with humility. Being able to make the comment is important in the lover's progress because he can have this exchange with the empirical woman exterior to himself. His reflection on the vari-

ous features of the lady's person are solidified in *Amor.* 14, where
he provides for them an object with which to identify—the
castle. From the "loftiness" with which he concludes 13, the poet
comes crashing to the earth with his own return to the love-as-
war metaphors. Writing in the long-standing courtly tradition,
the poet depicts himself as tempter of the castle-lady:

> Retourne agayne my forces late dismayd,
>> Vnto the siege by you abandon'd quite,
>> great shame it is to leaue like one afrayd,
>> so fayre a peece for one repulse so light.
> Gaynst such strong castle needeth greter might,
>> then those small forts which yet were wont belay;
>> such haughty mynds enur'd to hardy fight,
>> disdayne to yield vnto the first assay.

The situation is close to that described in the attacks on the
House of Alma (2.9.14–17), and the pun on "dismayd" is remi-
niscent of Britomart's experience with the taming of the croco-
dile (5.7.15), where Britomart goes to bed a maid (5.7.16) and
awakens "dismayd." The sonnet's submerged sexual allusions in
"dismayd," "belay," the "castles" and "forts," and subsequent
"dying" may be clever, but they get the narrator nowhere. He
calls on all his forces to batter her heart. One gets to the heart, he
feels, in precisely the way he has been attempting to do so:

> Bring therefore all the forces that ye may,
>> and lay incessant battery to her heart,
>> playnts, prayers, vowes, ruth, sorrow, and dismay,
>> those engins can the proudest loue conuert.

He has already tried "playnts" in *Amor.* 12 ("complaine"),
prayers in 10 (addressed to the "unrighteous Lord of loue"), vows
in 6 (to continue taking "litle paine, / to knit the knot"), "ruth" in
11, sorrow (implied throughout, but noted especially in 1, 2, and
11), and "dismay" in 6 ("be nought dismayd") and in this sonnet.
Contrary to what he claims, these devices have failed to "con-
uert" her, but he has not yet moved sufficiently away from his
"old" self to abandon these poses. Even his oxymoronic alter-
native plan is a throwback to earlier approaches: "And if those
fayle fall downe and dy before her, / so dying liue, and liuing do
adore her."

Yet the lady is becoming more objectified, even if she won't
permit the castle's being stormed. On the sequence's analogic

level she as a Christ figure will not permit such actions; one does not come to grace by storming a church. In a sexual sense she simply will not allow it.

What, we might ask, *will* she do? Thus far she has attracted and rejected. She has laughed (something sonnet ladies seem rarely to do) and soon she will actually respond (*Amor.* 18) with her own words. In the meantime, though, the poet's "adoration" takes shape in another poem in which he attempts to find the right means for expressing his love. *Amor.* 15, the lovely blazon cataloguing the lady's beauties (and later repeated in describing the bride of *Epith.* 167–203) draws heavily from numerous sources both outside and inside the Spenser canon. Its long list of jewels and rich minerals provides an example of the poet's trying-on of yet another style of love with which to win his lady.

> Ye tradefull Merchants that with weary toyle,
>   do seeke most pretious things to make your gain:
>   and both the Indias of their treasures spoile,
>   what needeth you to seeke so farre in vaine?

The earlier Petrarchan attempts have been unsuccessful; the neo-Platonic efforts somehow miss their mark; the *donna angelicata* and *dolce guerera* depictions result only in her laughing at him. From the rich sonnet literature itself, with its own images traceable from the Song of Songs through centuries of Italian, French, and English depictions of beautiful women, come these encomiastic euphemisms:

> For loe my loue doth in her selfe containe
>   all this worlds riches that may farre be found,
>   if Saphyres, loe her eies be Saphyres plaine,
>   if Rubies, loe hir lips be Rubies sound:
> If Pearles, hir teeth be pearles both pure and round;
>   if Yuorie, her forhead yuory weene;
>   if Gold, her locks are finest gold on ground;
>   if siluer, her faire hands are siluer sheene:
> But that which fairest is, but few behold,
>   her mind adornd with vertues manifold.

Donald Cheney[8] suggests that while such inventories as this are commonplace in love poetry, they are normally found ending with a description such as that which concludes the picture of Serena: "those daintie parts, the dearlings of delight, / . . . mote not be prophan'd of common eyes" (6.8.43). In these wittier

Amoretti poems, however, the poet leads the reader through a twelve-line buildup and then, amusingly, thwarts expectations with: "But that which fairest is, but few behold, / her mind adornd with vertues manifold."

Abruptly he moves from his catalogue to one of its subjects— the lady's eyes. He begins, as he had in *Amor.* 12, with describing what happened "one day." Now the poet relates in *Amor.* 16 the result of his own gazing on the eyes:

> One day as I vnwarily did gaze
>   on those fayre eyes my loues immortall light:
>   the whiles my stonisht hart stood in amaze,
>   through sweet illusion of her lookes delight;
> I mote perceiue how in her glauncing sight,
>   legions of loues with little wings did fly:
>   darting their deadly arrowes fyry bright,
>   at euery rash beholder passing by.
> One of those archers closely I did spy,
>   ayming his arrow at my very hart:
>   when suddenly with twincle of her eye,
>   the Damzell broke his misintended dart.
> Had she not so doon, sure I had bene slayne,
>   yet as it was, I hardly scap't with paine.

The allusion to Venus in her House (4.10.42), and thence to Amoret (a little love), is familiar; these same "loves" will accompany the lady later in *Amor.* 40 and will be with her on her wedding night in *Epith.* 357–63. The poem further telescopes; having started with "one day," having moved to the legions of little loves *(amoretti)*, his focus narrows to the action of one of the loves, an archer "ayming his arrow at my very hart." What in other poems, such as those by Watson and Sidney, becomes a cupidian digression is handled with conservatism and restraint in Spenser, and the focus is not so much on the figure of the archer but on the lady.

The poet's heart, he has already said in line 3, is a "stonisht hart [which] stood in amaze." Here again the heart/hart imagery appears, with the added impact of "amaze" referring not only to his bewilderment but also to his having been trapped within a maze. Significantly, the rhyme word for "amaze" in line 3 is "gaze" in line 1; the myriad of allusions to eyes in this and the previous sonnets, and the ample references to darts and arrows shooting from those eyes, have testified already to the eyes' effect.

This is life from the interior world of the sonnets, one in which the lover displays how he has worked himself into the labyrinth of various loves—courtly, Petrarchan, neo-Platonic, and literary. "Outside" the sonnet, that is, in the empirical action fictionalized in the poem, is a simple yet delightful part of the lover and lady's interaction: he has looked at her and has started to think about how delightful her looking at him would be (the "sweet illusion" of line 4). In the process of glancing around the lady turns until her eyes rest upon him. But with a "twincle of her eye" (line 11) she quickly looks away, and he is saved the embarrassment of being caught staring at her.

The amazement extends to the start of *Amor.* 17:

> The glorious pourtraict of that Angels face,
>   Made to amaze weake mens confused skil:
>   and this worlds worthlesse glory to embase,
>   what pen, what pencill can expresse her fill?
> For though he colours could deuize at will,
>   and eke his learned hand at pleasure guide,
>   least trembling it his workmanship should spill,
>   yet many wondrous things there are beside.

Here the significance of amazement becomes clearer, tied as it is with "confused." Like *Amor.* 3, this poem shows the poet doing what he says he cannot do—praising the lady well. In the author's metafictional game of manipulating the distance between the audience and his fiction, a work of art has become the subject of a work of art. The "pourtraict" has a definite effect on weak men, yet the poem itself is the product of the poet's artful depiction, intended, like the Masque of Cupid, both to deceive as well as to figure a kind of truth.

At the same time, the poet does not "expresse her fill," and the poem proceeds with a series of vague descriptions, unclear antecedents, and attempts to describe the indescribable. In the first quatrain, for example, the second line is unclear about what is "made to amaze." It is either the "pourtraict" or the face; the same holds true for the third line. The borderline between physical and spiritual reality becomes confused, amazed, as does the reference to weak men. Is it the poet whose skill at depicting is confused? or is it the reader, skilled in deciphering, who is confused?

Clearly there are items here that cannot be depicted in the ways one would describe a totally physical object:

> The sweet eye-glaunces, that like arrowes glide,
> the charming smiles, that rob sence from the hart:
> the louely pleasance and the lofty pride,
> cannot expressed be by any art.
> A greater craftesmans hand thereto doth neede,
> that can expresse the life of things indeed.

In one sense the poet's problem is the ongoing one of finding the right words and terms, "divizing colors," for expression. In another sense this poet's problem is that he has already tried and has been unsuccessful. "Expression" itself appears three times in the sonnet, the first time in the first quatrain's general statement about "pen and pencill" being insufficient for creating a complete portrait, the second time in the third quatrain's even more general statement that the lady's qualities "cannot expressed be by any art," and the last time in the couplet, where it is the "greater craftesman" who alone can "expresse the life of things indeed." Once again the poet is forced to confront his own poetic limitations. As in *Amor.* 9, the poet must turn to a divine "craftesman," a "Maker" (and "poet"), as the only one who can provide the right terms, the right means, for "expressing" the lady.

The last line also contains the poet's distinction about the kinds of expression possible. Lesser artists use pen and brush in making their portraits. The greater craftsman creates a living portrait, as in *FQ* 3, proem 1, where the narrator questions whether chastity might be portrayed "by any liuing art." His response is that "liuying art may not least part expresse, / nor life-resembling pencill it can paint." That is to say, the life of things is expressed in deed, in action. This becomes not only an important but a key concept in interpreting the *Amoretti* (as well as in reading all the Spenser canon). The poet's words and the painter's colors can capture only aspects; the real portrait is made up of that changing, developing, external, and empirical reality which the poet increasingly comes to recognize as the real object of his love. This is the reality that can be rendered only by depicting bodies in their ontological and teleological movements.

Undaunted in his efforts to "express," the poet opts for another approach. *Amor.* 18 adds new complexity to the sequence:

> The rolling wheele that runneth often round,
> The hardest steele in tract of time doth teare:
> and drizling drops that often doe redound,
> the firmest flint doth in continuance weare.

Yet cannot I with many a dropping teare,
　　and long intreaty soften her hard hart:
　　that she will once vouchsafe my plaint to heare,
　　or looke with pitty on my payneful smart.
But when I pleade, she bids me play my part,
　　and when I weep, she sayes teares are but water:
　　and when I sigh, she sayes I know the art,
　　and when I waile, she turnes hir selfe to laughter.
So doe I weepe, and wayle, and pleade in vaine,
　　whiles she as steele and flint doth still remayne.

In *Amor.* 11 he had tried "with reason [and] with rewth"; now he tries tears, entreaties, pleas, and sighs.

Yet before the clever play(ing) within the sequence drama, the poet comments on his own methods in this courtship. His effort is like that of the rolling wheel, which will wear down steel (the strongest of metals) during the tract of time. His method is also like that of the "drizling drops" (the alliteration of which continues in its verb "doe redound"), which wear away even flint, the firmest of rocks.

The poet's earlier comment about expressing the life of things in action ("indeed") is exemplified in 18, where the lady actually responds to the poet-lover's courting. Developed in terms of stage imagery, the lady's responses are appropriate to her comments about the "staged" courtship. The third quatrain presents some interesting possibilities. Each line contains the poet's "when I," followed by the lady's reaction. The lady's actions—bidding, saying, turning—may or may not precede her own direct discourse. Whether it can be read as such alters the meanings, although the effect is the same.

For example, in line 12 it makes a difference whether it is the lady who says "I know the art." If it is actually her comment, then it provides her observation to the poet that she ("I") knows what he is doing in his art of love; if it is the poet who speaks the whole line, then it refers to her comment ("she sayes") that the poet ("I") knows his art well—but it is still art, not sincere wooing. Even if the lines are not read as direct discourse, the lady's gentle mockery acknowledges her understanding of the whole procedure as a joke, as part of a game she refuses to take seriously.

Actually, the lady is playing as much a part in this game as is the poet. He does get responses from her, and he is the one who sets the play in action; his pleading gets a reaction, as does his sighing and wailing. And although she is part of the play, she condemns playing. When the lady leads the action, as she did in *Amor.* 7, the poet acts in consort with her: she smiled and then he smiled, she frowned and he followed suit. But his directing ability is not as good as hers; when he leads the action, she responds exactly the opposite way he would like, thus firmly refusing to "play" this way.

The couplet of this highly alliterative sonnet draws several things together; it picks up three of the earlier-noted actions—weeping, wailing, and pleading—and repeats them, noting they are all done in vain. The poet then brings back the subject of the steel and flint, presumably with a suggestion that the lady remains as "hard" and "firm" as they. Yet he has already said in the first quatrain that eventually both materials are worn down, and although the "rolling wheele" (time) moves "around" (a-round), at least the lady still ("yet" and "quietly") remains.

On the lover's wailing notes, the indefinite time sequence ends. The lover is suddenly alerted to the passing of calendric time (as he was earlier in *Amor.* 4):

> The merry Cuckow, messenger of Spring,
>> His trompet shrill hath thrise already sounded:
>> that warnes al louers wayt vpon their king,
>> who now is comming forth with girland crouned.

In *Amor.* 4, "lusty spring now in his timely houre" readied himself to come forth; here spring is coming forth. The poet-lover's problems in winning his lady are temporarily set aside as the king's entrance is announced. A potential forward motion is anticipated throughout all creation as all lovers are apprised to wait upon their king. This forward motion contrasts with the period of time just passed; the "cuckow . . . hath thrise already sounded" and has thus already announced the event now taking place.

To understand the time references here, the path must be retraced through the sequence and must take into consideration not just the surface developments but the analogic level. Doing so reveals the earlier progressions in another light.

This first spring sonnet (*Amor.* 19) appears in the sequence shortly before the poem commemorating the beginning of Lent (*Amor.* 22), marked by Ash Wednesday. Counting backward from that Wednesday poem finds the first spring sonnet falling on a Sunday, Quinquagesima Sunday, one of the three special Sundays calculated backward from Easter and preceding Ash

Wednesday. These three Sundays provide a countdown to Lent and ultimately to Easter. As part of ritual time they emphasize the cyclicality of ritual itself by looking, Janus-like, backward and forward. *Amor.* 19 parallels Quinquagesima Sunday, the third of the three notes preparing for the forthcoming Lenten section within the larger sonnet sequence. An early word for spring, "lent," serves as an internal reinforcement of the parallel.

These three Sundays before Lent serve a preparatory purpose in the Church calendar: they ready worshipers for the observance of Lent as well as providing a link between the Christmas and Easter festivals. *Amor.* 4 invoked the lady and the earth to "prepare [themselves] new loue to entertaine." With 4 representing 26 January, the preparations began immediately in 5, which in the sequence structure falls on Septuagesima Sunday, the first of the anticipatory Sundays. *Amor.* 12 is sequentially analogous with Sexagesima, the second Sunday before Lent. There is possibly more than a structural significance to the poem in that, thematically, its recounting of the lover's tribulations is similar to the message of the day's epistle in 2 Corinthians, which describes Paul's tribulations.

Spenser celebrates Quinquagesima Sunday in *Amor.* 19. The sonnet's connections with the propers of the day are closer than the connections between 4 and 12 and their respective propers. The subject of 19 is the cuckoo's announcement of the forthcoming King of Love. Paul's glorious encomium of Christian love in 1 Corinthians 13, which (in the words of the sonnet) raises "Loues honor," serves as the epistle for this Sunday. And Paul's comments on love help provide a perspective on the Christian love seen throughout the *Amoretti*. By Paul's noting that "when that, which is perfite, is come, then that which is in parte, shalbe abolished," the reader, at the beginning of Lent, is prepared for its termination, when all the preparation ends with the lady's acceptance of the then-readied love of her beloved. When Easter finally appears and finds the "unperfect" love gone, then perfect love can be celebrated as Christ's love manifested in sacralized human love.

Made clear not only by the poem's position in the sequence and by its structural reference to the "three soundings," but also by its analogies with the epistle, the religious overtones of *Amor.* 19 establish an observable correspondence between Christ and the allegorized King of Love. The cuckoo's "shrill trompet" reflects Paul's "sounding brass" or "tinkling cymbal." Moreover, the "girland" crowning the king possesses the double meaning of a garland and of glory,[9] used commonly in the description of Christ, who is crowned with glory. The trumpet, choir, and anthems of the second quatrain call the lovers as they do worshipers in a religious service to attend to that which is about to occur:

> With noyse whereof the quyre of Byrds resounded
>   their anythemes sweet devized of loues prayse,
>   that all the woods theyr ecchoes back rebounded,
>   as if they knew the meaning of their layes.

On the surface level much is transpiring. Although the major focus of the poem appears to be the coming of spring, the sonnet is actually part of the minor carpe diem motif underlying much of the early sequence. *Amor.* 4 introduced the secular temporal setting of the courtship; 19 reinforces it with this timely celebration of seasonal love, sanctified by the choir singing its anthems and lays. Echoing numerous spring poems with their choirs of birds ("The Kingis Quair," *Romance of the Rose*, "Parliament of Foules"), the poet sets nature in motion in anticipation of love. The cuckoo (here "merry," later, in 85, "witlesse") sounds his trumpet; the birds begin singing, and all the woods come alive with sounds. Syntactically, the second quatrain is ambiguous; its three "theirs" and one "they" echo and reecho one another, the birds "resound" their anthems with loud, resonant singing sounded again and again. The anthems are both sweet and sweetly devised. The resounded anthems are resounded again, this time by the woods, which not only echo them but "rebound" them, amplifying them as if the woods knew the meaning of the woods' songs. Alternatively, the anthems are rebounded as if the choirs knew the meaning of the choirs' songs. All is alive with singing; it is no wonder that all lovers wait ("await," "attend," "serve") upon Love.

After the allegorical description of coming spring in the first part of the sonnet, the extended Christian metaphor recedes to the background as the poet alters his tone, calling the lady (as in *Amor.* 6 and 10) a rebel. The change in tone between the earlier accusations and this one should be noted; it indicates development in the poet's perceptions of the lady and a more accurate view of his own presence in the situation. As part of the lover's "sermon" to himself, the lady's "rebellious pride" was treated seriously in *Amor.* 6; then, in a lighter but still partly serious mood, the poet complained in *Amor.* 10 of the lady's lording in "licentious blisse / of her freewill." Here, however, the poet's animadversions are markedly lighter, as indicated by the conditional mood of the last lines. By referring to her now in such a manner, he cannot hide his hope of eventual repentance:

> But mongst them all, which did Loues honor rayse
>   no word was heard of her that most it ought,
>   but she his precept proudly disobayes,
>   and doth his ydle message set at nought.
> Therefore O loue, vnlesse she turne to thee
>   ere Cuckow end, let her a rebell be.

This lightness of spirit continues into the next sonnet, with its seeking and suing for grace:

> In vaine I seeke and sew to her for grace,
>   and doe myne humbled hart before her poure:
>   the whiles her foot she in my necke doth place,
>   and tread my life downe in the lowly floure.

Whereas in 19 he complained of her indifference, in 20 the poet playfully transfers that indifference into a hyperbolic image of unusually cruel aggression, suggesting that she sees him as prey (when actually she might not seem to be interested at all). Earlier he had compared the lady to the most enduring member of the vegetative world, the "durefull oake" (6), while at another time he described her in terms of the hardest minerals, flint and steel (18); here the lady is compared with the king of the animal world:

> And yet the Lyon that is Lord of power,
>   and reigneth ouer euery beast in field:
>   in his most pride disdeigneth to deuoure
>   the silly lambe that to his might doth yield.
> But she more cruell and more saluage wylde,
>   than either Lyon or the Lyonesse:
>   shames not to be with guiltlesse bloud defylde,
>   but taketh glory in her cruelnesse.
> Fayrer then fayrest let none euer say,
>   that ye were blooded in a yeelded pray.

The lightness of tone is as evident as it was in 19. By comparing the lady with something as conventional as the lion, the poet exercises his poetic wit and thus takes pressure off the lover in him. His conscious humbling of himself in the form of the lamb adds more playfulness to the whole image, with its reminder of the biblical allusion to the lion and the lamb lying down together.

The poet again picks up the idea of the lady's pride (noted in *Amor.* 19) and cleverly uses that word in its connection with lions. He also reintroduces the image of seeking and suing, earlier (11) referring to peace but here suggesting grace, which on the analogic level the lover will need as he moves into Lent. The word "grace" reiterates the religious suggestions of 19 and adds to them this central idea. Heavenly grace becomes an essential support of the faith. It shines in Una's face, gives Contemplation his vision, and will be there in the Christ/lady's steadfast accompanying of the lover. Its echo is heard in the next sonnet's reference to the lady's "beauties grace."

The couplet of *Amor.* 20 addresses the lady; these efforts to talk to and with her are significant moves in the direction he must take if his courtship will be effective. In a confusing but witty last line the poet plays upon "blooded"; in its most obvious sense the poet warns the lady of being bloodied as she pursues her prey. But Elizabethans would know the word also as a hunting reference (the use of some blood so that dogs could find the scent of their prey). As such, the lady would be the huntress as well as the hunter, which is precisely what in *Amor.* 67 she turns out to be.

His wit in *Amor.* 20 changes to mild wonder in 21, where a number of the earlier themes are recapitulated and where the lover draws an important conclusion:

> Was it the worke of nature or of Art,
>   which tempred so the feature of her face,
>   that pride and meeknesse mixt by equall part,
>   doe both appeare t'adorne her beauties grace?
> For with mild pleasance, which doth pride displace,
>   she to her loue doth lookers eyes allure:
>   and with sterne countenance back again doth chace
>   their looser lookes that stir vp lustes impure.
> With such strange termes her eyes she doth inure,
>   that with one looke she doth my life dismay:
>   and with another doth it streight recure,
>   her smile me drawes, her frowne me driues away.
> Thus doth she traine and teach me with her lookes,
>   such art of eyes I neuer read in bookes.

The question with which the poem begins was a familiar Renaissance *topos*—the nature-art controversy. Philosophers, poets, and theologians in abundance examined the theme, agreeing on one significant point: art imitates nature, and nature, as Richard Hooker asserted, is the art of God. As in so many other elements of Spenser's thinking, nature and art are harmonious, divisible, and yet one. Additionally, nature as the art of God is usually, if not always, in the process of achieving the effects of art—design and pattern. Even God is seen as a "Maker," a greater craftsman. As Hooker writes: "those things which nature is said to do, are by divine art performed, using nature as an instrument; nor is there any such art of knowledge divine in nature herself working, but in the Guide of nature's work." Fallen nature can be redeemed by art, with the artist being the mediator between that fallen world and its potential golden qualities. As such, the contrast between art and nature[10] is not a matter of mere aesthetic theorizing, but is at the very heart of man's teleology.

This is the principle Spenser sets up against Mutability and her pageant of supporters; on a much smaller scale it is the principle Spenser uses to "dilate" a theme rather than to develop it. And as in *Amor.* 17, where the greater craftsman's hand alone "can expresse the life of things indeed," it is in deed, in action, that moving objects display themselves as they progress, and in doing so convey not only the process but the quality of movement.

At the outset of *Amor.* 21 there are difficulties; not only is Spenser dealing with a complex issue, but there is no way of knowing how carefully Spenser is suggesting the philosophical and/or theological implications of the terminology. The issue is complicated and has been treated well by other authors.[11] In brief, for Spenser (in general) the "natural" is good and the "unnatural" evil. Spenser sees the good as that which fulfills the law of its own kind (recalling the *Amoretti* motif of kind, kindle, kindling, etc.) within a universal order; often, as in *The Faerie Queene* and the *Epithalamion*, this is presented in terms of generation.

Nature can be bountiful, as it is in the Garden of Adonis and on Mount Acidale; it can be the green world of Sidney's and Spenser's shepherds. But it can also be a fallen nature where the Blatant Beast runs mad.

Likewise, art can be good, too, bringing nature to perfection and people to reconciliation. On the other hand, art can be sinister when it counterfeits nature, deceiving by a trompe l'oeil, as with Acrasia's bower or Busyrane's Castle, or when it is sterile and evil artificiality, as with the cannibals in the Mirabella episode.

In Spenser, art and nature have their connections with love. True love is praised because it is "naturall affection faultlesse" (4, prome 2), whereas false love, such as with Paridell, is an "art" in which one is trained to be "the learned lover." *The Faerie Queene* narrator's whimsical refusal to comment on the origin of Blandina's false courtesy picks up on this idea:

> Whether such grace were giuen her by kynd,
> As women wont their guilefull wits to guyde;
> Or learn'd the art to please, I doe not fynd.
>
> (6.6.43)

The art-nature dichotomy becomes a major motif in the *Amoretti*; it stands behind those poems expressing the inexpressible as well as those emphasizing the lady's mocking of the poet's artificiality. The distinctions Spenser draws between art and nature (in the Bower of Bliss and the Garden of Adonis episodes) he draws again here: the artificial that deludes is sterile, even evil, and must be refined or destroyed. C. S. Lewis investigates this matter at length and finds that the division is ultimately between reality and imitation: "like Life and Death, or Light and Darkness, the opposition of natural and artificial, naive and sophisticated, genuine and spurious, meets us at every turn" in Spenser's poetry.[12]

In *Amor.* 19 the poet was enraptured by the lady's beauty, as he also had been in 7 and 15. The "grace" for which he had sought and sued in 20 reappears in *Amor.* 21 in the lady's "beauties grace." The tempering of pride and humility (*Amor.* 13) now is recast as a tempering of nature and art. The problem of the "sweet illusion of her lookes" (*Amor.* 16) resurfaces in the pride and meekness "appearing" to adorn the lady's grace. The question raised in that earlier sonnet, and a key one here, is this: Does the lady really possess all that the poet claims she does, or is the beauty an illusion, an "appearance," of beauty?

The poem continues with the poet's amplification of his initial statement. But from the start Spenser blocks resolution. Nature and art are perfectly blended into even the sounds of the first quatrain, where "nature" and "feature" provide an Elizabethan aural connection, and where "art" and "part" are likewise conjoined. "Pride and meeknesse" may appear to correspond to "nature and art," but if they are in strict parallel juxtaposition, then pride relates to nature and meekness to art. If that is the case, then the lady's is an artificial meekness (certainly not a compliment to her at all). Likewise, if meekness relates to nature, then pride must be part of her art; again, the connection is not complimentary. Both pride and meekness, it is possible, only "appear" as adornments. Or it is equally possible that the two qualities make an appearance in order to adorn. And readers might also question if the "adorning" is art being added to her natural "beauties grace."

The poet provides exempla to support the two mixed qualities: with her mildness ("pleasance") she allures others' eyes (he already noted this quality in comments about her attracting others). This lovely, mellifluous line—"she to her loue doth look-ers eyes allure"—contains its own attempts to prevent an answer to the initial questions: does this mean that she allures the eyes to love, or to her, or to her love? And yet with her pride she repels "looser looks." The verbs are of interest: her "pleasance" dis-places pride; she allures eyes, she chases loose looks that stir up lusts. Verbs, by their nature, depict action, doing, performing. But readers are rather accustomed to descriptions of what the lady is like, not what she does. The unmoved mover of *Amor.* 18 now is doing something, and although the import of her action is not clear until the sonnet's end, her activity is noted as the poet amplifies the subject.

The third quatrain also establishes parallels; from talking about her face, the poet turns to discussing the lady's eyes, which "dismay" and "recure," repel and attract. Line 12 summarizes the alternating action of the first twenty-one sonnets: "her smile me drawes, her frowne me driues away." Yet no answer to the initial question appears. Is the frown the work of nature or of art? And what of the smile?

The couplet thwarts expectation. Instead of a direct answer to the question, another complaint about the lady's activities, or even a plea for change, the final lines reveal the poet's awareness of what the lady has been doing: she has been training and teaching him with her looks (both the approach and the re-proach, the drawing and driving-away, ones). The looks (of the first two quatrains) and the action of her eyes (of the third quatrain) are intended to lead him in another direction. They do this by nature ("her beauties grace") as well as by art (drawing and driving away), by means of a carefully orchestrated and modulated program (noted earlier in *Amor.* 18) that, with its training and teaching, eventually reveals its lesson in *Amor.* 68.

To reinforce the poem's pedagogical element Spenser gives the final rhyme to "lookes" and "bookes." Just as the lady was to "reade the sorrowes" of the lover's plight in the poetry (Amor. 1), so the lover is to read his lessons in her looks. The poet, well read in others' books, has looked in the wrong place as a source for his art and as a clue to her message. The secret is really no secret; her looks are both source and inspiration, both nature and art, in goodly temperature combined. The eyes themselves are natural, being God's gift to the lady; and the looking is artful in that the lady has learned how best to use the eyes. The poem concludes with a delightful pun apparent in Elizabethan pronunciation: "such artifice [art of eyes] I [eye] never read in bookes."

At this point in the sequence, although the poet has admitted understanding what the lady is doing, although he has made significant progress in relating to the empirical woman, and even though some of the poems clearly show his working himself out of the confines of Petrarchan imagery, the lady's lesson remains unlearned. Whereas in Amor. 21 she is an object of love, in 22, with the surfacing of the deeper analogic level of the sequence in the form of the Lenten references, she becomes herself an object of worship. Spenser parallels this change from love to worship by the changing of the "season." The cheerful playfulness of Shrove Tuesday (Amor. 21) gives way to the serious focus of Ash Wednesday (Amor. 22). Both the lover and, by extension, the Christian, are now about to enter the period of their greatest agon, a period of "fasting and praying," a period of soul-searching and of the soul seeking.

AMORETTI 22–68

"... Twixt earnest and twixt game. ..."

In the central panel of the *Amoretti* triptych are the forty-six sonnets making up the sequence's Lenten series. On both the surface and the analogic levels the sonnets in this section portray the major conflicts and struggles of the desirous lover/Christian; they also contain the most organized and demanding courting/ preparation in the sequence. By various means the lady encourages her suitor to a conversion—literally, a turning away from his self-directed, sterile "loves" and a turning to the life-affirming love taught and affirmed by Christ. Such turning implies eliminating the kinds of courting that reflect not the earnest, sincere wooer but the clever craftsman seeking by art, not the heart, to achieve his goal. It also implies yielding control, letting go of the "game" and "forsaking the chace" (*Amor.* 67).

By constantly thwarting the success of the ineffectual, Petrarchan lover, yet by continually encouraging the true lover's perseverance, the beloved purifies the poet and the penitent. As Fidelia and Speranza open the eyes of Red Cross and give him assurance before introducing him to Patience, Penaunce, Remorse, and Repentance, so the sonnet lady (and, metaphorically, Christ) encourages the lover and slowly "traine[s] and teach[es]" him to read the meaning of courtship. Simultaneously, the lady/ Christ fosters in him those same qualities (patience, penance, etc.) that accompany his "turning." In the *Amoretti's* Lenten segment the lover's development, sometimes retrograde but ultimately advancing, indicates the gradual laying aside of his various poses and the acceptance of his own ability to love his beloved properly; on both levels of the sequence this is necessary. During this segment the "contradictory impulses of the first twenty-one sonnets are reconciled, and the Lenten sequence ends with six sonnets celebrating a love that is simultaneously spiritual and physical."[1]

The Lenten segment is thus central to the *Amoretti*, not only in its being preceded by twenty-one sonnets and followed by twenty-one sonnets, but by its assertion of the centrality of the Lenten implications in human life.[2] Sanctified time, lived out in this life but nonetheless holy, indicates the movement of the lover/penitent from his anguished self-division to joyful reconciliation. The progress through Lent is similar for the lover and the penitent. While the experiences appear to be those of negation and difficulty, the impetus is actually a positive one—to remind humanity that God's creation is divine, that, although fallen, all creation is redeemable, and that in an imitation of Christ people can be conformed to the will of God. The liturgy Spenser follows in patterning and shaping the *Amoretti* is not an explanation but a series of signs, showing "in-deed" that creation is a language in which God both expresses and reveals himself. The analogues to the poet-narrator are clear, and his own emphasis on expression, on expressive discourse, its limitations and potentialities, is a direct reflection of the liturgy's own attempts to express and unfold. Lent, then, is an action, a transition absolutely essential in moving from the old to the new, from bondage to freedom, from death to life.

Although the Lenten progress has its "dark sides," the emphasis is not on the lover's failings or the penitent's sins, but on the overcoming of those failings and fallings through the redemption that occurs at Easter (*Amor.* 68). Always present in the *Amoretti* is the knowledge that the lady does accept the lover and that the betrothal eventually leads to marriage. For all the lover's complaints about the lady's cruelty and lack of interest, she is always concerned about the lover. Likewise, one of the points of Lent is the exemplification of God's continuing concern for mankind. Yet if humanity is to be sacralized, reconciled, atoned (the end both God and the lady have in mind), man must be held responsible for his actions. The lady's laughter, her frowns and smiles, all have a corrective pedagogical end; to those entering or already in the Church, Lent proposes a reformation of life and an advance toward divinization that is already theirs in principle but which they must make truly their own in an ever-more-conscious and radical way.

The Lenten segment offers an optimistic vision of a world in which human and divine love conjoin; though it portrays the lover's interior world as an agonistic expression of his outer reality, the truth is that the destruction of that inner world is linked to its transformation into a new world, just as the agon ultimately yields enlightenment and then redemption. Lent sum-

mons the poet-lover to something more than an artificial as-
ceticism and an inner-directed mode of expression; it demands of
him the courage of a *metanoia,* a radical turning of his life, and
hence his art, in a new direction.

In the sequence's Lenten segment the poet struggles with his
art (in itself an external expression of his Self). And the lover
wrestles with the kind of love appropriate to wooing and win-
ning this most resolute and determined young woman. On the
analogic level the penitent struggles with his own selfhood in an
effort to prepare for the gifts of grace and salvation that occur at
the end of this period. Neither the penitent nor the lover earns
the gift of grace, already prepared for him and already at hand.
Instead he rids himself of those elements which hinder accept-
ance of the gift. All of the characters now involved—poet, lover,
lady, and, metaphorically, the penitent—are deeply occupied
with this preparatory Lenten period and courtship, leading to a
turning and reconciliation in betrothal and Easter. Spenser does
not assert one-to-one parallels in these unfolding stories; his is
much too effusive a spirit to be confined in such a way. Instead,
the analogies he provides are often in the form of repeated or
paralleled words or phrases (glimpses of the one level inter-
penetrating the other) or even merely a general flow of modulated
highs and lows leading to the ultimate experiences at the end of
the segment.

Amor. 22 itself begins with a new direction; from considera-
tion in 21 of the lady's eyes and looks, the lover turns inward. The
image of the *donna angelicata* almost disappears from the early
part of this segment as the lover experiences unrelenting suffer-
ing as part of his spiritual, emotional, and poetic developm. t.

> This holy season fit to fast and pray,
>> Men to deuotion ought to be inclynd:
>> therefore, I lykewise on so holy day,
>> for my sweet Saynt some seruice fit will find.
> Her temple fayre is built within my mind,
>> in which her glorious ymage placed is,
>> on which my thoughts doo day and night attend
>> lyke sacred priests that neuer thinke amisse.
> There I to her as th'author of my blisse,
>> will builde an altar to appease her yre:
>> and on the same my hart will sacrifise,
>> burning in flames of pure and chast desyre:
> The which vouchsafe O goddesse to accept,
>> amongst thy deerest relicks to be kept.

In this excellent insistence of "Renaissance inconsistency in [the] . . . blending of paganism and Christianity, goddess and saint,"[3] the poet employs standard religious terminology to describe his worship of the lady. Yet it is important to note that by *Amor.* 22 the lover has begun his own self-conversion. He himself is committed to the task of enlightenment. He still has a long way to go, but he willingly has "inclynd" himself to the task. Like Red Cross at the House of Holinesse (1.10.52), the lover must "fast and pray" precisely because these are part of the purification and reconciliation processes. The poet includes himself among men of devotion, holy people who ought to be inclined "to fast and pray." He moves from the holy season to the holy day, from men to himself; implied as well is the movement from devotion to God, to devotion to the poet's "sweet Saynt." While the holy men "ought" to be inclined to service, the poet "will" find it, suggesting not only his awareness of obligations (on the sacred-analogical and on the secular-surface levels) but of his own determination. Likewise, both the season and his own service are "fit" ("made" as well as "suitable"). The "service" to which he refers is significant; he will do service to the lady through his poetry. He will seek to serve her in the courtship. And Spenser will *serve* his own lady through the analogy of love he presents, in which the liturgy itself is the service (Gr. *leitourgia*, "service").

The poem has moved from the larger world of seasons and men to the smaller world of a day and a man; now the poet moves into the man's mind, where a fair temple has been built for the lady's glorious image (both the idea of her and, in the context of the temple metaphor, a statue of her). The origin of the temple is not revealed; the poet does not say, and even when he later writes (lines 9–10) of the "author of [his] blisse" it is not clear whether it is the lady or he himself who is the controlling artist. The image of the temple is important in Spenser's poetry. In *The Faerie Queene* it provides a dominant recurring archetype; magic visions in all six books are presented in temples, which provide the sacred space for the interior dramas. The temples both include and exclude, and there, as in the sonnets, the temples allow the sacred to preside and the profane to be excluded.[4]

Amor. 7 had introduced the problem of reality and illusion, essence and appearance; in 16 the difficulty in dealing with the "sweet illusion of her lookes delight" had still been evident. Here the poet admits his idealization, which necessarily begins in the mind, of the lady. The lady is described as a saint, not a goddess, and it is her spiritual, not her physical, qualities he admires. She is the same "saynt" received "with honour dew" on her wedding day (*Epith.* 208) less than four months later.

His attendant thoughts, compared to priests "that neuer thinke amisse," now fulfill what the lady demanded in the previous sonnet when she drew attention but rejected any semblance of "lustes impure." And the "glorious pourtraict" he could neither paint nor describe in 17 here takes more "solid" form.

The third quatrain moves the reader out of the poet's mind and back to the empirical world, with the poet first declaring his intentions to build an altar and then noting the reason for doing so—"to appease her yre." What ire, we might ask, given that this element has not been noted earlier. And suddenly Spenser reminds us of the poet-lover's concerns for right wooing. He has just worked himself into the interior monologue concerning worship, which has suggested sacrifice, and which now has led to the Petrarchan image of sacrificing one's heart. True, the heart burns "in flames of pure and chast desyre." The burnt offering links the religious metaphor with the Petrarchan one and is accompanied by the couplet's prayer in which the burning heart (which neither consumes itself nor is consumed) is to be kept among the lady's relics.

While there is no reason to doubt the purity of the burning heart, the sincerity may be questioned. The following three sonnets (which Spenser places between Ash Wednesday, 22, and the first Sunday in Lent, 26) contain subject matter indicating they are still related to the poet's early stages of courting as recorded in the early sonnets of the sequence. But to the poet's credit the tone of these three sonnets suggests progress toward a better understanding of his situation and thus a clearer identification of his self. *Amor.* 21 and 22 define the suitor's relationship to the lady; seen as his teacher, she is also the object of his worship. But *Amor.* 23 and 24 present a half-humorous recognition that the poet's definitions of the relationship prove unacceptable to the lady. Ending with a prayer that the lady accept his heart, 22 contains the lover's hyperbolic praise and worship of his saint. *Amor.* 23 then suggests that the element of praise in the previous sonnet is not the type that pleases the lady, who refuses to be moved or persuaded:

> Penelope for her Vlisses sake,
>> Deuiz'd a Web her wooers to deceaue:
>> in which the worke that she all day did make
>> the same at night she did againe vnreaue.

Opening with the famous tale of Penelope's "weaving," the sonnet recalls the great number of entrapment metaphors scattered through the Lenten-segment sonnets. Penelope's web itself suggests the other great web Homer mentions in *Odyssey* 8.276–81, where Vulcan traps Venus and her lover. And we are reminded of the Palmer and Guyon, who throw "a subtile net" over lovers in the midst of their "lustfull game" in the Bower of Bliss. Interestingly, the pre-Lenten sonnets contain virtually no direct references to the entrapments. With the exception of "bands," noted in *Amor.* 1 and 12, the knitted knots of 7, and the allurement of the lady's eyes in 21, all the traps have been only suggested. From this point in the sequence forward, however, the lover will be caught in his own metaphors and allusions. Webs, chains, nets, snares, hooks, bands, mews, and lures all will be used to describe the lady's activities—as well as the lover's. By extension, all the poems—as *amoretti*—have built-in etymological associations with this image group, *amo* being Italian for "hooks." And in one sense the poems are indeed hooks for capturing the lady within the web of metaphor and the interweaving of rhyme and trope. Ultimately it is the marriage-knot that will bind the lovers.

The poet relates in *Amor.* 23 that Penelope "deuiz'd" a web, implying at the start the woman's craftiness and cunning, and making a connection between the woman and the spider, the female of which is the predator. In Homer's story, Penelope's web is a means of deceiving the suitors; in Spenser's sonnet the deception has the added emphasis of the word's Latin root, *decipere,* which means not only to deceive but to catch, to entrap. But Penelope is also the faithful wife, a model of constancy who does what she must do in order to preserve herself for her husband. Thus she assumes some of the lady's own characteristics (constancy, faithfulness, cleverness) just as the lady, in the poet's comparison, assumes some of Penelope's craftiness, ability to attract and then reject, and deceptiveness.

The second quatrain further details both Penelope's and the lady's actions:

> Such subtile craft my Damzell doth conceaue,
> th'importune suit of my desire to shonne:
> for all that I in many dayes doo weaue,
> in one short houre I find by her vndonne.

Penelope's "deceav[ing]" becomes part of the lady's "conceav[ing]"; the rhyming of the two words makes implicit their connection, just as "my damzell" connects the poet's lady with Penelope. The "web" of line 2 now assumes a different meaning. It is not just an object but is the "plot" Penelope wove.

Both women weave by "subtile craft," an appropriately ambiguous description given that "subtile" implies not only "finely done" (L. subtilis) but also "clever." Theirs is a fine craft and a crafty craft. But his craft is also subtle, as he himself suggests in the reference to his "importune suit," which is both importune (as in "persistent") wooing as well as "troublesome" suing.

In the first quatrain, the third and fourth lines explain the "web" of Penelope. In the second quatrain, the third and fourth lines explain the lady's subtle craft: all the poet has woven in many days the lady undoes in one hour. Once again the poem's rhymes are informative. Penelope's web deceives because every night she "vnreauve[s]" it (both "unweaves" and "takes away by stealth"); these words are rhymed with the crafty work the lady conceives, which in turn is rhymed with what the poet weaves. By his own subtle weaving, the poet makes a significant and witty shift in direction. At the start of the second quatrain the lady is identified with Penelope, the deceptive weaver, the artist who can attract and repel; yet by the end of the quatrain it is the poet who plays the part of the Penelope who weaves, while the lady takes the part of the Penelope who unweaves. Now the transposed Penelope-lady unweaves what the poet has woven; the suitor has become the suited, and vice versa. The conflict is not only between the lady/artist and the poet, but between two artist/lovers.[5] The crafty poet who has carefully plotted the courtship's course is not so clever as the lady who shuns and leaves undone his suit.

There are further subtleties in the Penelope-lady analogy. If the lover is now Penelope, then the lady becomes the suitor (which she is, as much as he). This lady/suitor, however, is undeceived, and it is she, not the lover/Penelope, who unweaves the web. Penelope never intended to complete the weaving; the poet does (as he has already noted in comments about planning his strategies). He described the function of the lady earlier in Amor. 18, where she laughed at the various roles the lover played. His has been a double-directed suit. He has attempted to win his lady and, concomitantly, has attempted to shape the poetic methodology he employs.

Rhetorically, the third quatrain employs some of the poet's own very fine and subtle craft:

> So when I thinke to end that I begonne,
>> I must begin and neuer bring to end:
>> for with one looke she spils that long I sponne,
>> and with one word my whole years work doth rend.
> Such labour like the Spyders web I fynd,
>> whose fruitlesse worke is broken with least wynd.

The poet's efforts to "end" have been implicit in the whole sequence, and, as will later be seen in *Amor.* 89, he does end where he began in *Amor.* 1. In the Spenser canon "never bringing to an end" has philosophic, moral, theological, and architectonic implications; his works do not "end," as such, but continue into yet other beginnings. The first line of the quatrain above gives the temporally reversed order of end-begun; this is corrected in the next line with begin-end. But the endings never occur; "end" finds a built-in commentary in "rend," just as "begonne" is something the poet has "sponne." Even the sonnet's time span is distorted; in line 9 the poet weaves for many days; by line 12 this becomes a whole year.

The poet as wooer and the poet as weaver/lover come together in the couplet, where the ambiguity and confusion of roles reveals the narrator's strategy: "Such labour like the Spyders web I fynd, / whose fruitlesse worke is broken with least wynd." The labor of the poet as wooer is "fruitlesse" if the lady continues deceiving wooers; the labor of the poet as weaver is fruitless if the lady continues rending his work. In both cases there is a comparison with the spider, but it is cleverly ambiguous as to whom "such labour" refers. If it is the lady's labor (of shunning, undoing, rending) that is like a spider's web, then the humorous implication is that the poet understands that he, ultimately, will devise the web that will capture her. If it is the poet's labor (of suing, weaving, thinking to end, spinning), then the more serious implication is that his work is fruitless. The poet "carefully avoids the creation of a position that explicitly either asserts his artistic superiority over his lady or succumbs to her control over him and his art."[6]

Finally, these images of knitting, weaving, and entrapment are complex. Judith Dundas's *The Spider and the Bee* argues that such "webs" suggest Spenser's view of the artist's task.[7] *Amor.* 23 picks up this concern, which already has been developing in the earlier poems about the writing process. In part, the weaving and unweaving are extensions of the poet's comments on his own craft, in which comments Spenser presents the poet in many forms—maker, craftsman, and weaver. The woven work, like the well-wrought poem, captures its beholders; the poet becomes the weaver, bringing into existence something that, before, did not exist. He spins his tales and holds the various strands before him as the tapestry (an image the poet will use later in *Amor.* 71) unfolds before us.

Penelope's, the lady's, and the poet's art give way in the next sonnet, *Amor.* 24, to another classical reference and another artist:

> When I behold that beauties wonderment,
>   And rare perfection of each goodly part:
>   of natures skill the onely complement,
>   I honor and admire the makers art.

Subtle craft yields to "skill" as the "makers art" (and indirectly God as Maker) is praised. The nature-art dichotomy of 21 is reintroduced and reinforced; nature is God's art. Yet a significant change has developed since *Amor.* 21, where the lover's thoughts, like sacred priests, waited upon his sweet saint. Here the lady is no longer worshiped as a saint; in fact, she is not worshiped at all. Instead it is God who is honored and admired for his works in the lady. She has become the mediary through whom the lover comes to God.

The lady's "essential" qualities, derived from "the maker," are here (as earlier) compared with those qualities of artificial and illusory appearance:

> But when I feele the bitter balefull smart,
>   which her fayre eyes vnwares doe worke in mee:
>   that death out of theyr shiny beames doe dart,
> I thinke that I a new Pandora see;
> Whom all the Gods in councell did agree,
>   into this sinfull world from heauen to send:
>   that she to wicked men a scourge should bee,
>   for all their faults with which they did offend.
> But since ye are my scourge I will intreat,
>   that for my faults ye will me gently beat.

The transition is swift from praise of the maker's art to complaint of the lady's cruelty; it is a reminder that the poet is in the midst of contradictory feelings and inner turmoil, yet his delicate mockery and gentle wit come through in the image of the lady as Pandora. The poet suggests only Pandora's negative, threatening qualities and fails to acknowledge her other distinction: as Pandora she is all-gifts and, by analogy, grace-giving. Like the lady, Pandora is in a mediary position between the gods and man; like the lady (who chases "looser lookes that stir vp lustes impure" and whose eye's dart out deadly arrows "at euery rash beholder" etc.), Pandora also becomes the scourge of wicked men who, like the poet, feel "the bitter balefull smart."

What he does not acknowledge is that if his analogy of the lady-Pandora is pursued, then he could be compared with Prometheus, the "fore-thinker," who was the specific reason for Zeus's punishing mankind by sending Pandora. The poet's role as fore-thinker is obvious; this has been his method of operation since the start of the sequence. But Prometheus is more than just a fore-thinker; from Hesiod onward, Prometheus is also associated with being a supreme craftsman—which is how the poet perceives himself and how he, in the weaving of *Amor.* 23, has just presented himself.

The sonnet ends gently and humorously in a direct address to the lady, who, as the lover's scourge, is asked to beat him gently.

The poet's "double-thinking," in which he proceeds by comparing and contrasting (drawing and rejecting, illusion and reality, essence and appearance, nature and art, cruel-fair and *donna angelicata,* death- and life-giving attributes, weaving and unweaving), continues into *Amor.* 25.

> How long shall this lyke dying lyfe endure,
>   And know no end of her owne mysery:
>   but wast and weare away in termes vnsure,
>   twixt feare and hope depending doubtfully?
> Yet better were attonce to let me die,
>   and shew the last ensample of your pride:
>   then to torment me thus with cruelty,
>   to proue your powre, which I too wel haue tride.

The poet complains that the scourging of 24 has become an endless "lyke dying lyfe," in which he "wast[es] and weare[s] away in termes vnsure, / twixt feare and hope depending doubtfully." Of the various possible meanings for the "termes vnsure," the two most fitting are that (1) the "terms" are part of the language he as poet uses to express himself and (2) his language has been shown to be unsure (at least as far as its efficacy in wooing is concerned). From 21 through 24 the poet toyed gently with definitions and praises of the lady. But such playfulness does not bring him closer to winning her; it succeeds only, in psychological time, to delay further empirical actions. Those things about which he has been so assured (his poetic abilities and his certainty that the lady would eventually give herself to him) are now doubtful; he hangs ("depending") between fear that she will leave and hope that she will yield.

The first quatrain of *Amor.* 25 concerns that fear and hope; the second quatrain focuses on fear and despair. Quatrain three telescopes to the hope. While *Amor.* 22 sought to freeze the lover-lady condition by having the lady accept and keep his ever-consuming heart, this third quatrain of 25 seeks to activate the situation:

> But yet if in your hardned brest ye hide
> a close intent at last to shew me grace:
> then all the woes and wrecks which I abide,
> as meanes of blisse I gladly wil embrace.

"Woes and wrecks," as means to bliss, are part of the courtly lover's stock-in-trade. They are expected, so much so that the desire is to intensify them—for very practical reasons:

> And wish that more and greater they might be,
> that greater meede at last may turne to mee.

The sonnet's contraries (life-death, fear-hope, woes-bliss, greater pains-greater rewards) extend to the next sonnet, 26, where the playful epigrams stress the lady's double aspect. In an emblematic blazon of oxymora, the poet accepts the challenge of 25 with a lighthearted catalogue of the "woes and wrecks" he will have to abide; yet in the praises of his beloved, he carefully combines the bitter with the sweet, reassuring himself that the contrarities are ultimately worth the efforts:

> Sweet is the Rose, but growes vpon a brere;
> Sweet is the Iunipere, but sharpe his bough;
> sweet is the Eglantine; but pricketh nere;
> sweet is the firbloome, but his braunches rough.
> Sweet is the Cypresse, but his rynd is tough,
> sweet is the nut, but bitter is his pill;
> sweet is the broome-flowre, but yet sowre enough;
> and sweet is Moly, but his root is ill.

In 25 he was hopeful yet serious when concentrating on the process that must be followed to attain the lady, admitting the uncertainty and pain of the task. Here he concentrates not on an abstract procedure but upon the "sweet" objectification of plants, just as in 15 his blazon had focused on gems. The sonnet's first two quatrains develop the traditional "bitter-sweet" oxymoron; each pair begins with "sweet," one of Spenser's most frequently used adjectives.

The third quatrain sums up his argument:

> So euery sweet with soure is tempred still,
> that maketh it be coueted the more:
> for easie things that may be got at will,
> most sorts of men doe set but little store.

The tempering of sweet and sour is a reminder of the lady's own goodly temperament (Amor. 13); it is also a reminder that the pain and pleasure noted here have the same goal as they had in 25, but now the poet ends on an even happier note: "Why then should I accoumpt of little paine, / that endlesse pleasure shall vnto me gaine?"

The "meade" of the previous sonnet now the "gaine" of this one, the poet wittily echoes both the sentiment and the rhyme of his couplet in Amor. 6: "Then thinke not long in taking little paine, / to knit the knot, that euer shall remaine."

It might be recalled that Amor. 26 marks the first Sunday in Lent, 17 February 1594. The balancing of the sonnet's lines echo the modulated rising and falling of the psalm (33) for this day: "Blessed is he, whose unrighteousness is forgeuen; and whose sinne is couered. Blessed is the manne unto whome the Lord imputeth no sinne: and in whose spirite there is no guile." The Sunday epistles and gospels originally served as instruction for the catechumens and were intended to draw a contrast between the old pagan life and the new Christian life upon which the converts were now embarking. Built in, then, is the kind of comparison/contrast we also find in the sonnet.

The first Sunday in Lent is the opening day of the great catechesis, during which the church is concerned with impressing on the catechumens both the essential attitudes to be remembered during this period of "fasting and praying," of "training and teaching," and with having the penitents be attentive to the basic reactions that must be awakened in the soul. The epistle from 2 Corinthians 6 provides Paul's grammatically and logically balanced discussion of his apostolic labors, with its good aspects and its bad ("in much patience, in afflictions, in necessities, in distresses, in stripes, in prisons, in tumultes . . ."). To be a Christian, Paul teaches, is to be prepared for suffering as well as for joy. The gospel lesson from Matthew treats Christ's temptation; but the temptation in the desert is a conflict that ultimately ends in victory. It is the prelude to the reconstruction and reunification of the world. In its agon are the seeds of "endlesse pleasure."

The *Amoretti's* analogic level surfaces here to suggest the lover-penitent's awareness of the task his next several weeks will entail. It will be a time of tribulation leading to triumph, a time of "paine" yielding to great "gaine."

The confidence displayed in *Amor.* 26 finds natural expression in *Amor.* 27's promises of poetic immortality. The hope expressed in the previous sonnet is now stated as almost a foregone conclusion. In the tradition of the *vanitas, omnia vanitas* theme, the poem disclaims against the lady's pride while arguing for poetic immortality. The sonnet exhibits the poet's continuing concern with his craft; as before, he proceeds by a definition of terms:

> Faire proud now tell me why should faire be proud,
>   Sith all worlds glorie is but drosse vncleane:
>   and in the shade of death it selfe shall shroud,
>   how euer now thereof ye little weene.

The poet's progress in the poem is both clever and witty. His address to the lady, commencing with calling her "faire proud," immediately focuses on the unclean dross of which the world's glory is constituted. From there he moves to death and shrouds, and in the following quatrain even the borrowed flesh is removed:

> That goodly Idoll now so gay beseene,
>   shall doffe her fleshes borowd fayre attyre:
>   and be forgot as it had neuer beene,
>   that many now much worship and admire.

(Ironically, he himself has just worshiped and admired her in *Amor.* 22 and 24.) To strengthen even more this grim progress, the poet claims that the ultimate destination of that "goodly Idoll" is oblivion: "Ne any then shall after it inquire, / ne any mention shall thereof remaine" (lines 9–10).

The "turn" in the sonnet comes not between lines 12 and 13, as it frequently does, but after line 10:

> but what this verse, that neuer shall expyre,
>   shall to you purchas with her thankles paine.
> Faire be no lenger proud of that shall perish,
>   but that which shal you make immortall, cherish.

His last line is cleverly ambiguous; "that which" refers both to the immortalizing poetry as well as, by extension, to the poet. Analogically the reference is a reminder of mortality and the true means of immortality through the word/Word.

The concern for poetry and its effects continues into the next sonnet, the first part of the first two-sonnet exchange between the poet and his lady. The interweaving of the two poems, 28 and 29, is complex. *Amor.* 28 picks up the situation begun in 23, where the poet wove and the lady unwove, and where both lover and lady were artists.

> The laurell leafe, which you this day doe weare,
>   giues me great hope of your relenting mynd:
>   for since it is the badg which I doe beare,
>   ye bearing it doe seeme to me inclind:
> The powre thereof, which ofte in me I find,
>   let it lykewise your gentle brest inspire
>   with sweet infusion, and put you in mind
>   of that proud mayd, whom now those leaues attyre:
> Proud Daphne scorning Phaebus louely fyre,
>   on the Thessalian shore from him did flee:
>   for which the gods in theyr reuengefull yre
>   did her transforme into a laurell tree.
> Then fly no more fayre loue from Phebus chace,
>   but in your brest his leafe and loue embrace.

The laurel leaf makes an interesting progress through this poem. Initially (in the first quatrain) both the lady and the lover appear to be in possession of it. But the laurel as poetic achievement is also associated (through the laurel tree, née Daphne) with pride, and the second quatrain gives the poet superiority in the situation.[8] The poetic powers attributed to the laurel are called on to do two things in the lady: inspire her gentle breast and put her in mind of Daphne.

In the third quatrain Spenser introduces his own metamorphosis of the leaf to the lady, to Daphne, to the tree. The classical reference, adapted to Spenser's purpose, is wittily handled; the laurel leaf the lady wears is now associated with her pride, while that sported by the lover symbolizes his associations with Phoebus. Accordingly, the proud Daphne-lady of 27 who scorned the Phoebus-poet will be transformed because of her trespass against the lover and against poetry.

Daphne's fleeing (line 10) is used to encourage the lady not to fly (line 13) from the chase (both Phoebus's chariot and the game, the chase, in which the lover is engaged). The admonition leads to his tender appeal that she "embrace" his leaf and love, reinforcing the association he has created between the poems as poems and the poems as "loves" *(amoretti)*. By extension, the line provides his request that, as she wears his leaf, so should she wear his love.

Apparently the lady is not as impressed with the poet's wit as is he. In *Amor.* 29 she "depraue[s]" his "simple meaning with disdaynfull scorne." In so doing she is in exactly the position she was in 23, where she "vnreaue[d]" his work and thus proved destructive to him as a poet. The reader is requested to inspect what has happened:

> See how the stubborne damzell doth depraue
> my simple meaning with disdaynfull scorne:
> and by the bay which I vnto her gaue,
> accoumpts my selfe her captiue quite forlorne.

Louis Martz sees in the phrase "stubborne damzell" evidence of the poet's tone: "it is intimate, smiling, affectionate, respectful, reproachful, and courtly, all at once: it strikes exactly the tone that an older man, of experience and wisdom (someone a bit like Emma's Mr. Knightley) might adopt toward a bright and beautiful and willful young lady for whom he feels, not awe, but deep admiration and affection. It is an attitude that also implies considerable hope and confidence that his suit will in time be rewarded."[9]

While in 28 he claims superiority in the relationship, in 29 she humorously reclaims it. The laurel leaf that, for the poet, had become the source of his Daphne-Phoebus allusion has become not so much a sign of his poetic superiority as the lady's own superiority in the relationship. In 28 she wore the leaf; in 29 the poet discloses that he had given it to her. In 28 he implied he was in the position of bestowing skills upon her; in 29 she asserts that such bestowing is done only by subordinates to superiors. In her own words:

> The bay (quoth she) is of the victours borne,
> yielded them by the vanquisht as theyr meeds,

and they therewith doe poetes heads adorne,
to sing the glory of their famous deedes.

In so saying the lady returns the subject of the "bay" to poetry,
where it signifies the poet's singing.

The transition back to the poet's voice appears in the third
quatrain:

But sith she will the conquest challeng needs,
let her accept me as her faithfull thrall,
that her great triumph which my skill exceeds,
I may in trump of fame blaze over all.

While noting the lady's "conquest," the poet maintains control
by suggesting that she has superiority only because he allows it:
"sith she will . . . [then] let her accept me." Simultaneously
implicit is the plea that she accept him, thus providing a con-
tinuation of the relationship, even if with unequal status.

The line beginning "that her great triumph" is far from the
"simple meaning" the poet claims at the start. The ambiguity of
"which" permits two readings: (1) my skill exceeds her great
triumph and (2) her great triumph exceeds my skill. The next line
extends the confusion: (1) his trumpet will sound for her great
triumph or (2) the trumpet will sound for the poet when he sings
of her.

The couplet suggests poetic development, even revision,
within the poem itself: "Then would I decke her head with
glorious bayes, / and fill the world with her victorious prayse."
The simplicity of "the bay which I vnto her gaue" (line 3) gives
way to the embellished "then would I decke her head with
glorious bayes." In a clever reversal, the poet adds that he will
deck her head with praise, by which action he both accepts her
earlier statement that the victor can distribute the bays and
reverses her intent. He says, in short, he will accept her (re)inter-
pretation of his actions but will do so in order to sustain and
maintain his own poetic assertions of superiority. In so saying, he
shows the ability of his art to transform; furthermore, he reasserts
the lady's ability to manipulate and modify his art.

Jacqueline T. Miller's observations on the last part of this son-
net are noteworthy:

The poet may be re-offering a poetic bay, or he may be assuming his
possession of the conqueror's bay; in addition, the reciprocity sug-
gested in lines 7–8 implies that even by relinquishing the bays to his

lady, the poet, by the lady's own admission and conditions, can expect to have the bays given back to him. The final line deftly claims victory for both the poet and the lady: 'her victorious praise' implies the poet's praise of the victorious lady, the poet's victorious praise of his lady (i.e., the victory of his art), and the lady's praise of the poet.[10]

The narrator thus balances his impulses to love and to create his poetry, never giving full allegiance to one or the other, and never denying the existence of both his roles.

After the jocular repartee of *Amor.* 28 and 29, in which the poet plays with defining the relationship in terms of classical and literary images, 30 returns to defining in traditional Petrarchan conceits. Refusing to be deceived or moved by the extravagances of his laurel/bay claims, the lady calls a halt to his poetic play; in doing so, though, she also refuses to permit his own self-deception concerning the efficacy of his poetic and amorous powers. After *Amor.* 25 he has increasingly become more confident; such confidence has led to some underestimation of what it actually will take to win her. Her refusal to play his game forces another approach, which comes in the traditional terms with which the poet is so familiar and to which he returns when seeking the safety and security of his craft:

> My loue is lyke to yse, and I to fyre;
> how comes it then that this her cold so great
> is not dissolu'd through my so hot desyre,
> but harder growes the more I her intreat?
> Or how comes it that my exceeding heat
> is not delayd by her hart frosen cold:
> but that I burne much more in boyling sweat,
> and feele my flames augmented manifold?
> What more miraculous thing may be told
> that fire which all thing melts, should harden yse:
> and yse which is congeald with sencelesse cold,
> should kindle fyre by wonderfull deuyse?

The image is everywhere among the Petrarchans, and its development through the three quatrains of 30 shows little more than Spenser's imitative and adaptive abilities—and his humor, when considering that Petrarchanism is one of the games being played. More important is the reemergence of themes the poet developed earlier: the harder-harden doublet of *Amor.* 6 and 18 (the former of which draws on the same images used here of hard-kindle-heart, and the latter of which employs the hart-heart cluster) and the kind-kindle combination (used in 3, 6, 8). Her "gentle breast" has already been mentioned twice (6 and 28); in the couplet of this sonnet the adjective "gentle" moves from a description of her heart to the quality of her mind:

> Such is the powre of loue in gentle mind,
>   that it can alter all the course of kynd.

Following the same pattern used earlier in *Amor.* 21 and 22, the poet states his relationship in one poem and then exaggerates it in the next one. The relationship poetically interpreted in 28 and 29, stated again in traditional terms in 30, is now exaggerated in the animal imagery of 31:

> Ah why hath nature to so hard a hart,
>   giuen so goodly giftes of beauties grace?
>   whose pryde depraues each other better part,
>   and all those pretious ornaments deface.
> Sith to all other beastes of bloody race,
>   a dreadfull countenaunce she giuen hath:
>   that with theyr terrour all the rest may chace,
>   and warn to shun the daunger of theyr wrath.
> But my proud one doth worke the greater scath,
>   through sweet allurement of her louely hew:
>   that she the better may in bloody bath
>   of such poore thralls her cruell hands embrew.
> But did she know how ill these two accord,
>   such cruelty she would haue soone abhord.

Drawing upon the beast imagery of *Amor.* 20 and the cruel warrior motif used intermittently throughout the early poems, the poet provides this mock-serious "inditement." Her "hard heart" picks up the hardness image of 30. Metonymically, the lady has the "goodly giftes of beauties grace" (the same "beauties grace" adorned by pride and meekness mixed in equal parts in *Amor.* 21). Her face ("louely hew"), he claims, is de-faced by pride, which depraves (distorts) it. His comparison of the lady to "all other beastes" leads him to the important contrast: nature gives other animals such dreadful countenances that they scare away others, but nature gives the lady so lovely a face that she attracts, rather than repels, those she will make her thralls.

Yet she is called "my proud one," just as she was "my loue" in 30, "the stubborne damzell" in 29, "fayre loue" in 28, and so forth. Real affection is always present in these appellations, these "pet names," even when the language appears serious. His movement from the initial "why" of line 1 to the example in quatrain two ("sith . . .") shows her in quatrain three to be the exception to all rules. No matter how disparaging the comments appear, she always is praised and recognized for her "alluring" qualities. This is a reminder that the "sweet allurement," with its paradoxical play on attractive entrapment, suggests the lady's ongoing, quiet, steadfast wooing of the lover, en"thralled" by his beloved.

Yet there is suffering in courtship, and the animal imagery of 31 reveals the serious element of the lover's poetic playfulness. The switch to inanimate imagery in 32 conveys the sense of even more suffering and reintroduces some familiar motifs:

> The paynefull smith with force of feruent heat,
>   the hardest yron soone doth mollify:
>   that with his heauy sledge he can it beat,
>   and fashion to what he it list apply.

The image of the smith, working painstakingly and painfully, connects with the craftsman, the maker, the fashioner, the poet. Working with "feruent heat," the smith (poet-lover) mollifies the hardest iron. Again the hardness motif enters, echoing the lady's hard heart (31) and the metaphorical hard ice (30), as well as those enduring oaks of earlier poems. The iron extends the earlier images of steel, flint, and other hard objects. "Mollifying" is an interesting choice of a word; the poet-smith can "mollify" (soften) with fervent heat and can "mollify" in the sense of allaying anger or righting some wrong.

The poet's approach throughout the sequence is depicted in the image of the smith fervently beating away at the iron in order to fashion it to what "he list apply." In the next quatrain he makes explicit this connection:

> Yet cannot all these flames in which I fry,
>   her hart more harde then yron soft awhit:
>   ne all the playnts and prayers with which I
>   doe beat on th'anduyle of her stubberne wit.

The "incessant battery to her heart" of "playnts," "prayers," "vowes," "ruth," and so forth (*Amor.* 14) neither affects her heart (passion) nor her will ("stubberne wit").

After revealing in the second quatrain what he cannot do, the poet gives the third quatrain to describing what the lady does:

> But still the more she feruent sees my fit,
>   the more she frieseth in her wilfull pryde:

> and harder growes the harder she is smit,
> with all the playnts which to her be applyde.

The couplet provides his exasperated resolution:

> What then remaines but I to ashes burne,
> and she to stones at length all frosen turne?

These six lines draw together many strands from the earlier lines of this sonnet and many images from earlier poems. The "feruent heat" of the blacksmith's fire, also applicable to the "feruent heat" of the poet and lover, is applied to the poet's "fit" in 9; his "fit," in turn, is an extension of the smith's effort at beating and fashioning as well as the poet's softening and beating. The lady's freezing clearly picks up the ice image of the previous poem, just as the lover's heat reflects that same poem's fire image, with the amusing twist that all the flames of passion may burn him to ashes. The lady's unnatural capabilities of being beyond ordinary natural laws (noted in *Amor.* 30) are again evident in her growing harder, the harder "she is smit." "Smit," in turn, both echoes the poet's "fit" and visually reflects the poet as "smith." The entire poem is one in which the end rhymes have significance, with the "feruent heat" being that with which the poet-smith "beat[s]." He does this ("apply") in order to "mollify," but he is so involved with the process that he ("I") fries in those same flames. What he cannot "soft awhit" is her "stubberne wit." And he has "applyde" his complaints precisely to attack her "pryde."

The respective directions the poet and lady take are depicted in the couplet. All the heat images, begun with the fire of *Amor.* 30, build up to his burning to ashes; all the cold images, begun with the ice of *Amor.* 30, build to her turning to stone. The threat, of course, is that he will burn himself out and that she will turn so hard that she will be petrified.

Yet another way into this poem is through the same imagery Spenser uses in describing another of his questing knights, Artegall, who engages in battle with Radigund (5.5.7–8):

> Yet still her blowes he bore, and her forbore,
>   Weening at last to win aduantage new;
> Yet still her crueltie increased more,
> And though her powre faild, her courage did accrew,
> Which fayling he gan fiercely her pursew.
> Like as a Smith that to his cunning feat

> The stubborne mettall seeketh to subdew,
>   Soone as he feeles it mollifide with heat,
> With his great yron sledge doth strongly on it beat.

> So did Sir Artegall vpon her lay,
>   As if she had an yron anduile beene.

Artegall fights a battle that eventually makes him thrall. The "smith" images, applied to the great Knight of Justice, are applied to a process that eventually upsets the whole system of justice when Artegall deals with Radigund as he does. Eventually, "So was he ouercome, not ouercome, / But to her yeelded of his owne accord." The *Amoretti* lover's path is too close to that of the knight's, and the wise sonnet lady is aware of the dangerous position the lover is in, whereby he is entrapped by his image of the proud, cruel, Petrarchan mistress.

During most of the highly emotional periods in the sequence, the poet alleviates his frustration by wordplay and by suspending empirical time as he withdraws into psychological time. In other instances the lover's anxious emotional condition quickly alters when he suddenly becomes aware of the "real" world's presence outside the sonnets. Spenser breaks the narrative frame as his characters look outward into "our" world, reminding the reader of the fictional nature of what is being read while simultaneously drawing readers further into the fiction by making them feel they are on the inside of the game.

This is what occurs at the start of the second week in Lent, *Amor.* 33; the radical departure from the narrative frame of the earlier sonnets provides a fine distinguishing mark for this second Sunday in Lent. The despair (mock or real) in which the poet found himself in *Amor.* 32 is suddenly interrupted by the poet's voice addressing the outside world. He did this indirectly in *Amor.* 5 ("Rudely thou wrongest"); here, however, he specifies the person addressed. The artist is responsible for his actions, both moral and artistic; here he accounts for them. The ludic nature of this interplay is fascinating. Spenser literally develops *Amor.* 33 "in terms" reminding us of Artegall and Radigund. But that redaction leads to its own narrative intervention, in which the narrator is reminded of Elizabeth I. That allusion, in turn, presumably leads the *Amoretti* narrator to remembrance of his epic task:

> Great wrong I doe, I can it not deny,
>   to that most sacred Empresse my dear dred,

> not finishing her Queene of faery,
> that mote enlarge her liuing prayses dead:
> But lodwick, this of grace to me aread:
> doe ye not thinck th'accomplishment of it,
> sufficient worke for one mans simple head,
> all were it as the rest but rudely writ.
> How then should I without another wit,
> thinck euer to endure so taedious toyle?
> sins that this one is tost with troublous fit,
> of a proud loue, that doth my spirite spoyle.
> Ceasse then, till she vouchsafe to grawnt me rest,
> or lend you me another liuing brest.

Ironically, love is detrimental to the poet's task, even if that task is depicted as "taedious toyle." But love itself produces "troublous fit[s]" (echoing the poet's "fit" of 32), at least a more honest appraisal of the situation than describing it as a war, a sickness, or worship. On the rhetorical level the sonnet forces us to view Spenser's "biography of a lover" as autobiography as well. The problem of Self, its creation, identification, and preservation, is thus greatly reduced. No longer is there a question about who is the speaker—Spenser inside the poems or Spenser outside. Here (and again later in the sequence) these "two" Spensers are presented as one. The creator is presented as equal to his creation, and together they create (generate) a mutual Self.

The suggestion of autobiography, like the later hint of it in *Amor.* 80, serves as a pretext for a "more detached and critical examination of the relationship between image and object, between the specific and the general, between the real and the ideal, than would be appropriate if [Spenser] were presenting a more inclusive and less 'private' view"[11] in the sonnets. By interjecting these poems (33 and 80) as he does, Spenser reminds his readers, just as the lover is reminded by the sequence's various time references, of a larger world beyond that of the persona's scope.

The poem is even more significant because of being positioned as the second Sunday in Lent. Structurally the sonnet coincides with the feast of Saint Matthias. While Christians offer prayers on this day, the poet offers apologies and explanations concerning his "troublous fit" and the weakening of his spirit. The poet, like the analogous penitent Christian, is already finding the Lenten "purification" no easy matter, and "love's" disturbing effects are carefully noted. The Collect for the second Sunday in Lent concerns "troublous" situations. While the sonnet's supplications are to Lodowick, that he "grawnt me rest, or lend you me another liuing brest" (in order to deal with the two problems—poetry and love), the imprecatory Collect beseeches God for deliverance from two kinds of enemies, outward "aduersities whiche maye happen to the body" as well as inward "euel thoughtes which maye assault and hurte the soule."

The tensions of the troublous fit, of the conflict between love and artistic creativity, are indirectly echoed in the next sonnet, *Amor.* 34. At various times in *The Faerie Queene*, Spenser uses the image of a ship to indicate the directions and plights of his epic progress. In *FQ* 6.12.1, the last canto of the last completed book, the book to which *Amor.* 33 and 80 refers, Spenser makes a claim that helps illumine the sonnet:

> Like as a ship, that through the Ocean wyde
>   Directs her course vnto one certaine cost,
>   Is met of many a counter winde and tyde,
>   With which her winged speed is let and crost,
>   And she her selfe in stormie surges tost;
>   Yet making many a borde, and many a bay,
>   Still winneth way, ne hath her compasse lost:
>   Right so it fares with me in this long way,
> Whose course is often stayd, yet neuer is astray.

Amor. 34 begins similarly:

> Lyke as a ship that through the Ocean wyde,
>   by conduct of some star doth make her way,
>   whenas a storme hath dimd her trusty guyde,
>   out of her course doth wander far astray.

The poet admits that, lacking his guide, he has been wandering; his love and his epic project (*Amor.* 33) have taken wrong turns. The "dimming" of the guiding star continues into the next quatrain, where the poet applies the ship-epic-courtship image to himself, projecting his inner emotional disorder onto nature's disorder. The literal storm of the first quatrain becomes a metaphoric and analogic one in the second quatrain, similar to Britomart's complaint ("Huge sea of sorrow, and tempestuous griefe, / wherein my feeble barke is tossed long"):

> So I whose star, that wont with her bright ray
>   me to direct, with cloudes is ouercast,
>   doe wander-now in darknesse and dismay,
>   through hidden perils round about me plast.

Significantly, the lover is strengthened by hope of the time when (not "if") the storm will pass:

> Yet hope I well, that when this storme is past
>   my Helice the lodestar of my lyfe
>   will shine again, and looke on me at last,
>   with louely light to cleare my cloudy grief.
> Till then I wander carefull comfortlesse,
>   in secret sorrow and sad pensiuenesse.

Yet images of wandering, darkness, and despair weave through the poem. The poem is structurally and characteristically self-involved (and Self is also its subject): the subject of line 1 reaches its predicate only in line 4; the new subject of line 5 does not reach its predicate until line 7. While there is a turn between lines 8 and 9, the couplet merely reflects introspectively on the preceding action, thus taking us back into the poem. The sequence at this point actually does appear to "wander now," and certainly does so during this treatment of its "darkness and dismay."

Spenser never reveals what the "clouds" obscuring the star actually are. Usually the term implies inner confusion or anger, but in this case it might be the lady's cold heart, which in Amor. 31 "deface[d]" her beauty and which here "ouercast[s]" her "bright ray." Or it might be the speaker's own confused emotions and wit (Amor. 33) that toss him with a "troublous fit."

An initial ambiguity remains unsolved: does the poem concern the lover and his lady, the poet and Elizabeth I, or a combination (and thus extension) of the two, as represented in the previous poem? And is this sonnet an elaboration of the conflict depicted in 33, with a commentary on the progress (or lack thereof) of the epic as well as with the courtship? If it is such an elaboration, is this echo of 6.12.1 to be considered an indication that the poet, no matter what his claims are here in 34, is in control of his ship?

There are no clear answers for these questions, nor do we know who "Helice" is, mentioned only once, here, in all the Spenser canon. In mythology she is one of Diana's nymphs and a daughter of the great Lycaon, king of Arcadia, the country named after the son (Arcas) Helice bore Zeus. Turned into a bear, she was then transformed into the constellation Ursa Major, the Great Bear. Helice can be read (and pronounced) as "Elis," that is, Elizabeth, who would be either the queen or Elizabeth Boyle, both of whom have connections with Amoret, described in 3.6.52 as the "lodestarre of all chaste affection," the guiding star who is also, as Hamilton wittily suggests, a center of attraction.[12] The sonnet's ambiguity is certainly intended, and suggests the continued blending of poetic obligation and personal concern.

Amor. 34 joins 35, 36, and 37 in providing a quartet of "eye" sonnets. In various ways all four treat either the poet's or the lady's eyes, thus voicing concern about the ability to see, to understand, to assimilate or synthesize. They illustrate the narrator's distracted and obscured sense and provide an example of the suspension of narrative action by psychological time.

While *Amor.* 34 treats the lady's starlike eyes (her qualities as a "lodestar"), *Amor.* 35 switches to the lover's eyes; *Amor.* 36 moves back to the lady's eyes and *Amor.* 37 to the lover's. The lady's eyes appear as cloudy guides in 34 and as cruel but thrilling conquerors in 36; his eyes are hungry, greedy, yet passive in 35, but in 37 they are warned against too much staring. The alternation between her eyes and his reflects an ongoing alternation and reversal of sexual roles, indicated by his passivity and her aggression. This reversal must be corrected before there can be proper love.

Amor. 35 begins with the poet's lament:

> My hungry eyes through greedy couetize,
>   still to behold the obiect of their paine:
>   with no contentment can themselues suffize,
>   but hauing pine and hauing not complaine.

While earlier sonnets contained numerous references to eyes, this is the first poem given entirely to his, not her, eyes. As with the other sonnets, this one presents a rather intricate interweaving of "eye" images and sounds, particularly in the pronominal phrases that either relate to the poet's eyes or to the lady's. Added to the sight motif is the hunger theme, which, at the very start, is interconnected with seeing: "hungry eyes" and "greedy couetize" relate not only by rhyme but by parallel structuring. The first contains an adjective followed by its noun, the second a clever play linking the adjective-noun combination ("greedy couetize") to "greedy covet eyes."

The poet's problem and its clarifying analogy appear in the second quatrain:

> For lacking it they cannot lyfe sustayne,
>   and hauing it they gaze on it the more:

in their amazement lyke Narcissus vaine
whose eyes him staru'd: so plenty makes me poore.

The lover as Narcissus appears a proper comparison. But Narcissus's abundance was in the love of himself; with the poet it is in his love of the lady. The famous reference to Britomart's looking in her mirror is instructive (3.2.44):

> But wicked fortune mine, though mind be good,
>   Can haue no end, nor hope of my desire,
>   But feed on shadowes, whiles I die for food,
>   And like a shadow wexe, whiles with entire
>   Affection, I doe languish and expire.
>   I fonder, then Cephisus foolish child,
>   Who hauing vewed in a fountaine shere
>   His face, was with the loue thereof beguild;
> I fonder loue a shade, the bodie farre exild.

The beldame responds by noting that Britomart has better fortune than Narcissus because behind the mirrored shadows upon which Britomart feeds lies a real knight. Narcissus directed his love toward himself, making it hopeless; Britomart directs hers to a knight who (even if with the aid of magic) can be found. In Spenser's poetry Narcissus's problem is not so much that he loves himself as that he is deluded by shadows. Britomart's search for the reality behind the shadow keeps her on the right quest. This is precisely the point the sonnet lady attempts to reinforce: she is not a shadow but a real woman, and must be approached as such.

The abundance the lover experiences in looking at the lady is, paradoxically, that which makes him poor. This is a continuation of the many contraries already listed in the sonnets—life-death, approach-avoidance, attracting-repelling, art-love, nature-art, bitter-sweet—and it is yet another example of love's disconcerting effects. Narcissus is held fast by an empty image and thus suffers a double torment; the lover, however, while suffering his double torment, at least is not really in love with only a shade.

The reminder here is of Marinell, who is also compared to Narcissus in being told (he by his mother, Narcissus by Tiresias) how he may live long and prosper by negation. Marinell's mother warns him about women; Tiresias warns Narcissus about not knowing himself ("si se non noverit"). Both Narcissus and Marinell are separated from their "significant others" by water, and in the *Amoretti* the water image of the ship on the "Ocean wyde" has just appeared. But in the *Amoretti* the ship eventually does come to port (*Amor.* 63), and in Faerieland Marinell and Flo-rimell are eventually joined.

Yet the *Amoretti* lover is a step ahead of Marinell, the true Narcissus of Book 3, whose sterile treasure is hoarded on the seashore and who will not share himself with anyone else. The third quatrain of *Amor.* 35 not only returns to the eye motif but indicates the important distinction:

> Yet are mine eyes so filled with the store
>> of that faire sight, that nothing else they brooke,
>> but lothe the things which they did like before,
>> and can no more endure on them to looke.
> All this worlds glory seemeth vayne to me,
>> and all their showes are shadowes sauing she.

Narcissus's eyes (8) are compared as well as contrasted with the lover's eyes at the start of line 9. Spenser has already prepared for the identification with "so plenty makes me poore," Narcissus's own statement, "inopem me copia fecit," as well as the poet's. But the "yet" that begins the sestet contains an objection; while it is through the eyes that he has become "poore," the eyes are also so filled with abundance that they require nothing else. With that objection in mind it is possible to see the rest of the sonnet as the lover's rejection of the lover-Narcissus identification: "I regard all this world's glory as vanity, all its 'shows' but shadows; Narcissus did not see these antitheses and therefore I am unlike him." Furthermore, the lady is a "faire sight" and is contrasted with the "shadowes" noted in the last line. Narcissus may have loved a shadow, but the sonnet narrator does not.

The sonnet's movement, then, is similar to that of the episode with Britomart and her nurse. First the resemblances to Narcissus are emphasized, then the differences are suggested so that a significant contrast may be made.[13] The poet's worship of the lady has brought progress in his vision; he has learned the lesson Narcissus failed to learn—that the world's glory is "vayne," and that there is an important connection (reinforced by the rhyme) between shows and shadows. But the connection does not lead to death, as it did for Narcissus, but to life with the empirical lady. Narcissus's unconscious seeking the innermost self of his soul, his quest to know himself (against which knowledge Tiresias warned him), is reflected in the poem's pool. Narcissus errs not in what he seeks but in how he seeks it. Our poet, by *Amor.* 35 and with the help of the lady, is in the process of correcting his own myopic vision. Out of context the poem might be read as another step "up" the neo-Platonic scala, but in context this is seen as a development in the purification of the poet's vision and as an element of his Christian ontology.

In *Amor.* 36 the poet's "pine" becomes, "pining languor"; his "hungry" yet full eyes yield to a focus on her "thrilling eyes":

> Tell me when shall these wearie woes haue end,
>   Or shall their ruthlesse torment neuer cease:
>   but al my dayes in pining languor spend,
>   without hope or aswagement or release?
> Is there no meanes for me to purchase peace,
>   or make agreement with her thrilling eyes:
>   but that their cruelty doth still increace,
>   and dayly more augment my miseryes?

The hunger/plenty, having/having-not ideas of the previous sonnet carry into this one; his attraction to her thrilling eyes only augments his misery ("plenty makes me poore"). The "couetize" motif of *Amor.* 35 ("couetize," "plenty," "poore," "store") is transposed to a spending motif in 36 ("spend," "meanes," "purchase," "increace"). The weariness noted earlier in *Amor.* 11 and 15, and to which the poet alluded in referring to the "taedious toyle" on his epic, is now applied to the courtship's "wearie woes."

The third quatrain and the couplet address the lady, reversing the idea that there is value in her "slaying" the poet:

> But when ye haue shewed all extremityes,
>   then thinke how little glory ye haue gayned,
>   by slaying him, whose lyfe though ye despyse,
>   mote haue your life in honour long maintayned.
> But by his death which some perhaps will mone,
>   ye shall condemned be of many a one.

Eyes appear again in *Amor.* 37; now, however, for the first time in the sequence, the real focus of the poem is on another of the lady's physical attributes—her hair. Here, too, is a change from mention of her (or his) eyes; now the eyes are "mens frayle eyes." So important have the eyes been that even the lady's hair assumes some of their characteristics:

> What guyle is this, that those her golden tresses,
>   she doth attyre vnder a net of gold:
>   and with sly skill so cunningly them dresses,
>   that which is gold or heare, may scarse be told?

Her "guilefull eyen" (*Amor.* 12) have certainly been sly, skillful, and cunning; like the tresses, her eyes also ensnare:

> Is it that mens frayle eyes, which gaze too bold,
>   she may entangle in that golden snare:
>   and being caught may craftily enfold
>   theyre weaker harts, which are not wel aware?

This is a return to the nature-art topos, and once again the lady is such a perfect blend of the two, using as she does her art to further nature, that that "which is gold or heare" is not distinguishable. There is also an extension here of the earlier entrapment theme, with nets, entangling, snaring, and being caught all furthering the image. Even eyes may be ensnared (as the lover knows). The metaphoric captivity described earlier becomes a literal entrapment from which he wishes to escape.

The third quatrain reintroduces the word "meanes" of the previous sonnet:

> Take heed therefore, myne eyes, how ye doe stare
>   henceforth too rashly on that guilefull net,
>   in which if euer ye entrapped are,
>   out of her bands ye by no means shall get.

Earlier he asked "is there no meanes for me to purchase peace," with a suggestion that there are no means to escape the lady's bands (a "banding" he actually desires). In both sonnets Spenser plays on "means," not just as ways and methods but as intermediaries (*media*, roughly equivalent to Pico's *temperamento*). The "means" refer to temperance, a topic he introduced several times. Although the poet wittily plays on the word, it is in truth through a temperate approach to the lady (not giving up his poetry but tempering it with judgment and truth, not giving up a "romantic" view of the lady but tempering that vision with reality) that he will find the means of success.

There is another side to this sonnet as well. At *Amor.* 37 the lover is over halfway to the bethrothal; his comment in the couplet about his condition—"Fondnesse it were for any being free, / to couet fetters, though they golden bee"—is perhaps a witty self-observation about the direction he is taking. It further concerns his desires for marriage, the "golden band" with which he would be fettered.

The cluster of eye poems ends in 37; in 38 the poet moves

ahead with a playful dictate to the lady, reasserting his role as
poet and restating his concern about her unyielding position:

> Arion, when through tempests cruel wracke,
>   He forth was thrown into the greedy seas:
>   through the sweet musick which his harp did make
>   allur'd a Dolphin him from death to ease.

Unlike the earlier allusion to Narcissus, this one to Arion
follows the traditional myth closely. Arion the poet is associated
with the poet who, in *Amor.* 36, apprised the lady he "mote haue
your life in honour long maintayned." The lover's abilities as
poet are reasserted by the connection with the seagoing Orpheus
of Herodotus, Ovid, and Pliny. Arion plays "sweet musick,"
which allures both sea and sea animals; his art represents har-
mony and order, and the ability to stay death as well as to
appease nature.

Following the pattern used in 35, once the poet establishes his
classical precedent he proceeds to qualify it:

> But my rude musick, which was wont to please
>   some dainty eares, cannot with any skill,
>   the dreadfull tempest of her wrath appease,
>   nor moue the Dolphin from her stubborne will.

Arion's sweet song is contrasted with the poet's "rude musick,"
just as the dolphin is compared to the lady. The seas' tempests
now become the lady's, and the dolphin that moved Arion to
safety now becomes an unmovable, willful woman. The in-
congruity of the willful dolphin is glaring: the animal is always
presented as friendly to men and, in fact, is occasionally a sym-
bol of salvation.

Having treated Arion in the first quatrain, and his own "rude
musick" in the second, the poet moves in the third to the lady:

> But in her pride she dooth perseuer still,
>   all carelesse how my life for her decayse:
>   yet with one word she can it saue or spill,
>   to spill were pitty, but to saue were prayse.

He appeals here to the same sense of honor he assumes she had
when he wrote in *Amor.* 36 of gaining glory; and he further
assumes that she wants praise, not condemnation:

> Chose rather to be praysd for dooing good,
>   then to be blam'd for spilling guiltlesse blood.

Those assumptions contain a part of the poet's continuing problem: he projects upon the lady what he would think, externalizing his own desires and approaches upon a lady who nowhere has indicated they are her wishes. The forward step taken in this sonnet is the poet's further questioning of his own ability to make "sweet musick," like Arion's. The backward step is that in his frustration he has reverted to the Petrarchan language of earlier sonnets, here presenting the lady in the old cruel/fair image.

In *Amor.* 39 he balances that image with a *donna angelicata* one:

> Sweet smile, the daughter of the Queene of loue,
>   Expressing all thy mothers powrefull art:
>   with which she wonts to temper angry Ioue,
>   when all the gods he threats with thundring dart.

One of a pair (39 and 40) concerning the lady's smiles, this poem is a delightful interlude in the midst of the poet's agon. The earlier poem concerning the lady's hair (37) depicted the hair as an external expression of the lady's abilities; this one on the smile expresses the lady's natural self. The poem not only describes how the lover feels (the language is almost as "sweet" and cheerful as his subject), it also depicts the smile's transforming power without even mentioning that effect. As Arion's sweet art tempered nature, so the lady (as her own natural "sweet art") tempers the poet's spirits:

> Sweet is thy vertue as thy self sweet art,
>   for when on me thou shinedst late in sadnesse,
>   a melting pleasance ran through euery part,
>   and me reuiued with hart robbing gladnesse.

The two-fold compliment aligns the lady's "vertue" with her smile; the two are inseparable. Actually, the sweetness is partly a result of the smile's virtue (which itself resides in the sweetness). The sweetness combines images of sight and taste; he sees the smile, tastes it, and its own two-fold nature is such that it both robs hearts as it vivifies (revives) them. In *Amor.* 35 his hungry eyes beheld the object of their pain; now the hunger is slaked as he

> fed on the fulnesse of that chearefull glaunce.
> More sweet than Nectar or Ambrosiall meat,
> seemd euery bit, which thenceforth I did eat.

The poem needs to be considered in light of those poems which compare the poet's art to the lady's; like the weaving and unweaving of 23, and the exchange of laurels and bays in 28 and 29, *Amor.* 38 shows the ineffectiveness of his art as craft. *Amor.* thirty-nine then asserts the effectiveness of her art as natural ability. Like Arion, the lady makes sweet music that carries from death to life; but if the lady is Arion, it is the poet who, as dolphin, is allured yet who must be moved from stubborn will. The poem, then, serves both as a commentary on previous poems as well as a further elaboration of (and variation on) several themes developing throughout the sequence.

Sonnet 40 does the same; it picks up the smile theme and explores it in another fashion. Whereas 39 provided the poetic, exuberant sentiment overflowing from the lover's emotion, *Amor.* 40 presents not a description of an experience but an expression of the joy of that experience and the feelings accompanying it:

> Mark when she smiles with amiable cheare,
> and tell me whereto can ye lyken it:
> when on each eyelid sweetly doe appeare
> an hundred Graces as in shade to sit.

As he has done in the past, once he has experienced a feeling, a situation, an occasion, the poet attempts to give it expression by likening it to something else, by attempting to capture it in a metaphor. The situation appears in the first quatrain, and the poet provides his own commentary, noting that

> Lykest it seemeth in my simple wit
> vnto the fayre sunshine in somers day:
> that when a dreadfull storme away is flit,
> thrugh the broad world doth spred his goodly ray:
> At sight whereof each bird that sits on spray,
> and euery beast that to his den was fled,
> comes forth afresh out of their late dismay,
> and to the light lift vp theyr drouping hed.

All nature responds to the sunshine/smile; its light-giving qualities are those which the poet has been seeking since *Amor.* 34, when "her bright ray" was said to be "with cloudes . . .

ouercast." In 34 he hoped "that when this storme is past / my Helice . . . will looke on me at last, / with louely light to cleare my cloudy grief." In 40, the "storme" apparently having passed, he concludes:

> So my storme beaten hart likewise is cheared,
>> with that sunshine when cloudy looks are cleared.

On the analogical level, *Amor.* 40 marks both 3 March and the third Sunday in Lent. Whereas Lent Two contrasted the old life with the new (and in the sonnet, the two tasks of writing and loving), Lent Three contrasts darkness and light. Its epistle comes from Ephesians 5, where verse 8 gives the key: "For ye were once darknes, but are now light in the Lorde: walke as children of light, for the frute of the Spirit is in all goodnes, and right-eousnes, and trueth." But before he discusses the darkness and light theme, Paul makes clear that his message concerns "walk[ing] in loue, euen as Christe loued us." By walking in love, Christians are to imitate God; Christian behavior is meant to be a reflection of God's action toward us. The lady's actions in the sonnet, then, may be read as imitations of Christ's actions, whose Son-shine revives and uplifts.

As the week of "fasting" and seriousness recommences, the joy of the Sunday "feast" day quickly disperses. *Amor.* 41 depicts a hasty return both to the tribulations of this prebetrothal period and to the war images. It also provides the poet a vehicle for analyzing the "tempest" of the courtship. He begins with a question:

> Is it her nature or is it her will,
>> to be so cruell to an humbled foe?
>> if nature, then she may it mend with skill,
>> if will, then she at will may will forgoe.

A third alternative is possible:

> But if her nature and her wil be so,
>> that she will plague the man that loues her most:
>> and take delight t'encrease a wretches woe,
>> then all her natures goodly guifts are lost.

The paradox is one of appearance and reality:

> And that same glorious beauties ydle boast,
>> is but a bayt such wretches to beguile,

> as being long in her loues tempest tost,
>   she meanes at last to make her piteous spoyle.
> O fayrest fayre let neuer it be named,
>   that so fayre beauty was so fowly shamed.

That is (in accord with standard neo-Platonic doctrine concerning outward beauty and inner goodness), her great beauty appears to argue her loving will and nature, although it is possible this lady (as he indicated earlier) does not respond to "natural" law.

In the following sonnet (*Amor.* 42), his being tossed "in her loues tempest" (just as he was "tost with troublous fit" in *Amor.* 33) becomes a cruel torment:

> The loue which me so cruelly tormenteth,
>   so pleasing is in my extreamest paine:
>   that all the more my sorrow it augmenteth,
>   the more I loue and doe embrace my bane.

The poet asserts "ne doe I wish (for wishing were but vaine) / to be acquit fro[m] my continuall smart." Experiencing joy in being her thrall, he begs to be bound with "adamant chayne," ending with:

> Onely let her abstaine from cruelty,
>   and doe me not before my time to dy.

In a sense the poem is wishful thinking. The poet asks the lady to give him the ultimate pleasure of the greatest possible suffering, yet hopes he can escape dying. Ironically, dying represents the greatest possible suffering.

The following poem, *Amor.* 43, continues the image of thralldom and death and introduces a new development in the poet's growing awareness of the need to withdraw from his Petrarchan pose, to turn into himself and there to create "in silence secretly" the proper speech.

> Shall I then silent be or shall I speake?
>   And if I speake, her wrath renew I shall:
>   and if I silent be, my hart will breake,
>   or choked be with ouerflowing gall.
> What tyranny is this both my hart to thrall,
>   and eke my toung with proud restraint to tie?
>   that nether I may speake nor thinke at all,
>   but like a stupid stock in silence die.

Yet I my hart with silence secretly
    will teach to speak, and my iust cause to plead:
    and eke mine eies with meeke humility,
    loue learned letters to her eyes to read.
Which her deep wit, that true harts thought can spel,
    wil soone conceiue, and learne to construe well.

The poet finds himself in the midst of an important decision: to speak (write) or not to speak (write). For him the matter is almost of existential significance, given that as a poet his "speaking" not only is the means of his craft but is what provides his identity. In one of the best meditative sonnets thus far, the poet expresses the niceties of his thought, the tenderness of his feelings, and the expectations of his love. The sonnet provides a network of images concerning expression: "silent," "speake," "thinke," "toung," "silence," "letters," "read," "wit," "spel," "conceiue," and "construe." Obliquely connected to these are images of his heart breaking because of silence, of tying his tongue with proud restraint, of dying in silence, of teaching in secret silence, and of pleading his just cause.

There is also here the recognition that the enthralled heart (his "poore captyued hart" of 42) is of his as well as the lady's doing; it is thrall to her precisely because he has "spoken" of it as such. His tongue, tied with proud restraint (as his heart was restrained in 42), is restrained because (1) he does not know whether or not to speak and (2) because the lady restrains him from speaking opaquely in the sterile metaphors he finds so expressive.

The sestet provides his witty resolution: he will both speak and not speak, redirecting his poet's craft to an inner language, teaching his heart to speak. His eyes, furthermore, will read "loue learned letters" to her eyes (as the birds will later, in *Epith.* 88, sing their "louelearned song" to her on her wedding day). He will, in short, provide his own secret language for her, a game only the two of them can understand or play. His heart and his eyes will tell her what he has been unable to say in words. Words transformed into pregnant silence (which her "deep wit" will conceive, spell, construe) thus begin a new kind of poetic expression through a process of interior dialogue. A bilevel kind of poetry is produced, as in an allegory (or as with the sequence's analogic level), which the lady's comprehending eyes can "spel."

The conflict between love and artistic creativity, noted particularly in *Amor.* 33, 38, and 43, and the poet's confirmation of silence, continues in 44 with the references to Orpheus and his music.

> When those renoumed noble Peres of Greece,
>   thrugh stubborn pride amongst themselues did iar
>   forgetfull of the famous golden fleece,
>   then Orpheus with his harp theyr strife did bar.

Like Arion in *Amor.* 38, Orpheus is said to quell tempests, the former in nature and the latter among "those renoumed noble Peres of Greece [who] / thrugh stubborn pride amongst themselues did iar." As in 38, the poet uses the classical image as a springboard for what he says of himself and his music. As in 38, the reason for the analogy is to show the differences in the effects of the respective musicians' music, not so much to suggest that the poet is less of a musician than his classical counterpart, but that the lady is so much more difficult to appease than are her analogues in the other poems.

While in his poetry Spenser uses various parts of the Orpheus myths, it is Orpheus the poet, the singer and restorer of order, who is of most interest to him.[14] In the sonnet's second quatrain the poet applies to himself Orpheus's ability to calm the Argonauts' civil strife:

> But this continuall cruell ciuill warre,
>   the which my selfe against my selfe doe make:
>   whilest my weak powres of passions warreid arre,
>   no skill can stint nor reason can aslake.

The Argonauts fought among themselves, forgetful of the golden fleece; the poet fights his own civil war between love and poetry, between silence and speaking. His "powres of passions" are weak because they are "warreid" (warred and wearied). The external search for the golden fleece (with its analogy to the lady's golden tresses) is thus transposed to an internal ethical and artistic quest.

The third quatrain and couplet find the poet aligning himself with both the warring Argonauts and Orpheus as he (the poet) attempts to use Orpheus's method of quelling strife:

> But when in hand my tunelesse harp I take,
>   then doe I more augment my foes despight:
>   and griefe renew, and passions doe awake
>   to battaile fresh against my selfe to fight.
> Mongst whome the more I seeke to settle peace,
>   the more I fynd their malice to increace.

The musical motif (bar, tune, augment) notwithstanding, the poetry has become "tunelesse." His "toung with proud restraint" (*Amor.* 43) is tied. Instead of stopping the fighting, the poet's music stirs it to fresh battle. His comparison with Orpheus (who is often depicted iconographically as a Christ figure)[15] proves fruitless. In *Amor.* 17 the poet simply deferred to the fact that "a greater craftesman hand" was needed for the expression he wished; here he takes responsibility for his lack of poetic ability and laments his condition.

In *Amor.* 45 the poet again addresses the lady directly. For several poems he has concerned himself with his inner turmoil. The poem is an outgrowth of that concern and focuses on the source of his artistic inspiration. But while the last two poems were dynamic expressions of the question "shall I then silent be or shall I speake?" and of his "continuall cruell ciuill warre," this sonnet depicts a static state mirroring, as it were, the outside world.

The poem involves the difficult yet common "mirror" motif popular among the neo-Platonists and Petrarchans:

> Leaue lady in your glass of christall clene,
>> Your goodly selfe for euermore to vew:
>> and in my selfe, my inward selfe I meane,
>> most liuely lyke behold your semblant trew.
> Within my hart, though hardly it can shew
>> thing so diuine to vew of earthly eye:
>> the fayre Idea of your celestiall hew,
>> and euery part remaines immortally:
> And were it not that through your cruelty,
>> with sorrow dimmed and deformed it were:
>> the goodly ymage of your visnomy,
>> clearer than christall would therein appear.
> But if your selfe in me ye playne will see,
>> remoue the cause by which your fayre beames darkned be.

The poet calls the lady away from the merely reflective vanity of the looking glass to use what in *Amor.* 43 he called "her deep wit, that true harts thought can spel[,] . . . conceiue, and learne to construe well." He makes another plea for his poetry and for himself as poet, insisting that in him (hence in his poetry) she will find more than mere appearance (such as that found in the "glasse of christall clene"); instead she will see her own "semblant trew," a "goodly ymage" that is "clearer than christall." The poem itself, he suggests, will provide a truer mirror than the glass in which the lady views herself.

But the image of the mirror is almost a standard Renaissance signal of a difficulty in perception; the mirror implies light and reflex, reality and appearance. In Renaissance epistemology the mirror emblem owes much to Paul's "glass": "videmus nunc per speculum in aenigmate, tunc autem facie ad faciem" (Now we see through a glass darkly, but then we shall see Face to Face). The glass was variously symbolized as mind, essence, understanding, or imagination; as a reference to any of these faculties, the spec- ulum was indispensable to the shaping of human knowledge. For Spenser, the glass is an objective piece of infinite facets, each of which darkly "signifies" the Creator.

Amor. 45 divides itself between the *speculum aenigmate* and a *speculum lucido.* For most Renaissance writers, Spenser in- cluded, to see *per speculum in aenigmate* (as the poet suggests the lady will do if looking at the image in his heart, where the lady's fair beams "darkned be") is to behold only distorted sim- ulacrums of reality. In the *Hymne of Heauenly Beautie* (113–19), having examined the essential attributes of the Deity (grace, truth, love, doome, mercy, etc.), Spenser explains how God dis- closes these qualities to mankind:

> Those vnto all he daily doth display,
> And shew himselfe in th'image of his grace,
> As in a looking glasse, through which he may
> Be seene, of all his creatures vile and base,
> That are vnable else to see his face,
> His glorious face which glistereth else so bright,
> That th'Angels selues can not endure his sight.

It in the great looking-glass of nature that we are allowed "to reade enregistred in euery nooke / His goodnesse" (*HHB*, 131– 32).[16]

In the sonnet, the poet calls upon the lady to look within him ("my inward selfe I meane"), acknowledging on the one hand a distinction between his inner and outer selves and, on the other, the superiority of the inner, while contrasting the "christall clene" with the even clearer crystal in his heart. The home of the image is the lover's heart (which in *Amor.* 43 he has taught to speak in silence secretly), to which he directs attention with "in," "inward," and "within." Just as he had claimed his eyes would "read" to her eyes, the implication is that through the poet's eyes the lady will see to his heart.

Yet the image within his heart is "with sorrow dimmed and deformed," perhaps a witty reference to the tears through which (either through his looking out of them, or of her looking into his heart through them) the image is deformed. As Desdemona says of Othello (3.4.137–45): "Something sure of state . . . hath puddled his clear spirit; in such cases men's natures wrangle with inferior things, though great ones are their object." Insofar as the puddled image thwarts high purposes (seeing the "goodly ymage . . . clearer then christall"), it frustrates the ability to become divine.

The lady is called upon to see more than her mere reflection; if that were all to be found in the lover's eyes, she would be in the position of Narcissus (*Amor.* 35), for which the "glasse of christall clene" would be quite sufficient. But she is called to an ex-stasis, a movement out of her self-containment into the heart of love. Yet the image is temporarily darkened, and that which the lady *would* see ("the fayre Idea of your celestiall hew") is not what she *will* see (a dimmed, deformed, and darkened representation). In the couplet, then, the poet calls on the lady to help him "remoue the cause by which your fayre beames darkened be" and provide the true resemblance. She is to use her art to reflect his art, which in turn will reflect her (etc.).

In *Amor.* 7 the poet wrote of the "fayre eyes, the myrrour of my mazed hart" and showed how he was reflected in her. Now she is reflected in him. Reflection reappeared topically in the narcissistic *Amor.* 35 ten sonnets before this one; there it was the poet who gazed, whereas here it is the lady called to see the poet as he mirrors her. The reflection is on and of the ideal, and the distinction is between that ideal and the mere appearance of it.

The poet has again made some progress; although still using images and language employed earlier in the sequence ("celestiall hew" goes all the way back to *Amor.* 3), he here acknowledges not only the distinction between his inner and outer selves, his reality and his appearance, but he acknowledges her "double reality" as well. Unlike other mirror poems of this type, where the Ideal beckons the lover toward it and away from earthly baseness, the lover in this one enlists the empirical lady to help give shape to the vision within him. It is not the lover who is asked to compare himself with the Ideal, but the beloved, whose real presence inside his heart actually mirrors her real presence. With her, appearance and reality are the same. The poet has been imagining an image that is not there; he himself has served an illusion. His turmoil and frustration, not the lady's cruelty, have caused the darkened image.

Like Narcissus, the poet loves an image; unlike Narcissus, this lover loves two images—the real lady and the image. He is yet unable to see the two as one, mirroring one another. As a mirror "clearer than christall," his heart only reflects; it does not create pictures ("fayre Idea") in it. He has yet to combine the inner and outer, appearance and reality, before he can see the unified woman and can accept her in all her humanness as "th'image of [God's] grace."

The heady metaphysics of *Amor.* 45 yield to the simple playfulness of *Amor.* 46. Although the lady is once again his "cruell fayre" she is also his *donna angelicata* (his "lower heauen"), and the tone is both light and witty. It marks the first time in the sequence that the lovers have apparently kept a prearranged appointment with each other. Its humor, especially as evidence of his turning a simple situation into a cosmically related directive, is evident:

> When my abodes prefixed time is spent,
>   My cruell fayre streight bids me wend my way:
>   but then from heauen most hideous stormes are sent
>   as willing me against her will to stay.

Despite her "cruelty," she obviously allows him to visit, although it is she who has "prefixed" the duration of his stay. The poet cleverly takes the natural situation of an unexpected rainfall to play upon the topic of storms and tempests, a topic he earlier used as a metaphor for his interior unrest. The poem describes a play of wills—the lady's, the poet's, heaven's.

> Whom then shall I or heauen or her obay?
>   the heauens know best what is the best for me:
>   but as she will, whose will my life doth sway,
>   my lower heauen, so it perforce must bee.

Heaven's will, he claims, conflicts with the lady's, but she as his "lower heauen," his heaven on earth, holds greater sway than the elements, and he must ("perforce") leave. The couplet ("Enough it is for one man to sustaine / the stormes, which she alone on me doth raine") provides the gentle and amusing conclusion concerning the situation, comparing her storms with those of heaven, and her rain with that of the clouds. Importantly, the poem also suggests the poet's growing externalization of the empirical lady; terms previously used to describe fictionally his interior situations now are applied to depict empirical, exterior events. And the lady's proper position, not only a "fayre Idea" or an ethereal being, but as his lower heaven, is first stated as the lover now moves into mid-Lent, which begins with *Amor.* 47.

"Trust not the treason of those smyling lookes, / vntill ye haue theyr guylefull traynes well tryde" initiates a poetic exaggeration of the playful and light mood of 46. Spenser utilizes here one of his favorite images, that of "baiting":

> for they [the smiling looks] are lyke but vnto golden hookes,
>   that from the foolish fish theyr bayts doe hyde:
> So she with flattring smyles weake harts doth guyde
>   vnto her loue, and tempte to theyr decay,
>   whom being caught she kills with cruell pryde,
>   and feeds at pleasure on the wretched pray:
> Yet euen whylst her bloody hands them slay,
>   her eyes looke louely and vpon them smyle:
>   that they take pleasure in her cruell play,
>   and dying doe them selues of payne beguyle.
> O mighty charm which makes men loue theyr bane,
>   and thinck they dy with pleasure, liue with payne.

While this is the second of four sonnets that specifically use the "bait" image (41, 47, 53, 72), the concept has appeared in various other forms as part of the "capturing" motif, the hunting imagery, the spider metaphor, the lion and lamb analogy, and so forth. Now the allusion is more closely associated with Circe, whose beguiling art (yet vicious nature) epitomizes the lady's actions as the poet depicts them, and whose "mighty charm" makes men "loue theyr bane."

The poem draws upon several familiar themes. Its "golden hookes" were seen earlier (*Amor.* 37) in the lady's golden tresses; the "bloody hands" appeared in *Amor.* 31. But there has been a definite progress, and the poet's present position in the courtship allows him to reuse old metaphors with new meaning. He writes now, for example, of treason's train, a term used as early as *Amor.* 12. And she has drawn "weake harts" to her several times. But he has already said in *Amor.* 21 that the lady trains and teaches with her looks, and the "traynes" and "guyde[s]" assume added associations when used again. The lady's ability to use her "charm" has already been alluded to in noting that through her "deep wit" she can "spel . . . [and] construe well" (*Amor.* 43); here she uses that talent to charm (both "delight" and "enchant") men to the "golden fetters" (37) of which he earlier wrote.

The poem also refers to *Amor.* 42, in which the poet expressed his masochistic situation: "the loue which me so cruelly tormenteth, / so pleasing is in my extreamest paine." Yet there is a clue in 42 to the action in 47, where one is not to trust the treason of the looks until they have been well tried, at which point one presumably may understand that the looks both teach and train and are therefore of a positive, not negative, nature.

The rhyme scheme is also instructive: the lady's looks (line 1) are hooks (line 3); they hide (line 4) their baits to guide (line 5), so she may kill with pride (line 7). The lady's cruel play (line 11) leads the wretched prey (line 8) to decay (line 6) so she may slay (line 9) them. Through her smile (line 10) she can beguile (line 12)—a rhyme partially repeated internally in "smyling" (line 1) and "guylfull" (line 2).

The poem marks the midpoint of Lent, the fourth Sunday, which in the *Amoretti* calendar falls on 10 March 1594. The fourth Sunday in Lent is peculiar in a number of ways. It has, for example, more names and more customs associated with it than any other of the Sundays in the whole year, being called (among other titles) Mid-Lent, Refreshment Sunday (a reference to the gospel lesson), Mothering Sunday (a reference to the epistle lesson), Laetare, Sunday of the Golden Rose, and *Dominica de panibus*. The tone of the day is one of restrained joy rather than the unbridled joy of Easter, the latter of which is sorrow turned into joy, while this one is joy in sorrow. Interestingly, *Amor.* 46 has Psalm 46 as its corresponding first *BCP* reading. The forty-sixth psalm provides a statement of trust in the midst of tribulation, "a helpe in troubles, readie to be founde." The epistle lesson from Galatians 4 concerns the theme of bondage versus freedom, just as Lent Three (*Amor.* 40) concerned light versus darkness. The pericopes provide for the *transitus* of Easter, which reconciles old and new, pain and pleasure, law and gospel, and which suggests the double nature of the sonnet theme.

The sequence continues with a playful address to a now-destroyed poem; the poem's letters are depicted as sinners burned for their heresy, and the poet here is able, once again, to make a claim for the artist's immortalizing ability.

> Innocent paper whom too cruell hand
> Did make the matter to auenge her yre:

> and ere she could thy cause wel vnderstand,
> did sacrifize vnto the greedy fyre.
> Well worthy thou to haue found better hyre,
> then so bad end for hereticks ordayned:
> yet heresy nor treason didst conspire,
> but plead thy maisters cause vniustly payned.

Although outwardly the poem appears more serious than the preceding one, the Petrarchan exaggeration of the lady's cruelty gives evidence of half-playful humor beneath its surface. Like *Amor.* 42, it asserts the lady's power to "kill": "Fayre cruell, why are ye so fierce and cruell? / Is it because your eyes haue powre to kill?" Yet it differs from the earlier one; he is not now resigned to a continued state of suffering (the Petrarchan lover's doom) but complains for relief. Contrary to his expectations in 43 that she "spel" true hearts, here she either cannot or will not "vnderstand" the poem's cause.

The content of the "innocent paper" is revealed in the third quatrain:

> Whom she all carelesse of his griefe constrayned
> to vtter forth the anguish of his hart:
> and would not heare, when he to her complayned
> the piteous passion of his dying smart.

Stating his love as "complaints" of "piteous passion" and of his "dying smart" reflects exactly that manner of artificial expression the lady has been attempting to dissuade. Understandably, she destroys the poem. "Constrayned" functions as one of those pivotal words: either the lady has been "carelesse" of the lover's constrained grief, or she has constrained him from uttering his anguish. Both possibilities illumine, although the latter provides a more humorous explanation of the action preceding the martyrdom.

The couplet, "yet liue for euer, though against her will, / and speake her good, though she requite it ill," asserts the power of poetry to immortalize its subject and to achieve its own immortality. The couplet draws together and then reverses the poem's heretic-death imagery, in which "innocent," "auenge," "sacrifize," "fyre," "end," "hereticks," "heresy," "conspire" (with its own play on breath, blow, spirit, fire), "payned," "griefe," "anguish," "passion," and "smart" all build a foundation undermined by the "yet liue for euer" in line 13. A further wordplay ties the paper's and heretic's "hyre" (recompense) to the lady's not "requit[ing]" the poem well—rewarding and, perhaps, echo-ing the requiescat of the funeral mass.

He suggests the poem is strong against its adversaries (even if they are his "lower heauen") and may exist, as do the heretics, in spirit if not in physical form. In Amor. 29 he asserted

> that her great triumph which my skill exceeds,
>   I may in trump of fame blaze ouer all.
> Then would I decke her head with glorious bayes,
>   and fill the world with her victorious prayse.

Now, as in 29 and again in 42 (where he noted acceptance of thralldom), he resolves to continue wooing, despite the problems and even though "she requite [repay] it ill."

Amor. 49 continues the poet's exaggerated claims of the lady's power to kill and, conversely, of his own ability to give life to her. Her cruelty, attributed to her hand in 48, is now directly applied to her. For the "maisters cause vniustly payned" (48) mercy is now pleaded. The "complaint" noted in 48, whether or not 49 is to be taken as the "resurrected" version of it, appears in 49 as

> Fayre cruell, why are ye so fierce and cruell?
>   Is it because your eyes haue powre to kill?
>   then know, that mercy is the mighties iewell,
>   and greater glory thinke to saue, then spill.

His focus on mercy is the same attributed to the lady's ability to "unwork" his artistry in 38: "yet with one word she can it saue or spill, / to spill were pitty, but to saue were prayse."

The poem's images are regressive; that is, the poet is picking up and reusing expressions of his "piteous passion" from numerous other poems. As far back as Amor. 7 he attributed death-giving qualities to the lady's eyes; her pride goes as far back as 2 and her cruelty to 10. The lady, he suggests, has been given power, but the crowning "iewell" is mercy, not power:

> But if it be your pleasure and proud will,
>   to shew the powre of your imperious eyes:
>   then not on him that neuer thought you ill,
>   but bend your force against your enemyes.
> Let them feele th'utmost of your crueltyes,
>   and kill with looks, as Cockatrices doo:
>   but him that at your footstoole humbled lies,
>   with mercifull regard, giue mercy too.

> Such mercy shal you make admyred to be,
> so shall you liue by giuing life to me.

It is the same argument used earlier in 36 when trying to show that the lady would gain little glory

> by slaying him, whose lyfe though ye despyse,
> mote haue your life in honour long maintayned.
> But by his death which some perhaps will mone,
> ye shall condemned be of many a one.

The poet once more plays on vision and looking. The lady's powerful, imperious eyes, echoed in "enemyes" and "crueltyes," are metamorphosed into the killing looks of the Cockatrice. Opposed to those looks is the "mercifull regard" of the truly mighty.

The couplet affords the poet the opportunity to assert the artist's power to grant immortality, a claim obliquely made in 48 but directly stated as far back as 27 ("that which shall you make immortall, cherish").

The quality of mercy is an important theme introduced by *Amor.* 49. While there have been frequent complaints about injustice and many pleas for just treatment, this is the first time mercy has been mentioned, and presumably the first time the lover has recognized that her treatment of him actually has been just. That being the case, he no longer can speak seriously of justice or injustice, and those words never appear in the sequence after this point.

Giving life to the poet (his request of the lady in 49) is further treated in 50. Love can bring about dis-ease, as the references to Cupid's arrows and wounds suggest; in *Amor.* 50 the "malady" is discussed and a physician prepares to treat it, but the lover rejects the physician's prognosis and proposed remedy. The lover makes his own diagnosis and seeks a second "medical" treatment:

> Long languishing in double malady,
>   of my harts wound and of my bodies griefe:
>   there came to me a leach that would apply
>   fit medicines for my bodies best reliefe.
> Vayne man (quod I) that hast but little priefe,
>   in deep discouery of the mynds disease,
>   is not the hart of all the body chiefe?
>   and rules the members as it selfe doth please?
> Then with some cordialls seeke first to appease

> the inward languour of my wounded hart,
> and then my body shall haue shortly ease:
> but such sweet cordialls passe Physitions art.

He described one form of his double malady earlier as "troublous fit" (his "harts wound") that affected his spirit and caused him to question whether he had the endurance to complete his "tae-dious toyle" (his "bodies griefe"). The pains of love, his "dis-ease," have expressed themselves fictionally (in his "harts wound") and empirically (in his "bodies griefe"); their only (and mutual) cure is the lady, whom he addresses in the couplet:

> Then my lyfes Leach doe you your skill reueale,
> and with one salue both hart and body heale.

As the Great Healer, his "lyfes Leach," the lady will bring "salve-ation" to him, a "salue" better than any others. Like Britomart, who can become a woman only after having been wounded in Castle Joyous, by Gardante's keen arrow, the lover can be sa(l)ved only after experiencing love (in this case both human and di-vine). The wound is therefore both formative and reformative, as it is for Marinell, who changes from a static emblem to a man only after being wounded. The poet will never change or even transform his Petrarchan pose and static artificiality until love's wound provides the salve to heal his (he)art and body.

"Wounds" occurred twice earlier in the sequence, the first time in *Amor.* 6, where they "dint . . . the parts entire / with chast affects" and re-form "the gentle brest." The second occurrence is in 8, where the blind guest, shooting out "darts to base affections wound," recalls Malecasta's attempt (3.1.49) to "wound" Brit-omart by darting glances at her, an attempt that yields the follow-ing address to the reading audience:

> Faire ladies, that to loue captiued arre,
>   And chaste desires do nourish in your mind,
>   Let not her fault your sweet affections marre,
>   Ne blot the bounty of all womankind;
>   . . . .
>   For loue does alwayes bring forth bounteous deeds,
> And in each gentle heart desire of honour breeds.

True love, therefore, is productive; it forms and reforms, generat-ing "bounteous deeds." The heart struck by true love is a "gentle" one, which is not really "wounded" but is pregnant with the seed of moral action.[17] In both *Amor.* 6 and 8 this is the case, the former suggesting productivity in marriage, the latter the framing and fashioning of the poet. In *Amor.* 50 the love-wound is necessary for a healing of heart and body, a making whole of that which is diseased. Its product will be more than a healing; it will be a true salvation, a new heart that, in *Amor.* 58 (containing the next occurrence of "wound"), will soon suggest making peace and granting "timely grace."

In *Amor.* 51 the doubleness that has been heard of (directly and indirectly) results in the narrator's self-examination of his role as artist and lover. The images and motifs (hardness, endurance, artistic endeavors, the lady's stubborn heart, the poet's resolution to continue) draw heavily upon earlier sonnets:

> Doe I not see that fayrest ymages
>   of hardest Marble are of purpose made?
>   for that they should endure through many ages,
>   ne let theyr famous moniments to fade.
> Why then doe I, vntrainde in louers trade,
>   her hardnes blame which I should more commend?
>   sith neuer ought was excellent assayde,
>   which was not hard t'atchiue and bring to end.
> Ne ought so hard, but he that would attend,
>   mote soften it and to his will allure:
>   so doe I hope her stubborne hart to bend,
>   and that it then more stedfast will endure.
> Onely my paines wil be the more to get her,
>   but hauing her, my ioy wil be the greater.

Most of the sentiments are already familiar. In 6 the poet observed that "such love, not lyke to lusts of baser kynd, / the harder wonne, the firmer will abide"; in 26 he added that "for easie things, that may be got at will, / most sorts of men doe set but little store. / Why then should I accoumpt of little paine, / that endless pleasure shall unto me gaine?" In 18 he noted that "the rolling wheele, that runneth often round, / the hardest steele in tract of time doth teare." But now there is a change from these earlier statements; in those the narrator wrote with determination and resolution as a poet. Here he questions whether the poet's view is accurate. This again is a sonnet about the artist's art.

The analogue he presents appears to be to the Pygmalion myth, in which the artist has purposely made the "fayrest image" of his *donna pietra*. The lady (Pygmalion's and the sonnet poet's) is the cruel fair, the hard-hearted woman, because he has fashioned her thus, not because she necessarily is that way. In the second quatrain he comments that he is "vntrainde in louers trade," the first example in the sequence of such an admission. Artists know their trade, and as an artist he has felt competent even when asserting his inability to express as he would like. But as a lover he is less experienced, attributing to the lady through art those things which perhaps were more artificial than natural. The artist's business is to fashion an "enduring moniment" of his hard lady; the lover's is to soften and give flesh to that fair image so she may be loved as a woman, not as an image or a marble monument. As a poet he could suffer all the slings and arrows of Petrarchan love; but that is all he could do. Even neo-Platonism provides only a spiritual relief from the suffering. The Christian "loving" on which the lover (both on the surface and analogic levels) has embarked gives a rationale for the devotion and the "salving" of body as well as heart.

The third quatrain provides insight into the artist's process. "Ne ought so hard" refers to the image, to the lady's hardness, and to the achieving. The artist's determination, his attending to the task, makes these less hard, softening them and "allur[ing]" them to his will. This is the first time "allure" has been used to refer to the poet; previously it has been the lady who has allured, and usually with negative connotations. But the allusion to the lady is a reminder that she indeed has been steadfast through all this courting. The poet's softening and bending are a reflection of the lady's own attempts to transform him. The *Hymne in Honor of Loue* (162–68) provides a useful comment that is applicable to the lady's role in the lover's progress:

> Yet herein eke thy glory seemeth more,
> But so hard handling those which best thee serue,
> That ere thou doest them vnto grace restore,
> Thou mayest well trie if they will euer swerue,
> And mayest them make it better to deserue,
> And hauing got it, may it more esteeme,
> For things hard gotten, men more dearely deeme.

This is one of the reasons for Lent, and clearly one of the reasons for the empirical lady's behavior throughout the sequence.

The sonnet narrator's language takes us out of the poet's realm and into the lover's, moving from images of marble, monuments, and the achievement of artistic endeavors to softening, alluring, bending, and "having" her (instead of a monument). The lover's resolve, as well as the transition from unfading monument ("hard") to steadfast heart ("enduring")—and the important distinction between the two—are completed by the end of the third quatrain. The couplet, with its play on "get her" and "greater," makes the point that the lover's pains are directly proportional to the quality of love he eventually hopes to win. There is also in this couplet a sense of determination and an underlying belief that his suffering is neither pointless nor interminable. His joy will be the greater for the greater pains (both "sufferings" and "efforts").

The reference to the greater joys he will (not "might") receive, as well as the reference to bringing to an end the assays and attempts (line 8), reinforce the surface continuity and progression of the sequence as a sequence. He *is* moving (albeit slowly), *is* making progress, and *is* deepening as a poet and a lover even as the penitent deepens spiritually the further he gets into and goes through Lent.

The narrator's confidence apparently renewed, his new perspective and resolution to take greater pains to win the lady immediately manifest themselves in Amor. 52, where he picks up the "joy" and "paines" of 51, the "languor" of 50, and the warfare image of 49;

> So oft as homeward I from her depart,
>   I goe lyke one that hauing lost the field,
>   is prisoner led away with heauy hart,
>   despoyld of warlike armes and knowen shield.
> So doe I now my selfe a prisoner yeeld,
>   to sorrow and to solitary paine:
>   from presence of my dearest deare exylde,
>   longwhile alone in languor to remaine.
> There let no thought of ioy or pleasure vaine,
>   dare to approch, that may my solace breed:
>   but sudden dumps and drery sad disdayne
>   of all worlds gladnesse more my torment feed.
> So I her absens will my penaunce make,
>   that of her presens I my meed may take.

Progression is again evident in the poet's resuming the use of earlier metaphors—but with new uses. The love-as-war image appears with a change; the battle now is over, but whereas in earlier poems the poet depicted himself as being in the midst of the battle, he is here a soldier who has lost the field and is being led away.

This is an echo of his earlier visit to her home (Amor. 46), when storms attempted to stay him. She who had prefixed the duration of the visit sent him away. Here, however, he is not being sent but is being led. Furthermore, he is now "dispoyld" of warlike arms and shield; giving those up is a far cry from giving up his life, as he previously claimed he would do. Most important, it is the leaving, not the confronting, of her that is defeat. In defeating him this way the lady actually frees him and makes him more eager to return.

The couplet provides a lighter resolution, recalling the poet's continued wit and the serious nonseriousness, the sense of *serio ludere*, with which the poet's game is played. "Her absens" is tied by rhyme and meaning with its qualifier, "my penaunce." Her "presence," noted earlier in line 7, is repeated and tied in with these other internal rhymes, culminating in his comment on taking his "meed"—his reward for the penance (as well as, in Elizabethan pronunciation, his "maid").

In *Amor.* 53 the "cruel fair" image returns, although now in a rather distant, unreal fashion, perhaps as a result of the "absens" noted in the previous sonnet:

> The Panther knowing that his spotted hyde
>   Doth please all beasts but that his looks them fray:
> within a bush his dreadful head doth hide,
>   to let them gaze whylest he on them may pray.
> Right so my cruell fayre with me doth play.

In 47 the poet denounced the lady's treasonable luring and killing, where by craft the woman baited her lovers. Here in 53 the comparison to such activities is made in terms of the panther. In addition to suggesting baiting, the image adds the element of fierceness and cruelty described in 49. Spenser emphasizes the viciousness of the panther's game, depicted as the way the lady plays with the lover, by conjoining "pray" and "play." As in 49, the poet moralizes on mercy, drawing on an earlier image (*Amor.* 9) in which the lady and God ("the Maker") were connected: "But mercy doth with beautie best agree, / as in theyr maker ye them best may see."

Yet the lady's play does not cease. It is redescribed, along with the poet's own playing, in the next sonnet, where the *theatrum mundi* motif reasserts the underlying theme of role playing, of discovering one's self through staging actions, of love as an action staged and restaged by a continuous stream of new actors/"acters." The sonnet's images of audience (spectator, staying, sitting, beholding), combined with those of player (masking and

playing) and drama (pageants, comedy, tragedy), echo the inter-
play of the lovers throughout the sequence, beginning in *Amor.* 7
with the lady's smiling and "louring." They also echo in their
own ways the numerous pageants, masques, spectacles, inter-
plays, and dramas of Spenser's canon, in which virtually every-
thing is presented as though enacted on the stage of the poet's
vast imagination. Of great significance among those passages is
the narrator's observation in 3.5.1:

> Wonder it is to see, in diuerse minds,
>> How diuersely loue doth his pageants play,
>> And shewes his powre in variable kinds . . .
>> But in braue sprite it kindles goodly fire . . .

This comments well not only on *Amor.* 54 but on the entire
sequence. In 54 the rich variety of the earlier sonnets is summed
up in the lover's complete recognition and acknowledgment that
he deliberately has been playing many parts in order to woo and
win his lady:

> Of this worlds Theatre in which we stay,
>> My loue lyke the Spectator ydly sits
>> beholding me that all the pageants play,
>> disguysing diuersly my troubled wits.
> Sometimes I ioy when glad occasion fits,
>> and mask in myrth lyke to a Comedy:
>> soone after when my ioy to sorrow flits,
>> I waile and make my woes a Tragedy.
> Yet she beholding me with constant eye,
>> delights not in my merth nor rues my smart:
>> but when I laugh she mocks, and when I cry
>> she laughs, and hardens euermore her hart.
> What then can moue her? if nor merth nor mone,
>> she is no woman, but a sencelesse stone.

The poem is filled with play, beginning with the ambiguity of
"stay" in line 1 (to reside or, possibly, to wait until moving on)
and continuing through the sonnet to the petrified woman of the
last line. But there is confusion as well. Line 2 relates that the
lady sits "ydly" like a spectator; presumably she sits idly, pas-
sively, watching the lover, but it is soon evident that this spec-
tator (formerly "fayre Idea" and "goodly Idoll") is part of the
audience as well as part of the play. She has played several times
earlier, particularly in 18, where she functioned both as *magistra*

ludens and a *magistra ludi,* and in one way or another she has directed the lover's actions throughout the sequence.

The poet also plays now on his "wits," in the sense that he disguises his emotions and his witticisms. Additionally, as far back as *Amor.* 3 he has associated "wits" with his poetry and the poetic process, when he marked "the wonder that my wit cannot endite." He did this again in 33 when questioning "how then should I without another wit, / thinck euer to endure so taedious toyle" (completing his epic project). His troubled wits have been his various poems as well as his diversely presented emotions. Both the poet and his poems (the antecedent is cleverly ambiguous) have played out their functions as "pageants," a term Spenser applies to the entire *Faerie Queene* (Dedicatory Sonnets, 1. line 6) in which all the characters play their roles. As in the sonnets, those characters experience both mirth and moan, comedy and tragedy, and have their times on the stage.

The second quatrain is especially instructive, particularly in looking back through the sequence at the various fluctuations of mood and exaggerations of temperament. It has never been the case that the poet should not "ioy" when "glad occasion fits"; it is "fit" that he do so. But his own artistic embellishments have deterred his progress. His joy is "mask[ed] in myrth" instead of being expressed as the joy it is. Likewise it is not unnatural that his joy should turn to sorrow; in love, honey without gall is an impossibility. But the sorrow expresses itself with "wail[ing] and mak[ing his] woes a Tragedy." His bad acting and acting badly, therefore, have resulted in his critic's scorn.

The sonnet subtly supports the unsure thespian qualities of the lover, who in 51 told us he was "vntrainde in louers trade." Line 5 ends in "fits," by which he means seemly, proper or suitable. But the word also suggests irregular movements or uncontrolled action. Likewise "flits," clearly indicating the quick movement from joy to sorrow, also suggests abrupt, fluttering motion. It is possible that the actions at the secondary level of their meanings are a result of his "troubled wits," but even if this is not the case, the words suggest his ineffective efforts at playing roles.

By contrast with the lover's fits and flits, masking and wailing, the lady, with constant eye, sits beholding him; she counters his theatrical expressions with opposite ones in order to indicate her displeasure with the exaggerated roles he plays. His laughing and crying, conversely, lead to her mocking and laughing. In this world's theater all play their parts, even the lady.

Despite the confession about role-playing, the poet nevertheless concludes this sonnet with yet another set piece by declaring that if the lady will not, or cannot, be moved by mirth or moan, "she is no woman, but a sencelesse stone." He is playing upon the image he used in 30, when the cold lady was exaggeratedly "congealed with sencelesse cold," and in 32, when he burned to ashes while she "to stones at length all frosen" turned.

His playing serves as a reminder that at this point in the sequence his pageants, in their own way, have almost achieved their end (both their purpose and their conclusion).[18] With *Amor.* 54 begins the fifth week in Lent, a week that starts with a dramatic appellation of its own—Passion Sunday, 17 March 1594. Modern versions of the *BCP* mark off the last two weeks of Lent as Passiontide and the fifth Sunday as Passion Sunday. While the term does not appear in the Tudor prayer books, it was well known. In the sonnets' Lenten segment, as in Lent itself, this period marks the beginning of the end, although the narrative of Christ's Passion itself does not predominate until Palm Sunday and Holy Week. While there appear no clear thematic analogues between the *BCP* propers for this day and the sonnet, a linguistic connection appears in the sonnet's last word—stone—and the last line of the gospel lesson (John 8): "then tooke they up stones. . . ."

The following sonnet, *Amor.* 55, continues the witty rhetorical playing. In a reductive attempt at analogy, the poet tries to discover of what substance the lady is formed that would have made her simultaneously cruel and fair. Just as the lady carefully observed him in 54, here he now observes her and turns that scrutiny into his rhetorical exploration. As in *Amor.* 52, the poet begins here with "so oft as"; like *Amor.* 9, 15, and 21, this sonnet provides a catalogue. As in 46, 49, and 53, she is his "cruell fayre." And, as often before, the poet cleverly and carefully fashions his argument while distorting information to suit his purposes. His octet sets the situation, which concerns its own quest for analogy:

> So oft as I her beauty doe behold,
>> And therewith doe her cruelty compare:
>> I maruaile of what substance was the mould
>> the which her made attonce so cruell faire.
> Not earth; for her high thoghts more heauenly are,
>> not water; for her loue doth burne like fyre:
>> not ayre; for she is not so light or rare,
>> not fyre; for she doth friese with faint desire.

His list of "nots" is worth examining. Beginning with the lowest of the elements he moves hierarchically to the least "earthly"—fire. But a close reading indicates his playful intermixing of elements, a poetic sleight-of-eye trick to further his cause. In order to build in the third quatrain to his praise of the "heavenly" lady, he has made his ladder of "noncomparisons" out of rearranged items. That is, the things he says of her in the second part of comparative lines are true when placed properly with the correct element. They do not work as comparisons here because he aligns them with the wrong elements. For example, she *could* be made of fire because "her loue doth burne lyke fyre." She could be fashioned of water because she "doth friese with faint desire." Her basic substance could be air because her high thoughts are heavenly, and she could be made of earth precisely because she is neither "so light [n]or rare" that her humanity removes her from earthly matters.

It might also be noted that symbolically and alchemically both earth and water were considered passive elements to which were appointed feminine gender; conversely, air and fire were thought of as active and masculine. The active and passive qualities reappear in the dichotomized cruel (active) and fair (passive) combination, the contrarieties of which provide a basic motif in this sonnet. The third quatrain presents his solution:

> Then needs another Element inquire
> whereof she mote be made; that is the skye.
> for to the heauen her haughty lookes aspire:
> and eke her mind is pure immortall hye.

He concludes with a request for mercy, a continuation of the request he first voices six sonnets earlier, in 49, and two sonnets back, in 53: "Then sith to heauen ye lykened are the best, / be lyke in mercy as in all the rest."

In the wordplay that begins *Amor.* 56 he acknowledges her "fairness," referring both to her beauty and to her freedom from exhibiting injustice. The sonnet's unusual structure, in which each quatrain commences with the same term, suggests that more might be going on here than first appears.

Such is the case in this highly artificial, rhetorically balanced, and symmetrical poem—which appears to say nothing new at all.

> Fayre ye be sure, but cruell and vnkind,
> As is a Tygre that with greedinesse

> hunts after bloud, when he by chance doth find
> a feeble beast, doth felly him oppresse.
> Fayre be ye sure, but proud and pittilesse,
>   as is a storme, that all things doth prostrate:
>   finding a tree alone all comfortlesse,
>   beats on it strongly it to ruinate.
> Fayre be ye sure, but hard and obstinate,
>   as is a rocke amidst the raging floods:
>   gaynst which a ship of succour desolate,
>   doth suffer wreck both of her selfe and goods.
> That ship, that tree, and that same beast am I,
>   whom ye doe wreck, doe ruine, and destroy.

The poem's effect is purely intellectual; it appears to be almost a rhetorical exercise asking the reader to recollect the sequence's major similes, metaphors, adjectives, and motifs.

Yet the sonnet sums up the poet's Petrarchan pose to this point. Jammed into its fourteen lines are all the chief complaints the poet expressed earlier. Even a partial list of its source within the sequence suggests the poem's composite nature: the lady is

"fair" in *Amor.* 4, 5, 7, 8, 13, 14, 15, 16, 24, 27, 28, 35, 41, 45, 46, 49, 53;
"cruel" in 11, 12, 20, 31, 41, 46, 47, 48, 49, 53, 55;
"proud" in 2, 5, 6, 10, 13, 14, 17, 19, 27, 28, 31, 33, 49;
"hard" in 18, 31, 51;
"stubborn" (obstinate) in 29, 32, 38, 44, 51;
"greedy" in 11;
a "rock" in 32; and
a tiger, panther, and lion in 20 and 53.

And storm-tossed ships, blood-seeking animals, feeble beasts, oppression, comfortless trees ruined by storms, wrack, ruin, and decay have also been encountered numerous times. The poem is filled with its own rhetorical repetitions: "Fayre ye be sure" (line 1) is rearranged as "fayre be ye sure" in lines 5 and 9; the second line of each quatrain begins with "as is a." Each of the "fayres" is qualified by a pair of adjectives: "fayre . . . but cruell and vnkind"; "fayre . . . but proud and pittilesse"; "fayre . . . but hard and obstinate." And each of the adjectives ties the lady to the particular object of the simile—a cruel and unkind tiger, a proud and pitiless storm, a hard and obstinate rock. Line 13 picks up all the passive objects ("that ship, that tree, and that same beast") and compares them to the poet; line 14 balances this by compar-

ing the forceful verbs ("wreck," "ruine," and "destroy") to the
lady's actions.

The opaque artifice and the rich interplay of rhetorical balance
and structuring indicate the poet's delicate mockery and lack of
seriousness. The lines are emotional only insofar as they serve as
part of his final outburst, and as elements of the purging of his
Petrarchan stance. Drawing together the similes, metaphors, epi-
thets and motifs he has utilized thus far, he stimulates his, the
lady's, and the reader's, intellect(s). Realizing now that his Pe-
trarchanisms are only a pose, he finds himself free to pursue
them with humor and lightness.

Amor. 57 continues the "purging" by focusing on the one
major metaphor he did not include in 56—love as war.

> Sweet warriour when shall I haue peace with you?
> High time it is, this warre now ended were:
> which I no lenger can endure to sue,
> ne your incessant battry more to beare.

No longer forced by convention to pursue her in his old manner,
no longer needing prolonged retreat into his own psychological
time, and no longer required to play a fictional role at all, the poet
reminds the lady that the time is at hand to move ahead with the
real courtship: "Make peace therefore, and graunt me timely
grace, / that all my wounds wil heale in little space." With the
ship, tree, beast, and warfare, the poet has drawn together his
"substance" images; he now moves on to time and space, which
interact here in important ways. The "timely grace" he seeks
refers to receiving grace "soon." It also suggests "timely" in the
sense that it is now time. And it serves as a pivot; the lover is
moving into the "fastest" period of the sequence, when time
becomes more and more important in the poet's progress, in the
poetic imagery, and in the analogic references.

"Grace," too, is timely; Spenser uses it as a noun but views it as
something that only really exists as a verb; as such, grace is
enacted in time and is thus "timely grace." Finally, there are ten
sonnets until 67, where the betrothal will occur and where
"grace" will come to the lover. The "little space" between this
sonnet and that one will encompass those poems which heal his
wounds and find him healing hers as well.

Time is echoed in *Amor.* 58, the only sonnet with a subtitle:
"By her that is most assured to her selfe." Since the poet as actor
is no longer a role the poet feels is necessary, the lover is now free

to speak in his own person. His newly felt assurance in his position, in his ability, and in what he feels is his forthcoming acceptance by the lady all find expression in 58 and its companion piece, 59. Immediately after his regenerative experience in 56 and 57 the poet shifts to the most basic of rational methods, the pro-and-con discourse, although here he provides first the negative side and then the positive. The lady's self-assurance is the subject, one treated neither flippantly nor in the Petrarchan images of earlier poems:

> Weake is th'assurance that weake flesh reposeth
>   In her owne powre, and scorneth others ayde:
>   that soonest fals when as she most supposeth
>   her selfe assurd, and is of nought affrayd.
> All flesh is frayle, and all her strength vnstayd,
>   like a vaine bubble blowen vp with ayre:
>   deuouring tyme and changeful chance haue prayd
>   her glories pride that none may it repayre.
> Ne none so rich or wise, so strong or fayre,
>   but fayleth trusting on his owne assurance:
>   and he that standeth on the hyghest stayre
>   fals lowest: for on earth nought hath enduraunce.
> Why then doe ye proud fayre, misdeeme so farre,
>   that to your selfe ye most assured arre?

Some critics have suggested that the heading of 58, "by her that is most assured to her selfe," belongs with 59, and thus leads into the lady's response to the lover who, in 59, raises questions about her self-assurance. However, as Martz suggests (following William Nelson and Leicester Bradner), Spenser uses the word "by" in the sense of "concerning," as Gascoigne used it in the headings of several of his poems. "Thus [Spenser] has composed a pair of sonnets on this problem: rebuke and palinode; and he has phrased the second in a way that allows it to be taken as a representation of the lady's point of view."[19]

With a didactic voice more familiar in Reformation sermons or even in Sackville's "Induction" than in the *Amoretti*, the poet speaks out against the folly of self-assurance. The repetition of "weake" in the first line connects assurance and flesh; flesh, in turn, is connected with the lady through the pronoun "her" in the second line. The lesson to her flesh, hence about her assurance, and to her, is presented in the second quatrain, which introduces the allegorized figures of "deuouring tyme" and "changeful chance," terms that appear elsewhere in the Spenser canon with the same kinds of connections intended here. Both time and chance (which Spenser interchanges with "change" in the first and second editions of *The Visions of Bellay*, 11.12) prey upon the flesh, even though (as the poet is later to apply to himself in 75) "on earth nought hath enduraunce."

That same assurance of *Amor.* 58 has another side, put in balance in the adversative *Amor.* 59. The value Spenser places on a quality such as self-assuredness is reasserted and then exemplified in the following lines:

> Thrise happy she, that is so well assured
>   Vnto her selfe and setled so in hart:
>   that nether will for better be allured,
>   ne feared with worse to any chaunce to start,
> But like a steddy ship doth strongly part
>   the raging waues and keepes her course aright:
>   ne ought for tempest doth from it depart,
>   ne ought for fayrer weathers false delight.
> Such selfe assurance need not feare the spight
>   of grudging foes, ne fauour seek of friends:
>   but in the stay of her owne stedfast might,
>   nether to one her selfe nor other bends.
> Most happy she that most assured doth rest,
>   but he most happy who such one loues best.

It is possible to read these lines as the lady's response to the poet's comments in 58. It is also appropriate to read them as the poet's further elaboration on the subject, with evidence of his clearing understanding. While F. W. Bateson criticizes this sonnet for its "non-committal tautologies," its "repetitions, and amplifications,"[20] the repetition of subject matter can be viewed as an important part of Spenser's poetic process. In the *Amoretti*, as in *The Faerie Queene*, "each recapitulation and reexpression sheds a different light on the 'primary meaning,' entailing the further exploration of the original idea. It is only by reducing the 'primary meaning' to the barest and least interesting of formulae that either poem can truly be called tautological."[21]

The poem, then, is not just a reevaluation of the theme presented in 58, but a suggestion of the poet's awareness that perhaps the lady has not "misdeeme[d] so farre" after all. Just as there had been a noticeable difference in tone between 57 ("Sweet warriour . . .") and 58, so is there a marked difference between the didactic distancing of 58 and the pleasing assurance of 59. The ponderous development and weighty amplification (with five trisyllabic words) of 58 yields to the swift movement and steady development of 59.

The poem begins strongly with Spenser's often-used "thrise happie." Just as the merry cuckoo had thrice sounded its notes in *Amor.* 19, just as Red Cross had been declared a "thrise happy man" when entering the House of Holinesse ("high heauen to attaine"), and as Agape, mother of Priamond, Diamond, and Triamond, is declared a "thrise happie mother," so the sonnet lady is "thrise happie" for being well assured in her Self and in her heart. The remainder of the sonnet develops the "happinesses."

In the first quatrain she is happy because of her well-balanced position between extremes. Neither driven nor allured by the desire for betterment, she does not live in fear of change for the worse. Her via media is literalized in the metaphor of the second quatrain, where she parts the waves and "keepes her course aright," not swerving in bad or good weather. In Spenser the sea is often "fortune," which in turn is mutable; the poet has just noted that the lady is unmoved by the prospect of "chaunce" (change). He then proceeds to one of Spenser's favorite images both of stability and change—the ship at sea. *Amor.* 34 ("Like as a ship that through the Ocean wyde") has already shown that the sonnet narrator uses this image to depict both his life and his poem.[22] (In 34, however, the poet was the ship of "succour desolate" who suffered destruction of its goods because of the raging floods and hard rocks; here, by contrast, the lady is "like a steddy ship" who finds the right path.) The lady's image as "a steady ship" is therefore quite important; not only is she steadfast and well assured, but she possesses that same sense of single direction the poet (who has a "double malady," is "tost with troublous fit" between artistry and love, and who pines when he has love and complains when he doesn't) so ardently desires.

In the third quatrain the lady is further made happy by not being restricted by fear of foes or the favor-seeking of friends, bending to neither in her own self-security. This is a significant acknowledgment that the poet's previous statements about having to defend the lady's pride, having to protect her from others' statements, and warning her that others would be upset were he to die of unfulfilled love are of little import to her.

The couplet repeats his theme; it also echoes the "reposeth" of *Amor.* 58 ("Weake is th'assurance that weake flesh reposeth"), just as 58's "strength vnstayd" now becomes the "stay of her owne stedfast might." The poem concludes with a witty ambigu-

ity in which the poet, once again and now with his own "cor-
rected" self-assurance, comments by using a "superlative
superlative." She is "most happy," "but he most happy who such
one loues best." That is to say, although she is most happy, the
one she loves is even happier; alternatively, although she is most
happy, he is happier yet for loving such a one. Both interpreta-
tions serve well, and the line's dual possibilities reflect the same
double examination he has given to the term "assurance."

Having completed his contemplation of the lady's self-as-
surance, the poet moves ahead with an abrupt announcement:

> They that in course of heauenly spheares are skild,
>> To euery planet point his sundry yeare:
>> in which her circles voyage is fulfild,
>> as Mars in three score yeares doth run his spheare.
> So since the winged God his planet cleare,
>> began in me to moue, one yeare is spent:
>> the which doth longer vnto me appeare,
>> then al those fourty which my life outwent.
> Then by that count, which louers books inuent,
>> the spheare of Cupid fourty yeares containes:
>> which I haue wasted in long languishment,
>> that seemed the longer for my greater paines.
> But let my loues fayre Planet short her wayes
>> this yeare ensuing, or else short my dayes.

In 57 the poet has just requested "timely grace"; here in 60 time
is the subject, a reminder that historical time still moves swiftly
even though the poet's amatory experiences have lengthened and
shortened psychological time. In 58 and 59 he completed the
interchange concerning, or at least the meditation on, the lady's
self-assurance, ending with the witty comment about who is
most happy. The dalliance in those poems contrasts with the
fresh progression here; an excitement, an academic teasing, per-
meates the poem, marking an end of one period and anticipating
the start of the new. The tension created is partly because of its
positioning; like the Janus reference in *Amor.* 4, sonnet 60 looks
behind and ahead. It comes right after a "yeare" of loving and
forty years of "long languishment," and right before a shortening
of days and, on the analogic level, immediately before Palm
Sunday and Holy Week.

Spenser's elaborate time game is now in full play; he has
inserted various indicators among the earlier poems (suggesting
calendars, both civil and liturgical), but now "time" itself be-

comes the focus. Its reference in 57 is picked up in 60; as the sequence gains momentum in its movement toward the betrothal (67) and Easter (68), time will come up again in an important function in 62 and then again metaphorically in 63. In 60, various concepts of time are played against one another, mixing and blending calendars until they merge during the Holy Week poems and Easter. "Spheares" and "circles," mentioned nowhere else in the sequence, intersect in this witty, brilliant poem, which is important in itself and within the sequence.

The poet prefaces his personal comments by the explanation provided in the first three lines and the example given in the fourth. The first "year" presented is a relative one appointed to each planet according to the period of its orbital restitution. It varies, therefore, from subject to subject. Conversely, the "yeares" noted in line 4 refer to "earth-bound" years, sixty of which constitute Mars's planetary year, although the "whole years work" of *Amor.* 23 was presumably a metaphoric application of the word "year."

The second quatrain personalizes the topic: Cupid now has circled (moved his planet in) the poet for one year, now spent. But this third mention of a year could be either the relative (planetary) Cupidean year or the "objective" earth year that has passed since the poet fell in love. There is no need to tie this year to *Amor.* 4 (as some have done) and the new year mentioned there. That earlier poem promised "new delight" as the poet moved into the courtship represented by the early sonnets; on the analogic level it prefaced the start of the pre-Lenten segment. In 60, the year noted in line 6 is a "year" of loving; it may be a period that is psychologically a year in length (as he suggests later) or may be an actual period of 365 days, taking it outside the sequence frame to before the sonnets begin marking time. The suggestion in lines 7–8 is that the year in line 6 is a relative planetary year that appears longer than the forty earth years of the poet's life.

On first reading these poems one is taken aback by the poet's revelation of his age. Discovering the poet is forty explains a great deal about what may have been puzzling concerning the lover's manner and tone. "It confirms our impression that the . . . sonnets are written from the broad, experienced view of maturity, written with a witty and mature consciousness that has mastered all the modes of courtship."[23] The break in the narrative frame, by which the empirical Spenser reaches and through which this mature narrator suggests autobiographical references, is another part of the fiction; it takes readers further into the game and provides a means of association with this clever, mature, practiced lover whose age only adds to the delight of playing his experienced, amorous, poetic game.

A part of that game has been the long languishment and greater pain, which have made the Cupidean year seem even longer. Because his year has seemed longer, he requests that the lady, as his "loues fayre Planet," shorten her ways (her orbit, the coming earth year) or shorten his days (so the year will seem shorter). As the sonnet concludes, there has been a movement from astrological/astronomical years to chronological years and then to psychological days.

Still there is more. The poet's example in the first quatrain is to Mars's planetary year being composed of sixty chronological years. In Spenser's poetry, Mars appears in four different aspects: as the bloody god of war, as the adulterous lover of Venus, as Venus's "gentle knight" and courtly lover, and as the planet. Here, although the reference is to the planet, the imagery of Mars as god of war as well as courtly lover is suggested. As Mars takes sixty years to run his planetary sphere, so in this sixtieth sonnet Mars, god of war and turmoil, has indeed run his course. After this sonnet, with only one exception (and that being a reference in *Amor.* 69 to the memory of conquest) there is no more martial imagery in the sequence. The "fierce warres" that make up half *The Faerie Queene* narrator's song (proem, line 9), and of which the sonnet narrator has written so much, are completed. Mars, as patron of "lover-knights," is no longer needed. There remains the "other half" of the epic song, "faithful loues," a reference that takes us to the second and third quatrains' notation of Cupid and his year.[24]

But while a year's a year, love is disruptive of progressive time, and even the cyclicality of the spheres, by their repetitions, creates mirrors among the cycles. As a natural concept, circularity ties man to nature; in doing so it promises freedom from time's yoke if man surrenders to the natural community and merges with history. Likewise, the liturgical year, like the civil calendar, moves round and round in that "rolling wheele" (18). The liturgical analogy transposes the reader from "objective" time to eternal time. Cupid's year in *Amor.* 60 is out of sync with objective and eternal time, being a subjective, psychological time running parallel to, but not temporally with, the other times. The sonnet's last lines compare the lady to a planet; this transition has already been prepared for by the pronominal change between "his" and "her" in lines 2 and 3. As a planet, she is enjoined to align her planetary year with the chronological year, synchronizing and sacralizing the times and the poet's life.

The lady's celestial qualities are further elaborated in the following sonnet, 61, which celebrates not only her beauty but marks the end of the "accusations" of the lady's pride. The poem corresponds to Palm Sunday; as such it also marks a pivot—the end of most of the Lenten agon and the start of Holy Week.

> The glorious image of the makers beautie,
>   My souerayne saynt, the Idoll of my thought,
>   dare not henceforth aboue the bounds of dewtie,
>   t'accuse of pride, or rashly blame for ought.
> For being as she is diuinely wrought,
>   and of the brood of Angels heuenly borne:
>   and with the crew of blessed Saynts vpbrought,
>   each of which did her with theyr guifts adorne;
> The bud of ioy, the blossome of the morne,
>   the beame of light, whom mortal eyes admyre:
>   what reason is it then but she should scorne
>   base things that to her loue too bold aspire?
> Such heauenly formes ought rather worshipt be,
>   then dare be lou'd by men of meane degree.

Like 59, 61 is a poem of self-assurance and praise; religious imagery pervades the sonnet, with terms such as "the makers beautie," "my souerayne saynt," "brood of Angels," "crew of blessed saynts," and "heauenly formes," supporting a bilevel reading and the analogy of the poet's love for the lady and the penitent's love for Christ.

By beginning his poem with the reference to "the glorious image," the poet looks back to the Ash Wednesday sonnet, *Amor.* 22; here it is not the lady's glorious image but the lady herself, as the glorious image of the Maker's beauty, who is celebrated. The beautiful lady as a reflection of God's beauty is noted in her being an "image" of the divine beauty (she appears in God's image); but she also is a creation of God's imaging powers. From God's fashioning and imagining the idea of woman, this lady was created. And she is also a "souerayne saynt" with whom an "Idoll" is associated. As an idol, she might be thought of as the image of a saint, both in the sense of a physical representation (a statue or even a poem) or as an idol of his mind as he mentally envisions the "image" of the Maker's beauty. And she has also been, throughout the sequence, his idyll, the subject of romantic reveries.

The compound predicate "dare not . . . t'accuse . . . or rashly blame" appears in lines 3–4, but the subject is left ambiguous. It is either his injunction to himself, in which case the poem is one of his own reflections, or it is a directive to those others who earlier found fault "with her too portly pride" (*Amor.* 5). It is significant that "henceforth" he will not accuse or blame; implicit is the poet's recognition and admission that he has been doing both and that the accusing and blaming have been rash and "for ought." Given that the various years have already ended in 60 and that the new one will start in 62, 61 provides, in a way, the lover's New Year's resolution.

There follows a grammatically complex six-line prepositional phrase (lines 5–10) in which lines 6 and 7 refer to the "is" of line 5 (she is of the brood of angels and is brought up with the crew of saints), and in which lines 9 and 11 refer to the "she" of line 5 (she, the bud of joy, blossom of the morn, etc.). The phrase itself begins with a play on "being," in which the word may be read either as a divinely wrought Being or as "being, as she is. . . ." But the lengthy structuring of the phrase, which delays the subject until line 11, subtly distances the reader from the earlier topic of the lady's pride. No longer does the poet talk about the pride, or even actually accuse her of it; now he discusses those others who accuse her of pride, which is quite different from making the accusation itself. Even the pride has already been dismissed when paralleled in line 4 with "ought." Just as martial imagery ceased after its dismissal in 60, so pride as a negative aspect is no longer depicted. Henceforth, except in jest, the lady's pride will be viewed as the proper scorn of base things "that to her loue too bold aspire."

His compact wordplay in the second quatrain is worth noting. The lady as "Being" or "being as she is" is "diuinely wrought," implying both the point of her origination as well as the quality of her creation. Even the rhyme words point to her ethereal qualities; she is divinely "wrought" and "vpbrought" by saints; "borne" (both "carried" and "created") aloft by angels and "adorne[d]" by saint's gifts. Furthermore, the lady's being "wrought" by the "maker" connects her to "the brood of Angels," suggesting her angelic quality (with celestial peers) and also providing an alternative source of her origin—her being "wrought" by angelic contemplation (brooding). Una (1.3.8) is described in just such a way when called "the virgin borne of heauenly brood." Even "heauenly," paralleling the clever pun on "diuinely," is ambiguously employed, allowing it to describe the angels, the lady, the type of quality of her birth, and the location in which the lady was born. "Of the brood of Angels" also stands in parallel construction with "with the crew of blessed Saynts." This "crew" returns us to "brood" and also suggests the cruet used in communion, a term Spenser uses in S.C. February 209, "and often crost with the priestes crewe."

Finally, "vpbrought" has its own multiplication of meanings. Quite literally, it associates the lady with the blessed saints. In one sense she was brought up, raised as a child in the church, with the saints; in another sense she has been raised, canonized, to the level of "souerayne saynt." Not only divinely wrought, she has been elevated to the rank of sovereign saint.

The third quatrain moves from the lofty heights of heavenly adoration back to the earth. The lady, after all, is not a saint (except insofar as all Christians are part of that communion of saints), and she is not divine (except insofar as being created by God). The third quatrain shows the poet retreating from those elevated images which, earlier in the sequence, would have kept him in the airy realm of Petrarchan exaggeration. At this point in the sequence the lady's true divinity is put in perspective with her true humanity. She is on the one hand the art of God and is "diuinely wrought"; on the other, she has been graced with the gifts of nature and the saints—she is (and has the gifts of) the bud of joy, the blossom of the morn, the beam of light.

The couplet provides the poet's reflection on what he has just said: "such heauenly formes ought rather worshipt be, / then dare be lou'd by men of meane degree." The lady as a "form" (image, idol, divinely wrought being, angel, saint) ought to be worshiped, not loved by men of "meane degree" inclined to aspire too boldly to her love. Which is not to say that he will not love her, but that she is deserving of more than love; she is worthy of worship.

Such worship, and the poet's humble acceptance of his relationship, parallel the worship and humility of the Collect for Palm Sunday, in which God's love is not just a benevolent sentiment but a concrete event embracing both the incarnation and the crucifixion. The sonnet's emphasis on origin and birth (divinely wrought, heavenly born) perhaps reflects this part of the thought. Yet the Collect also emphasizes the exemplarist nature of Christ's passion ("that all mankynde shoulde folowe the example of his greate humilitie . . . and be made partakers of his resurreccion . . ."), thus focusing on humility and patience.

The *BCP* psalm for the day *(Exaudi, Deus deprecationem)*, for this sixty-first sonnet, is 61. The epistle for the day, from 2 Philippians, concerns the preexistence of Christ who, "being in the forme of God, thought it no robbery to be equal with God." The epistle moves us from Christ's divine nature to his incarnation, in which he voluntarily surrendered the divine image and took upon himself the mode of human existence. At the time of the resurrection, Christ is exalted on high; he is also "giuen . . . a Name aboue euerie name" so that He may be worshiped "bothe of things in heauen, and things in earth, and things vnder the earth."

The Palm Sunday epistle balances Christ's heavenly with his human nature. The cross is viewed as the culmination of Christ's humiliation and at the same time as the basis for his triumph; that which was negative ultimately becomes positive. Likewise the gospel is the Passion according to Matthew 26 and 27, emphasizing Christ's mighty majesty; it twice calls him "Son of God," but at the same time depicts him as humble, lowly, innocent, and obedient. It also compares the mystery of the new covenant with the old, calling followers in their penitential journey to a worship, through imitation, of Christ.

The analogues with the sonnet are fairly clear; a rereading of the poem in light of even these short selections from the epistle and gospel lessons, combined with a knowledge of the day's general theme, shows the sonnet/Palm Sunday parallel in which lover, lady, and Christ all partake in the "humble exaltation."

The sonnets immediately following 61 constitute the *Amoretti's* analogue to Holy Week. In the sonnet sequence these poems celebrate the completion of the actual courtship; at the end of the "week" they culminate in the betrothal and exhibit the poet's transformation as he moves away from the sterile, false *amoretti* of Petrarchan conceit, neo-Platonic leaders, courtly idealization, and rhetorical opaqueness. And they show the lover's increased (and finally full) acceptance of the lady as a real woman, not as an expression of his desires to fashion a woman as he would have her be. On the analogical level the sonnets mark the culmination of the penitential journey as Christ's Passion is depicted analogically through his suffering, death, and (on Easter) his resurrection. In the church this is the week of reconciliation, the time toward which the penitents have been striving (fasting and praying), and the time in which they are finally admitted into full fellowship. The reconciliatory nature of the sonnets is every-where evident; all of them, from 62–68, suggest the reconciled nature of the two lovers.

By the end of 61 the poet has been freed from the bondage of restrictive traditional language; his spirit and his words have soared. But he also stops himself and returns to more realistic language and to a more humble attitude. By the end of 61 the lover, too, has come to an understanding of his right relationship with the lady who, by now, is a real lady and not just a literary expression of the poet's imagination. His "lower heaven" is still worthy of worship—but as a human incarnation of God's beauty, not as a Platonic Ideal. Likewise, the penitent has left behind his affected and ineffective attempts at securing Christ's love by winning his own salvation. All that has passed is now ready to be left in the "old year," replaced by a new approach, a renewed anticipation, a transformation of old into new.

Hastened by the ending of Cupid's year in *Amor*. 60, the calen-dar year makes its own turn in 62 (25 March, the Feast of the Annunciation and New Year's Day, Old Style). The old year hav-ing run its course, the new begins with promptness. As in *Amor*. 4 ("New yeare forth looking out of Ianus gate"), the poet uses the occasion of temporal change to envision a new season of love. In just two lines he moves from the old year to the new. Nature responds, and the poet sees the response as a positive significa-tion of what will come:

> The weary yeare his race now hauing run,
>   The new begins his compass course anew:
>   with shew of morning mylde he hath begun,
>   betokening peace and plenty to ensew.

The suitor, now using "us," and thus suggesting that the amend-ing of lives has already begun, applies nature's situation to his own and calls for his own beginning:

> So let vs, which this chaunge of weather vew,
>   chaunge eeke our mynds and former liues amend,
>   the old yeares sinnes forepast let vs eschew,
>   and fly the faults with which we did offend.

The lady is now separate from, yet a part of, the lover; the "us" becomes "we" as he permits his old self to expand, to incorporate the lady as another being, and then generate a new self made of the two of them. Nature influenced them; now they will influence nature:

> Then shall the new yeares ioy forth freshly send,
>   into the glooming world his gladsome ray:
>   and all these stormes which now his beauty blend,
>   shall turne to caulmes and tymely cleare away.
> So likewise loue cheare you your heauy spright,
>   and chaunge old yeares annoy to new delight.

The poet takes the previous sonnet's natural images and re-places them in the natural world: the "ioy" extends the "bud of ioy" in 61; the gladsome ray" reflects the "beame of light" (61); and the "morning mylde" suggests a generalizing of the "blossome of the morne" (61).

Noticeable here is the tender freshness of language and the unstilted nature of expression. No longer is the lover rhapsodic about "fresh loue" and "lusty spring"; there is now found a more mature, a more realistic acceptance, that their new joy will bring "gladsome ray[s]" into a world still beset with storms but into which love can bring "caulmes." No longer is heard his brash challenge to "prepare your selfe new loue to entertaine"; "instead of awakening a lusty hour, these more experienced lovers are both enjoined to amend their lives, eschew old faults, and cheer their heavy . . . spirits."[25] The wordplay is gentle, witty, and more controlled than it was in Amor. 4. At the end of the second quatrain the poet directs to "fly the faults with which we did offend." In a regressive assimilation of sound, in which the second element (here the s sound) anticipates the first (here the t), the word "faults" is pronounced as though it were "false" (also a "fault," to be sure, but of a different sort). The falsities, pretensions and exaggerations exhibited throughout the sequence have caused much of the lover's distancing; it is time, he suggests, that such things were left.

The end of the third quatrain moves from storms to calms; such a movement, brought about by "new yeares ioy," will "tymely cleare away" the storms and, in time, clear a way for the joy. The "clearing" suggests by internal rhyme the "chearing" referred to in the couplet. The final line ends the poem gently, simply, and clearly with an affectionate admonition to "chaunge old yeares annoy to new delight," the tenderness of the line reinforced by the Elizabethan pronunciation of "annoy," which would render it close to "an I," thus yielding "and change old years, an[d] I, to new delight."

Twice earlier in the *Amoretti* Spenser used the ship to sym-
bolize the journey through the courtship (34 and 56). He uses it
again in 63, but this time the ship, like the lover, is in sight of the
happy shore. Analogically, the penitent catches a metaphoric
glimpse of paradise and is in sight of the "fayre soyle" of heaven
toward which (through his belief and forthcoming baptism) he
has been moving. With religious overtones as reminders that this
poem is part of Holy Week in the sonnet-week pattern, the lover
announces:

> After long stormes and tempests sad assay,
>   Which hardly I endured heretofore:
>   in dread of death and daungerous dismay,
>   with which my silly barke was tossed sore:
> I doe at length descry the happy shore,
>   in which I hope ere long for to arryue:
>   fayre soyle it seemes from far and fraught with store
>   of all that deare and daynty is alyue.
> Most happy he that can at last atchyue
>   the ioyous safety of so sweet a rest:
>   whose least delight sufficeth to depriue
>   remembrance of all paines which him opprest.
> All paines are nothing in respect to this,
>   all sorrowes short that gaine eternall blisse.

The poet's fresh start in the new year is evident as he takes one
of his old images, that of the ship, and readjusts it to mean
something new. In 34 the poet wandered in darkness and dismay
like a ship out of course; in 56 the poet was like "a ship of
succour desolate" when beaten by the lady's waves of obstinacy.
In 63, however, the image of the lover's journey through courtship
coalesces with the poet's attempts to complete his poetic nar-
rative, an image Spenser uses with similar meaning in *The
Faerie Queene*.
   The poet gives the first quatrain to things of the past—the
storms and tempests that tossed his "silly barke" as the tem-
pestuous waves of passion tossed the sonnets. He moves swiftly
from past to present and to the sight of the happy shore, observ-
ing who is most happy and playing on the safety of "so sweet a
rest" ("arrest," as in the place of rest, as well as in the lady's
having arrested him so sweetly). The import of the action is not
merely that he will have so sweet a rest but that the consolation
depicted in 10–12 is so much greater than the pains, that he is
willing to forgo remembrance of the pains for the promise of

future bliss. Such a consolation appears to be stock for the *Amoretti* poet (he expressed it in 26 and 51, and he will remind himself of it later on his wedding day, *Epith.* 32–33). But the difference here is that while formerly he used the idea in the midst of turmoil in order to bolster his flagging spirit, now there is no despair. The happy shore is in sight, and the observation is less a consolation than an affirmation of current happiness.

In the next sonnet, *Amor.* 64, the poet picks up on his own image of the "fayre soyle . . . fraught with store / of all that deare and daynty is alyue." In the sequence's third, and last, extended blazon (76 and 77 will have much shorter catalogues) the poet celebrates the only kiss recorded in the *Amoretti.* With distinct echoes of Belphoebe, the sonnet's imagery unmistakably derives from the lush eroticism of the Song of Songs. Baroway observes that the beauty of this passage, like that of the garden passage of the Canticles, derives "not from the singling out of details, but from the sensuous and sedative suggestiveness of the whole group."[26] The blazon itself will be echoed in the tenth stanza of the *Epithalamion* (167–84), where it combines with the jewel images of *Amor.* 15.

Earlier the lady had been compared with flowers and plants, but in 26 ("sweet is the rose . . .") the purpose of the comparison was to show their sweetness in contrast to the bitterness accompanying them. In 64 there is no bitterness; all the flowers are employed to suggest parts of the lady's body:

> Comming to kisse her lyps, (such grace I found)
>   Me seemd I smelt a gardin of sweet flowres:
>   that dainty odours from them threw around
>   for damzels fit to decke their louers bowres.
> Her lips did smell lyke vnto Gillyflowers,
>   her ruddy cheekes lyke vnto Roses red:
>   her snowy browes lyke budded Bellamoures,
>   her louely eyes lyke Pincks but newly spred,
> Her goodly bosome lyke a Strawberry bed,
>   her neck lyke to a bounch of Cullambynes:
>   her brest lyke lillyes, ere theyr leaues be shed,
>   her nipples lyke young blossomd Iessemynes:
> Such fragrant flowres doe giue most odorous smell,
>   but her sweet odour did them all excell.

The poem's frank sensuality is unconcealed and appears refreshing after the scores of stilted conceits that did more to detract from, than to describe, the real lady. Instead of intellectual conceits the poet uses embroidered fantasy of Spenser's richest type, and the poet so loses himself in the rhapsodic response to the kiss that the octet-sestet division is blurred without significantly (or even noticeably) enjambing it. The flower analogies, like a garden itself, suggest not only a great natural display but one that hints at both fragrance and color, appealing thus on two counts. While her cheeks are like roses, fragrant and sweet as those flowers are, the cheeks are also "ruddy." The highly perfumed jasmine is held up to comparison with the nipples (the shape of the buds suggesting the shape of the nipples).

The "sweet" flowers and sweet lady are reechoed when the poet returns to the now-practical courtship at hand. Earlier the poet contemplated his possible loss of freedom in the bands of betrothal; in 37 he realized it was folly "for any being free, / to couet fetters, though they golden bee." *Amor.* 47 found him "charmed" by his Circe-like lady, yet caught by her baits. These playful descriptions revealed themselves as mere coverings for his real desires for marriage. Now the situation is reversed; he will accept the "bonds," but the very-human young lady must now herself be convinced. In *Amor.* 65 the poet reassures her of the freedom within "bounds" and "bands," explaining that any misgivings she might have are unwarranted:

> The doubt which ye misdeeme, fayre loue, is vaine,
>   That fondly feare to loose your liberty,
>   when loosing one, two liberties ye gayne,
>   and make him bond that bondage earst dyd fly.
> Sweet be the bands, the which true loue doth tye,
>   without constraynt or dread of any ill:
>   the gentle birde feeles no captiuity
>   within her cage, but singes and feeds her fill.

Unmentioned in the poem are two important developments. First, the poet has not just "courted" the lady but apparently has proposed marriage. Second, the lady has apparently expressed her fears of losing her "liberty" through marriage.

The poem's lines provide a fine example of the lover's radically reformed use of previous images; the captivity, bondage, and entrapment metaphors employed so frequently are brought into play. The literal captivity noted earlier transforms into something both positive and productive; the caged bird eats, and sings, her fill, though the bird itself is generally associated with freedom. Freedom is the issue, and the poet has already provided his clever paradox in which "losing" becomes "gayne." Reciprocity in love ("mutuall good will") not only nourishes but flourishes. In love, the old definitions no longer hold. That which formerly limited actually provides for growth; that which seemed to take away actually adds.

The lady's doubts recall a frightened Amoret who, after having been wooed and won by Scudamour, tries to "woo" her own "wished freedom" from her betrothed. And the ensuing allegorical depiction of the situation is a reminder of Dante, who, in media vita (the *Amoretti* poet being only slightly past that age), began his own allegory on a day exactly corresponding to this one in *Amor.* 65—Maundy Thursday.

> There pride dare not approch, nor discord spill
>   the league twixt them, that loyal loue hath bound:
>   but simple truth and mutuall good will,
>   seekes with sweet peace to salue each others wound:
> There fayth doth fearlesse dwell in brasen towre,
>   and spotlesse pleasure builds her sacred bowre.

In the "bond" or "cage," pride and discord have no effect. The "bands" become a "league" "bound" with "loyal loue." Truth, good will, peace, faith, and spotless pleasure provide Spenser's idealized image of the good marriage toward which the sonnets lead. The somewhat metaphysical (albeit accurate) explanation of gaining two liberties by losing one and the somewhat homely (albeit gentle) example of the caged bird feeling no captivity and singing her fill are displaced by the real consolations the lady will enjoy: mutual goodwill, simple truth (perhaps as opposed to the veiled truth he has displayed throughout the sequence), and the salving of each other's wounds. "The cage in which a captive songbird expands its soul in sanctified freedom has become a tower of faith without fear and a prelapsarian bower of erotic bliss."[27]

The mention of wounds is a reminder of various other wounds noted earlier. In *Amor.* 50 the poet called upon the lady, his "lyfes Leach," to "salue both hart and body." A notable development between that sonnet and this important one is that now, with mutual goodwill, they will salve each other's wounds. Wounds, potentially life-negating, now have life-affirming ability; those who engage in the wounds' salving benefit mutually.

Another significant development is that the poet-lover has now become the lady's teacher, a reversal of the earlier role in which she trained and taught him (*Amor.* 21). This is a position toward which the lady has been urging him throughout the sequence. The assurance he so much praised in the lady in 59 ("Thrise happy she") is now his own. Earlier the roles had been reversed; the cruel lady and *donna angelicata* were in control of all situations. That is strikingly altered now as the poet assumes what Spenser views as a man's proper role. Artegall has been rescued from Radigund, and Britomart is prepared to abandon her aggressive, assertive command in favor of the "mutuall good will" of betrothal. The lover's language is firm and controlled; the poet paints a picture that, although artificial in the sense of its being an allegory, is nonetheless as straightforward as one could wish. His rhymes are instructive: the paradox of "gayne" and "vaine" reinforces the lines' internal meaning; "liberty" does the same with "captiuity," as do their parallels in "fly" and "tye." "Bound" and "wound" support the mutual effects of mutual salving.

The calendar analogue is Maundy Thursday; the epistle lesson is Paul's injunction in 2 Corinthians 11 concerning reconciliation and mutual benefit in the Christian community. In the church this is the great day of Lenten teaching; the penitent presents himself in church to be (1) instructed in the final mysteries before beginning the Good Friday observations and (2) allowed into fellowship through communion. In the *Amoretti* this is also a time of instruction, the lessons having their analogues in mutuality (of which Paul wrote) as well as in the benefits of living life in community.

Maundy Thursday is the first of the Triduum Sacrum, the last three days of Holy Week. For centuries these three days not only represented the unitary paschal celebration but, in three separate ways, displayed its component parts. Maundy Thursday represents the total feast of redemption, brought about through reconciliation and at-one-ment; Good Friday celebrates the redemption, with special emphasis on God's act of becoming, being, and dying a man. And the Easter Vigil (Holy Saturday) celebrates the redemption not as an isolated event in Christ's biography but as the transitus of Christ from death to life, the turning point between the old law and new, and the meaning such "turning" has for all believers.

In the sonnets, *Amor.* 65, 66, and 67 mark this same period. They conclude the Lenten sequence, and the period of the lover's agon in courtship ends as the betrothal begins. The three poems represent the transitus, starting in 65 and continuing in the following two poems. The action commencing in 65 continues through 66 and culminates in 67. All three suggest movement from old to new and a reinterpretation of the past in light of the future.

Good Friday, 29 March 1594, is represented by *Amor.* 66; the poem continues the "reformed" love and revised poetry of the last several sonnets as the lovers move closer to that point of acceptance which will occur soon. The lover has asked for the lady's hand, has attempted to convince her that in the bonds of marriage she will find a greater freedom, and the lady has declared her love to him. In 61 he noted that "such heauenly formes ought rather worshipt be, / then dare be lou'd by men of meane degree," a topic reintroduced here at 66. However, in 61 he was still hovering between the old and the new year. Having displayed an astonishing degree of assertiveness in 65, he now is free to praise the lady and exhibit his humility in a way he was unable to do earlier. No longer is his "unworthiness" a hyperbolic effect of the "too-poetic-lover." It is true humility in the presence of the woman he loves. Yet he does not contradict what he has just said in 65 about the ideal marriage; in fact, 66 grows out of 65 as an exemplification of that mutual goodwill.

He begins with a compliment, qualifies it, and then explains the qualification:

> To all those happy blessings which ye haue,
>> with plenteous hand by heauen vpon you thrown,
>> this one disparagement they to you gaue,
>> that ye your loue lent to so meane a one.

He referred in *Amor.* 46 to heaven's intervention in sending a rainstorm, but never to heaven being involved in their love. Now he wittily suggests divine action, an idea reinforced by the second quatrain, which also begins with a compliment:

> Yee whose high worths surpassing paragon,
>> could not on earth haue found one fit for mate,
>> ne but in heauen matcheable to none,
>> why did ye stoup vnto so lowly state?

As one surpassing paragon, the lady's high worth has neither a rival nor a pattern; even that "brood of angels" and "crew of blessed Saynts" (56) are not fit ("worthy" or "made") to be compared to her. Yet the lover's admiring, gentle, and humble question remains: how could the lady have stooped to loving him?

His humility asserted, his awe of the lady restated, he is ready to qualify his and his lady's roles:

> But ye thereby much greater glory gate,
>> than had ye sorted with a princes pere:
>> for now your light doth more it selfe dilate,
>> and in my darknesse greater doth appeare.
> Yet since your light hath once enlumind me,
>> with my reflex yours shall encreased be.

Her action in stooping to love him will be reciprocated by his own love; by extension, she will be immortalized by increasing her "light" in his poetry. But those mutual lights are more complex. In Spenser's scheme goodly light does not just shine; it illuminates the physical, moral, and spiritual worlds. And the light does not merely increase; it dilates and expands, as it does in the cantos of Mutability (7.7.58):

> I well consider all that ye haue sayd,
>> And find that all things stedfastnes doe hate
>> And changed be: yet being rightly wayd
>> They are not changed from their first estate;
>> But by their change their being doe dilate:
>> And turning to themselues at length againe,
> Doe work their owne perfection so by fate.

In an Aristotelian sense the dilating is a fulfilling of one's nature, a becoming of who one actually is. Mutability thus works positively toward the perfecting and the perfection of being. The end of one's teleology is one's ontology, and the lady's light not only radiates into the lover, illuminating his darkness, but in turn shows the lady who she is.

In an action suggested earlier in 45 ("Leaue lady in your glasse of christall clene"), in which the lady was directed to see herself in the poet, the last lines of 66 suggest the mutual reflexivity of the lovers' respective lights. The dilating of her light will "enlumine" the lover; illuminated, he will by "reflex" increase her light. The process continues ad infinitum, with one light reflecting the other, which in turn dilates, which in turn reflects—the same process Spenser describes in the *Hymne in Honour of Beautie* (176–82):

> But gentle Loue, that loiall is and trew,
> Will more illumine your resplendent ray,

And adde more brightnesse to your goodly hew,
From light of his pure fire, which by like way
Kindled of yours, your likenesse doth display,
Like as two mirrours by opposd reflexion,
Doe both expresse the faces first impression.

In short, reciprocated faithful love enhances beauty and reveals its true nature. The reflexive light does not diminish but grows. The "reflexive" nature of the action is important; it clearly suggests that the poet will reflect the lady's light.

"Reflect" also means "to turn" (L. re-flectere), and on another level of the sequence is the reminder that Spenser has already connected turning with dilating in the stanza (above) from Mutabilitie. "Turning" itself has various meanings for Spenser. As early as the "Ruines of Rome" (18.14) he used the term to suggest ontological development ("all things turne to their first being"); but he also associates it with the poetic process (in "Mother Hubberds Tale" [line 68] the poet intends "to turne the next leafe of the booke"; and Alcyon, in "Colin Clouts Come Home Againe" [386–87], is said "for Daphnes death" to "tourn sweet layes of loue to endlesse plaints of pittie"). The poet, then, will increase the lady's "light" by his turns, his poems.

There have been other "turns" that have been seen during the sequence; old years have turned to new, planets have turned in their orbits and returned to their starting points, ships have turned toward safe ports, things have threatened to turn to other things (the lady to stone, storms to calm), and the lady has bent (flectere) herself, turned herself, to laughter. Turning is intrinsic to the Amoretti as old yields the way to new, as the poet turns from one kind of poetry to another, as old texts in new contexts yield new texts, fresh life, and light. The lover is poised on the major "turn" he will make in the sequence; that movement in itself provides the chief pivot, the major turn, in the sonnet action, and will be accompanied by the lady's own (re)turn to the lover.

On the analogic level, Lent indicates the penitent turning his life around, converting; the pericopes lead one through the drama of the Passion to the final "turning," in which death turns to life. Spenser chooses to focus on the "good" aspect of Good Friday, the felix culpa, not the crucifixion. The gospel lesson for this day, from the Passion of Saint John (18 and 19), differs from other gospel narratives of the Passion by focusing on Christ's sovereign and unqualified majesty (Matthew stresses the humble king; Mark, the lonely warrior wrestling the powers of darkness; Luke, the loving savior sympathizing with those who are lost). The second petition of the second Collect for the day asks that all "should be conuerted [i.e., turned] and liue."

The entire sonnet may be reread (without straining) by substituting Christ for the lady and taking the lover's witty resolution in the couplet as the penitent's statement of dedicated service and determination. Christ, who stooped to so low a state, will receive through his act of submission a greater glory; his enlightening of the penitent, by the penitent's dedicated life, will reflect Christ's act. His preparation complete, the penitent (poet and lover) now turns ("reflex") to Easter Even.

Undoubtedly one of the finest poems in the sequence, *Amor.* 67 is one of the most important in the narrative structure.

> Lyke as a huntsman after weary chace,
>   Seeing the game from him escapt away,
>   sits downe to rest him in some shady place,
>   with panting hounds beguiled of their pray:
> So after long pursuit and vaine assay,
>   when I all weary had the chace for forsooke,
>   the gentle deare returnd the selfe-same way,
>   thinking to quench her thirst at the next brooke.
> There she beholding me with mylder looke,
>   sought not to fly, but fearlesse still did bide:
>   till I in hand her yet halfe trembling tooke,
>   and with her owne goodwill hir fyrmely tyde.
> Strange thing me seemd to see a beast so wyld,
>   so goodly wonne with her owne will beguyld.

The sonnet resounds with old images newly used; the hunt, pursuit, and chase employed in various forms throughout the earlier sequence, are now past matters. Captivity and tying transform to positive conditions; wildness becomes beauty, and beguilement productive. The "game," both as object of quest and as process of play, is completed when the dear-deer herself re-turns to the re-formed lover and is taken by the hand in betrothal, preparing for her later being led by the hand into the bridal chamber.

The sonnet is rich in echoes, some of which shed light on the lover as the "huntsman" and some on the lover himself as the deer. Such is the paradox that throughout the long metaphorical hunt, the lover has acted as hunter when in fact he was simultaneously the hunted. Britomart, likewise, is the deer brought to bay by Artegall's long pursuit, although she, like the sonnet lady, has been as much pursuer as pursued (4.6.41):

> So well he woo'd her, and so well he wrought her,
> With faire entreatie and sweet blandishment,
> That at length vnto a bay he brought her,
> So as she to his speeches was content
> To lend an eare, and softly to relent.

Her being brought to bay is not the same condition as in the sonnet where the lady-deer-game has "escapt away," but Britomart's submission is as much her doing as Artegall's.

The sonnet begins with a "lyke as" simile; it appears between only two others in the sequence (34 and 89) beginning in this manner. Immediately we are in the midst of the hunt metaphor, an extension of the love-as-war motif used earlier. But the poet never makes the expected hunt-courtship comparison; instead he works out comparisons between the hunt in general and this particular hunt, in which the lady is the quarry. The traditional Petrarchan love-hunt topos is challenged by Spenser's conclusion that love cannot be a hunt if it is really love. The early lines are significant; the warfare eagerly pursued in the past has now become a "weary chace." It is especially so because he apparently has lost. The game escaped, he sits down in the pastoral "shady place" (which, in Spenser, almost always juxtaposes the world of experience with some form of a sacred, magic circle). The earlier external labyrinth of circuitous and meandering ways is replaced by the present interior temple of reflection and rest, aligning the situation with Sidney's violent world of Asia Minor and the Arcadian retreat, Lodge's Bordeaux and the Forest of Arden, Sannazaro's Naples and Arcadia, and Montemayor's stylized Spain and the fields of Ezla.

The inner pastoral circle always is presented as the place where natural and supernatural join, where earth and heaven mingle, and where supernatural and supernormal are the order of the day, overturning the commonplaces of the nonarcadian world. Such will be the case here in the second quatrain, where the hunt analogy cannot cope with the facts of this particular courtship or of this particular lady. William Bowman Piper observes the careful and subtle shifts with which Spenser has shaped the syntax of these lines to suggest the inadequacy of the lover's image "by tucking the lover in the subordinate clause, 'when I', etc., and balancing 'huntsman,' the subject of the first quatrain, with 'the gentle deare.' Syntactically, the first two quatrains read: 'As a huntsman sits down, so did the deer return.' What Spenser has done is to oppose the flow of the poem's syntax to its speaker's obvious drift of meaning. By so doing, he has loosened the second quatrain's first line, allowing it to go with either the lover, as the lover intends, or the deer, as the syntax implies. This syntactical erosion of the lover's analogy, which reveals the force on his mind of the deer's strangely undeerlike return, suggests that the mistress may be and may always have been as much the huntsman as the lover was."[28]

The futility of the lover's game, partly a "weary chace," is supported by its other qualifiers: it has been a long pursuit and a "vaine assay," something noted all along but something that assumes another meaning, considering that it has been the poet's own vanity which has misassured him that he could win the lady by the methods he, until recently, continued to employ.

It is in the very middle of the poem that the sonnet, and the relationship, turns. The pivotal transitus occurs only after the game has been given up as lost, only after the hunter-poet has abandoned the long pursuit. Like the poet's "reflex" in Amor. 66, the lady makes her own "return" in 67. His game "escapt away," she, as game, returns "the self-same way."

The third quatrain dissolves the poet's Petrarchan hunt image by virtually destroying it. "In specifying the mutual redirection of the will away from egotistical conflict by both poet and Lady as the key condition for the existence of love, as he does explicitly in sonnet 67 and implicitly throughout the Amoretti, Spenser is striking at the very heart of Petrarchism."[29] The deer-dear beholds the hunter-lover; "with mylder looke" fluidly refers both to the lady and the lover, both the deer and the hunter. The "doubt[s] which [she] misdeeme[d]" in 65 have been allayed; now she, fearless, "still" ("quiet" and "yet") remains. Earlier it was the lover who had bid the lady "make him bond that bondage earst dyd fly" (65); now the lady agrees not to fly but to accept the "bond" of the next lines.

The lady "beholding" him is reflected punningly in the lover's taking her "in hand," and in a profoundly quiet sylvan ceremony the gentle lady, yet half-trembling, is "fyrmely tyde." Amor. 54 contained the line: "Yet she beholding me with constant eye"; here the qualifier "yet" becomes the definite "there," and the lady's constant attention yields to a milder look. In similar fashion Scudamour leads Amoret out of the Temple of Cupid (4.10.55), her hand trembling in his like a "warie Hynd." At the same time Spenser leaves open the antecedent of "yet halfe trembling"; it is the lady as well as the lover who, with anticipation and reserve, take each other.

The sonnet poet thus plays on the traditional male-female "game," in which the man chases the lady until she catches him. But the poet proceeds with the utmost gentleness. He exhibits a sense of wonder at her action, as well as a sense of the great mystery embodied in that act. The couplet supports and continues that state of wonder, doing so with the mature lover's bemused yet mild and charming observations, in which the "wild" beast (the gentle deer) is "so goodly wonne" (both "won" and "so goodly a one"). In line 4, the exhausted hounds were beguiled of their prey; in line 14 the lady herself, who, like the hounds, has also been hunting, is "with her owne will beguyld." The defeated lady is the successful lady, just as the conquered lover is the conquering hero. Both, with "mutuall good will" (65), have relinquished the game, both having lost and both having won, being joined together in a "league . . . that loyal loue hath bound" (65). The deer is tamed less by the hunter than by her own will.

Spenser draws his deer-lady from an enormous body of "deer" literature, from the Bible, from Pliny and Horace and Virgil, through medieval religious allegory into many varieties of Renaissance literature.[30] More important in the overall *Amoretti* than these sources are those elements tying the poem to its analogical level. In the Church calendar Easter Even is one of the most significant times of the year, marking the transitus from death to life, from the old being to the new, from slavery to freedom. It makes the transit by a focus on "both" sides—the old and the new—in what Tillich calls the "Gestalt of Grace." In the sonnet, for example, the old captivity imagery assumes new meaning, the old beguilement leads to new winning, and "yielding" itself leads to victory.

The great paradox of Easter is depicted in the transition. By focusing on only the new there would be resurrection without passion, life without death. Making the focus a point of transit, a "turning," provides the necessary negative as well as positive poles. "It is the dialectic of the 'No' of the 'boundary situation,' the 'No' to all human attempts to absolutize the finite, and the 'Yes' that comes to man when he relinquishes all the props and feels the full brunt of despair over finitude as the basis of existence."[31]

What Spenser depicts in the sonnet (with the poetic license

allowed a poet writing poetry, not dogma), is the "turning" to, and of, grace. Try as the lover did to win his lady, she turns to him only when he gives up trying; similarly, try as one might to obtain grace it only comes freely, as a gift, not as a reward for our efforts. All the "teaching" the lady and the poet do, all the exerting of power of her word and his word, are beneath the power of the free gift bestowed in the grace-full act presented poetically here as "yielding." As a Protestant, Spenser does not admit to a doctrine of works; nonetheless, he suggests that while on one level there is a choice whether to hear the call of grace, on another level it seems clear that God does the choosing and not man. Implicit in all this is the paradox that man both chooses to allow himself to be chosen and is simultaneously chosen by grace.

This extends into the amatory situation presented in the sonnets by suggesting that while the lover wishes to be loved, he must make himself lovable, must prepare himself to be loved, lovable, and loving. But as long as his object is only to be loved, he is dependent and self-serving, and not himself genuinely loving. Only when nurturing himself without a primary concern of finding reward does (and can) he become lovable by the lady who, all along, has loved him. Once he becomes lovable, his "unsought" reward is that he is rewarded with love. Arthur, descending into Orgoglio's dungeon to free Red Cross, imitates Christ's harrowing of hell (*Amor.* 68) and indicates the efficacy of grace that comes undeserved. But "once Red Cross undergoes penance and purgation at the House of Holiness and once he comes to an understanding of the nature of his fall and the glorious hope that awaits the baptized man, he becomes like Arthur, and freely binds himself to the divine command to love both God and man. Then, in his turn, he too is capable of playing the role of liberator."[32] It is so with human love *and* with God's love; what one "does" to "prepare" for grace is to "un-do" (or not "do") preparation.

The essential "action" the lover learns is "that the individual should abandon the pretense that he can act in any way pertaining to salvation: he must experience the full realization that salvation belongs to God, that nothing he can do either by faith or works can help."[33] The conversion implicit in the early sonnets, in which the lover already turned to the lady, was not enough; it is necessary to supplement this with regeneration and a willingness to abandon all that the old life entails. The surrender of the hart-lady to the hunter-lover celebrates the final triumph of prevenient grace (which in Spenser, as in Hooker, does not destroy nature but perfects it) over man's will, no matter how cooperant the latter appears to be with the former.

Yet the sonnet depicts the lady as the one who "returns" to the lover, is taken in hand and firmly tied. The lover sits passively, acting only when the lady does. In the poem's Christology, the Christ-lady, by his own goodwill, has firmly tied himself (herself) to the penitent; but the tying is a reciprocal process implying that the penitent is now tied to the Christ-lady through an imitation of Christ that binds them to one another. The relationship is confirmed by the taking of the hand, possibly Spenser's chirograph implying a relationship between "chiro" (hand) and "Christ."

Augustine's comment on the catechumens chanting Psalm 42, *Sicut Cervus,* as they prepared for baptism on Easter Even helps focus the significance of the hart-lady image, as does Jerome's comparison of the hart to the penitent going to the font: "Desiderat venire ad Christum in quo est fons luminis, ut ablutus baptismo accipiat donum remissionis."[34] The *BCP* epistle for this day (1 Pet. 3) focuses on Christ's baptism; the gospel (Matt. 27) concerns the deposition from the cross and burial. Baptism itself is a transitus, beginning with a death and then rebirth and thus fittingly connected with Christ's death and subsequent resurrection.

Even closer to Spenser's age than Augustine's and Jerome's comments on the deer-baptism connection is the Sarum Missal's elaboration of the topic. Though no Roman Catholic, Spenser would have known the importance of that missal in the English tradition and in the development of Anglican liturgy, and it would have been readily available to him. Prescott keenly observes that the missal as well as the *BCP* are "so rich in intratextuality that at the end of each day in the church calendar the reverberating complex of scriptural references merely rotates forward a notch in its emphasis. Anticipation and reiteration are central to the liturgy and to Spenser's sonnets as well. . . . The storm-tossed ship of *Am.* 63 is found in Sarum's Maundy Thursday blessing of the oil as well as in Palm Sunday's celebration. The shiny lady of *Am.* 66 responds to the Passion Sunday prayer, 'Emittee lucem tuam' almost two weeks late, and on that same Sunday the dogs of Psalm 22 are already out, if briefly, looking for an animal like the deer of *Am.* 67." It is Sarum's use of Psalm 42, with its cervidological image connected to the baptism of penitents on Easter Even, that carried the old tradition forward. It is no coincidence that in *Amor.* 67 the hart and the hunter, lover and beloved, penitent and Christ, meet at the water's edge. As Prescott observes, "it seems safe to say that incorporated into the deer of *Am.* 67 are the most famous Old Testament harts and hinds, all thought by one or another authority to represent Christ, the Christian, or the Church, and by some to signify more than one of these."[35]

The lady's central act as lady and as deer is one of willing submission. The particular "hunt" of which the poet writes, instead of resolving in great triumph or total defeat, ends quietly, calmly, tenderly as the lady turns and accepts the lover's hand. Given that the lady, in fact, has been the one who actually did her own hunting, the whole action may also be viewed in reverse, with the penitent-lover now accepting the offered hand of the Christ-lady. Spenser would have known "deer," both female and male, and commentators on Psalm 42 have associated the deer both with Christ and with the penitents. The panting deer of the liturgy is the accepted one, not the one who accepts. But in the poeticized analogy the lady both accepts and is accepted. By extension and by analogy, Christ, who always accepts, is now accepted by the penitent. As for the hunt, it provides a metaphor that, altered and expanded, includes one of Christianity's major tenets: *caritas vincit omnia*—love conquers all.

It must not be forgotten that the poet in 67 compares himself to the huntsman; it is he who "sits downe to rest him in some shady place." The poet has perceived himself as a hunter and pursuer, images implicit in the warfare imagery even when his hunt and pursuit have left him conquered. It is when the analogical level of the sequence is considered that the possibility exists for the lover to be the deer as well as the hunter. But the resting hunter is important, too, and Christ may be perceived as the pursuer, with the hunt now completed, in the first quatrain. The epistle lesson (1 Pet. 3) refers to the difficult situation of Christians amid the world; it encourages persecuted Christians to bear witness to their hope. It also notes the implied action of the Holy Spirit, who raised Christ from the dead and gave him victory over the powers of sin and evil. The same Spirit is to be man's hope, since he also gives man a rebirth. The rebirth first occurs, in this lesson and the sonnet, by water—initially by means of Noah's ark, and "lyke as Baptysme also nowe saueth us." Man is born again by water and the spirit, then, is the message the Church teaches catechumens on Holy Saturday.

The gospel (Matt. 27), with its connections to the Church's

practice and traditions, is more complex. The lesson tells of Joseph of Arimathea begging Pilate for Christ's body, preparing it, and laying it in his new tomb. Easter Even celebrates Christ's resting in the tomb (Psalm 88, the Communion psalm for this day, recounts the narrator's life "draw[ing] nere to the graue" and being "counted among them that go downe vnto the pit"). With the holy women sitting at the tomb, the Church sits, waits, and meditates on the resting Christ. Penitents are invited into their own rest with the women and with Christ.

The sonnets have noted "rest" since *Amor.* 8, where "Angels come to leade fraile mindes to rest / in chast desires on heauenly beauty bound." The narrator longed for the "ioyous safety of so sweet a rest" as he saw that happy shore in 63. In the Church, the Easter Vigil meditation is on the Creator's resting on the seventh day, the rest promised to the Hebrews but not obtained because they lacked faith and disobeyed, and the great sabbath rest at the end of time. Christ's death is not viewed as an act of completion; it is merely a "rest" that, as in Spenser's poetry, prepares for further action. The "weary huntsman" in 67 sits down to rest—as Christ is laid to rest. For both huntsman and Christ, though, there is implied a repose, not stasis.

Traditionally, Christ's entombment itself was viewed as a transitus. As Dante well described them, Christ's "activities" during the "rest" were numerous and significant. Spenser possibly suggests Christ's descent into hell by referring to the "shady place," the land of shadows; the "panting hounds beguiled of their pray" might then be an allusion to those underworld hounds powerless to attack Christ as he harrows hell, an act recalled in *Amor.* 68.

Amor. 67 abounds in liturgical and archetypal images evoking responses from deep within the human psyche: death and life, chaos and order, slavery and freedom. The sonnet, while not as symbolically evocative as the lengthy liturgy, nevertheless conveys in the sequence this profound sense of its significance. It reverberates in its own movements, in its language and special pivotal position. It culminates the Lenten sequence by drawing together Christ's last words. From "forgiveness" (in the eschewing of "old yeares sinnes" in *Amor.* 62), to the "paradise" of "fayre soil" in 63, there are lead-ins to this sonnet's "beholding," "forsooke," "thirst" and "hands," echoing words from the cross; "it is finished" is reflected in the completion of the lover's game, the end of the chase, the abandonment of the hunt.

Both in the sonnets and in the liturgy, the Lenten sequence concludes with quiet, solemnity, and wonder. Its purposely low

tone sets the stage for the contrast found and heard at the start of
the next sonnet, which ushers in Easter.

What *Amor.* 67 accomplishes by quiet movement, subdued
tone, and gentle depiction, 68 effects by freshness, jubilation,
and exuberance. Synchronizing the lovers' new love with the
divine love of Christ, Easter Sunday shatters the quiet of the
previous night's vigil with a glorious strain:

> Most glorious Lord of lyfe that on this day,
>> Didst make thy triumph ouer death and sin:
>> and hauing harrowd hell didst bring away
>> captiuity thence captiue vs to win:
> This ioyous day, deare Lord, with ioy begin,
>> and grant that we for whom thou diddest dye
>> being with thy deare blood clene washt from sin,
>> may liue for euer in felicity.
> And that thy loue we weighing worthily,
>> may likewise loue thee for the same againe:
>> and for thy sake that all lyke deare didst buy,
>> with loue may one another entertayne.
> So let vs loue, deare loue, lyke as we ought,
>> loue is the lesson which the Lord vs taught.

The psychological and historical time spent during the courtship
now assume new meaning as they align with the time of Christ's
passion and resurrection. The sequence's teleological movement
and ontological quest, its "farther up and further in" motion (as
C. S. Lewis uses the term), conjoin. The human love story is now
clearly a part of the divine love story, a play enacted repeatedly,
cosmically, and eternally. Human love is important here both for
itself and, as with the sequence's various time patterns, as a
reflection of its divine counterpart. Cycles of time give scope to
man's life, but Christ's resurrection and its liturgically symbolic
cyclical return give life its meaning. All the games played in this
theatrum mundi are merely part of the "entertayne[ment]" en-
acted daily.

In this sixty-eighth sonnet[36] the *Amoretti* loves and time sys-
tems merge. The cycles correspond; the loves correspond. That
which people do is viewed entirely in light of the divine model,
in whose figure divine and human combine. The lady is no
longer viewed as merely human nor solely divine; like Christ,
she is a "lower heauen" on earth, and her simultaneous human-
ity-divinity are both important.

G. K. Hunter observes *Amor.* 68 as a "tissue of biblical echoes;

these and the sacramental occasion (the feast day) are used to enlarge the relationship between the lovers into the analogical relation between Christ and the world. . . . The parallel and overlapping patterns of life against death, freedom against captivity, joy against purgation, salvation against sin, take their place in a skillful and lucid structure of concepts."[37] Those biblical echoes are themselves reechoed through centuries of liturgy; for Spenser's purposes, they produce, especially in the *BCP*, not a dogmatic statement or a creed but a poetic celebration of the meaning, on a very basic human level, of Christ's action. Tempting as they might be to catalogue, the analogues are quite secondary in import to the transformative effect Christ's love has on the lovers, the poetry, and the sequence.

For the purposes of this study it is unnecessary to attempt an enumeration of the numerous biblical passages from which the sonnet draws. It is sufficient to note that more than any other poem in the *Amoretti*, this one derives its language from familiar Easter Collects, gospels, and epistles. It blends with and transforms the Petrarchan and neo-Platonic terminology of the early sequence. Death not only yields to life (itself a reversal of the human pattern); death is transformed into life. "Captiuity" no longer means only non-freedom; it is transformed into an entirely new kind of captivity, in which the old meaning has no application. Metaphors, allusions, and analogues open one upon another, dilating as did the lady's light in 66. "Such freeing of [semantic] place[s] and of the literal vocabularies that places give rise to is itself a poetic imitation of Christ's redemptive act. For the Christ who frees love opens the space in which love is imprisoned in literal dichotomies [and] transforms that place into a metaphor that voids all dichotomy. Christ's freeing love thus frees as well all ways of expressing love."[38] The "closed" language used in the early sonnets is not, in itself, "wrong"; but in being closed it is viable in a human community only when opened by and accommodated to the "lesson which the Lord vs taught"—loving one another as he loves us.

Christ's unmistakable entrance into the sequence breaks the narrative frame just as his resurrection breaks the old laws and the Old Law. The center intervenes in the circle as the timeless comes directly into time. In an even more dramatic act than the narrator's interventions in *Amor.* 33 and 80, Spenser shatters and then transforms the sequence's frame. Here the analogic level, running somewhat parallel to the surface through most of the sequence and slightly tapping that surface at various points (not-

ably the Sunday sonnets and other "liturgical" days), pierces that
surface with unmoderated force. Human action, human life,
human love can never be the same by virtue of the sacralizing
ramifications of the divine activity. The sonnet sequence, con-
cerned with the lover and his lady, takes second place to this
encomium of Love, making that Love a model for all future
aspiration. It does so in the poetry itself, which celebrates by
delighting and teaching. It does so in the *Amoretti* love, which
centers now on the very core from which all love, and all of love's
metaphors, derive—the literal fact of Christ's sacrifice and resur-
rection. All things would stray to their confusion, as Boethius
writes, but that God's purpose, through his love, draws them back
where they are "by love returned" to their sources and goal.
Amor. 67 showed the returning; *Amor.* 68 points out the source
and goal.

The sonnet's ties to the *BCP* were observed over a century ago
when James Ashcroft Noble (who, ironically, found the *Amoretti*
"deficient in body, frigid in tone, and altogether wanting in . . .
graces of manner") noted its "very appreciable affinity to the
style of the collects."[39] Its syntactic pattern, as Carole Kaske sug-
gests, is the syntactic pattern of about half the Collects—name-of-
God + relative-clause + "grant that we" + petition.[40] Prescott,
however, shows that the "on this day" formula is in fact very rare
in the 1 and 2 Edward and the Elizabethan prayer books, al-
though the Sarum rite provides rather interesting parallels:

> Sarum's chief Easter prayer, ancestor of the *Book of Common Prayer*'s
> Easter collect, is much closer to the syntactic pattern and content of
> Am. 68, as though Spenser had its shape and rhythm in the back of
> his mind: 'Deus, qui hodierna die per unigenitum tuum aeternitatis
> nobis aditum devicta morte reserasti: vota nostra quae praeveniendo
> aspiras, etiam adjuvando prosequere.' Several prayers later we hear,
> 'Concede nobis famulis tuis ut in resurrectionis eius graudiis semper
> viavmus.' Combining and condensing these two Eastern prayers in
> effect gives us a structure and even a thought quite like Spenser's:
> 'Lord who on this day didst open for us the gate of eternity, having
> conquered death (an English equivalent to the Latin ablative abso-
> lute), . . . grant that we (concede nobis) may live forever in the felicity
> of his Resurrection.' No prayer . . . in the *Book of Common Prayer* is
> as close to Spenser as this, further evidence that whatever his the-
> ology he remained moved by the patterns and language of an older
> time.[41]

The sonnet's initial quatrain addresses Christ as "most glorious
Lord of lyfe," a life celebrated throughout this sonnet and one

which makes living (line 8) an object of the petition. His "triumph," a word used only once earlier and then in connection with the lady's "great triumph" over the lover (29), is echoed later in the *Hymne in Honour of Beautie*, "Io tryumph" (267); there its Latin origin as part of a celebratory shout is a reminder that "trimpe!" was a classical victory cry.[42] It also suggests a shout, as does "glorious" (Gloria) in line 1, and it is recalled that the Easter celebration is the first time since the start of Lent that the "Alleluia" is used in the service.

The alliteration of Christ's harrowing hell (an act nowhere mentioned in the Bible) parallels the alliterative structure of "captiuity thence captiue." The reference may be found in Ephesians 4:8 and Judges 5:12; and there may be found a parallel for this sixty-eighty sonnet in the sixty-eighth psalm. The reference to "lyfe" (line 1) triumphs (and is structurally "ouer") death and sin (line 2). The descent into hell (line 3) moves toward the ascent out of the depths and the winning of "vs" (line 4). Thus the victory and triumph are both Christ's and man's.

The significance of such an act leads to the second quatrain, where the day's joy becomes the individual's joy. The "Lord of Lyfe" is now "deare Lord," suggesting (through "deare") the incredible cost and worth of his purchase. Then follow the petitions, where the personalization of Christ's act ("we for whom thou diddest dye") is made explicit. Spenser repeats "deare," this time in connection with Christ's "deare blood" (again, both "beloved" and "costly"). Captivity opens to a wholly transformed meaning as "the conventional thraldom of love [transforms] into an exhilarating spiritual liberty in which fulfillment is an effortless attainment, a caged bird [as in *Amor.* 73] singing and feeding its fill, and filling the world with its gifts."[43] As the lady is "fyrmely tyde" by her "owne goodwill" in a bond that is not really bondage, so man's own willing captivity to Christ is no captivity but a triumph that overcomes the past ("washt from sin") and prepares for a future of everlasting happiness ("may liue for euer in felicity," such felicity perhaps being Spenser's extension of *felicitas*, the "joy" in line 4). Once Christ pays for man's sins, death becomes the threshold to the joyous liberation of eternal life. The octave, beginning with a descent to hell, ends with its *O altitudo* of eternal bliss.

The sestet returns to earthly matters, in which Christ's love is again portrayed as mimetic. As in the seventh canto of "The Book of Temperance," it is seen that behind all truly worthy actions lies the pattern laid down by the greatest hero, Christ. Man, "weighing" Christ's love worthily, will love Christ. Again, the wordplay on "worth" emerges; man weighs "worthily" and loves the same "againe." The verbal play continues in the next lines, where man becomes not only a lover of Christ (line 10) but a lover like Christ (line 12), because Christ "didst buy" man's purchase from sin and death. His "buying" may be a reflection of Acts 20.28, in which God purchases the Church with "his own blood." "Deare" appears for the third time here; the term is first applied to the resurrected Christ (line 5), then to his human blood (line 7), and now to the God-man as well as to humans, persons-God. Line 11 may be read "and for thy sake that all of us, as dear [beloved and costly] to God as you, didst buy. . . ." It may also be interpreted as "and for thy sake that all of us, as being dear to you, didst buy . . ."; or it could be read as "and for thy sake that all of us, like the deer [*Amor.* 67], didst buy. . . ." What matters is that in all of this the human and the divine commingle, the mundane and heavenly conjoin; the great price the penitents paid during Lent was really only a human reflection of the greater price Christ paid on the cross. Christ's transformation from death to life becomes man's as well as his.

The alternating between sacred and secular, between divine and human, is noted in lines 1–11. Its action is completed in line 12, where people "with loue may one another entertayne." The antecedent of "one another" is purposely unstated. It is either that man and Christ will "entertayne" one another with love, or that mankind, the lady and the lover, will do so. The line supports both meanings and both are appropriate. The "entertayne[ment]" is a reminder that the entire sequence is an unfolding drama on both the surface and the analogic levels, that humans "play" with loves lovingly just as God played with the great comic ending of the crucifixion's near-tragedy. "Play" as masque, drama, interplay, verbal play, amorous play, even as "game" in the deer-dear hunt, has marked the surface level; "play" as liturgical drama, as the game of bistructural significa- tion, as God's playing with love, through love, and by love in the Christ narrative, has marked the analogic level.

The third quatrain ends with yet another ludic display: the wordplay of "entertayne" is etymologically linked to holding (L. *tenere*). Once again the captivity and bondage motif is intro- duced, this time with a wonderful transformation that makes constraint and constriction a playful liberation, an entertain- ment, in which man is bound to Christ, and he to man, "with loue," and in which people thus hold one another in those same bonds. The lady and lover (who "bondage earst dyd fly") now find such captivity the supreme form of liberation. Corruption of the will and, in the case of the sonnets, corruption of the form and the object of love, caused the first imprisonment; now released from those bonds, people may be guided by "goodwill" (67) and may freely commit themselves to the liberation of a higher captivity, bragging with Paul of being a prisoner for and of Christ (Eph. 3:1).

Spenser never allows his readers to remain long without a turn to the lady; the couplet marks such a turn, both serious and playful, urbane and tender. Human love becomes a religious duty in which man's *imitatione Christi* (recalling that Christ, too, imitated man by becoming like him) calls people to a life of unselfish, liberating love. In his gentle way the lover calls his lady (again using "vs") to love. The fourth use of "deare" appears, bringing all the other dears into the context of the lady. The love of the divine Lord (line 5), the love of the human lord (line 7), the reciprocal love between Christ and man, and man and Christ (line 10), now become the mutual love between lady and lover. Christ's love is lived out "in-deed" among people, and the movement toward this reciprocal human love establishes the community as the playing field, and the sacred space, for that entertainment. The phrase "deare loue" merges agape with eros, recalling Spenser's assertion of the "rightness" of human sexual love in the wider context of Christian marriage.

Kaske notes that these last lines echo John 15:12–13: "This is my commandement, that ye loue one another, as I have loued you. Greater loue than this hathe no man, when any man bestoweth his life for his friends." "The verses are of course already intrinsically appropriate to Easter because they concern Christ's death. The liturgy recognizes this by assigning them . . . [as] those exact verses [which] begin the Gospel for Holy Communion on St. Barnabas's Day . . . the day of the poet's wedding with this same lady. . . . Thus God Himself would seem to have originated the application of Christ's words to the sexual love of this particular pair, whether in Spenser's mind alone or also in the minds of his church-going readers."[44]

There is a further suggestion in line 13 connecting the lovers' obligation to love one another as Christ loved them to their obligation as husband and wife. They are to love "lyke as we ought." How they ought is depicted in the "causes for which matrimonie was ordeined," as indicated in "The Forme of Solemnizacion of Matrimonie." The BCP lists as one cause for marriage the "procreacion of children," another as a "remedie agaynst sinne, and to auoide fornicacion," and a third, "for the mutuall societie ["mutuall good will," Amor. 65], helpe, and coumfort, that the one oughte to haue of thother, both in prosperitie and aduersitie." As a prelude to the Epithalamion, then, Amor. 68 assumes that we know "as we ought." But not only does "as we ought" imply Christ's model as well as God's commands, it suggests that such love, in a fashion, is the recompense for the gift of Christ's redemption. Christ's command to love one another extended beyond couples; it was a call for reconciliation, for unification, and for community. In this sense there is an added "ought" to the loving: people are to love one another individually and collectively. Thus a third love, philia, is implied. And, looking back to the third quatrain, it is possible to see in "thy loue" (God's love for man) agape, eros (in the religious sense of longing for God), and, in the entertaining of "one another," philia.

Earlier we saw the "costly" imagery of "deare," "worthily," (possibly) "againe," and "buy." Likewise "ought" can be read here as the past tense of "owe" or as the perfect tense or passive voice of owe, thus meaning: "let us love one another by the same amount that we have owed [to Christ]."

The sonnet's last line, with its fifth mention of "love," draws in the imagery of teaching, employed earlier in the sequence. Love becomes the lesson, just as it is found in the liturgical lessons that Christ taught. God's gift anticipates a countergift, not just the receiver's love of the giver, but love for the other recipients as well. On one level the sequence has concerned itself with right reading. The lady is to "read" the lover's leaves, lines, and rhymes, and learn to read through them just as she is to read through his actions. The lover, too, has had to learn to read the lady (both as text and as a real woman). Thus, reading as information appears here. What the Lord teaches is love, which in turn is his lesson, with its etymological connections both to legere (read) and lectio (a reading). Thus we read the lesson of Christ's life, and in reading we find the lesson is love—descending, ascending, and communal.

4

AMORETTI 69–89

"They all agreed, so turning all to game,
And pleasant bord, they past forth on their way . . ."

Easter is not part of the Lenten sequence, coming as it does at the end of that period and marking the beginning of its own church season. But Spenser uses *Amor.* 68 to conclude, and then begin, two major sections of the *Amoretti* architecture. Twenty-one sonnets precede the Ash Wednesday poem (22); twenty-one sonnets follow the Easter poem.

The first sonnet after Easter represents 1 April 1594. A notable change in language and pace occurs in the sonnets following Easter; its triumph puts all the earlier poems in a new perspective and changes the focus and meaning of all events following it. The long sonnet-days of courtship (longer than usual, the poet wrote, because of his "greater paines") give way now to the fresh, exuberant, quick-moving sonnet-days that immediately follow the lady's acceptance and that anticipate the forthcoming marriage. These final twenty-one sonnets present the lovers in a number of situations, some tender, some amusing, some troublesome, all of which reflect the concerns and diversions of a couple filling time before their wedding day. Preparations for matrimony, declarations of love, walks on the beach, attempts to fill the empty hours of separation, even small disagreements, moments of elation, and moments of sadness make up the various subjects of these twenty-one poems. They have in common that, no matter what happens, the lady has accepted his proposal and the couple will be married.

Using ancient victory metaphors, *Amor.* 69, Easter Monday, begins the last section of the *Amoretti* triptych with a reminder of the "anticke world." The poem also picks up the victory theme of *Amor.* 68, transforming the praise of Christ's triumph, with its subsequent immortality for all believers, to a witty play on poetic immortalization.

> The famous warriors of the anticke world,
>   Vsed Trophees to erect in stately wize:
>   in which they would the records haue enrold,
>   of theyr great deeds and valarous emprize.

The poet transposes the warrior-trophies motif to a poet-poem one:

> What trophee then shall I most fit deuize,
>   in which I may record the memory
>   of my loues conquest, peerelesse beauties prise,
>   adorn'd with honour, loue, and chastity.

The analogy is not difficult, and the poet engages in a bit of wordplay as he develops it. He is to be compared to the warriors, his trophy to theirs. They enrolled their records in trophies; he, too, will record the memory of his own conquest. Their trophies were erected "in stately wize" after the battles; he, as poet, will find a "fit deuize" to record his own victory. But line 5 is ambiguous; "most fit" floats between modifying "I" and "deuize" and functions well for both. The poet, most fit among all famous warriors, must find the most fit device to record his conquest.

The variorum editors read this poem as one of the love-as-war poems. In the sequence context (and given that the "war" ended almost ten sonnets prior to this one, and that the ultimate victory of Easter has just been experienced) such a reading is unjustified. The poet may use the same motifs, may write on the same topics, but they no longer have the same meaning. In this poem, "warfare" is but a metaphor based on the "anticke world," employed to get him into the present, playful situation.

The poem concerns poetry and marks the "transformed" poet's use of old images in new contexts, which has been one of his major themes all along. He returns to it here not only in the larger analogy of the conquering hero/conquering lover but in his play on the "trophee" and "fit." "Fit" functioned earlier as a play on "making poetry"; in that sense it would now be a play on creating the most fit poem he, most fit for the job, could make. But the question he asks concerns the "trophee," which etymologically (Gr. *trepein*) refers both to "turning" (which connects here with "turning a poem") and with "trope." The warrior's "records" (noun, line 3) now become activated as his poetry "records" (verb, line 6) the great events.

Lines 7–8 actually do record the memory, with further playfulness as a reminder that the poet, transformed as he is, is still in part the lover in the pre-Easter poems. "The memory / of my loues conquest" is exactly the kind of gentle humor in which he engaged in 67 when toying with his tying her and winning the victory. Here it is his conquest over the lady that he wishes to memorialize; but it is also the conquest of the lady over him ("my loues conquest"). Such a conquest is the prize of "peerlesse beauty"; either the prize or the conquest, or both, is "adorn'd with honour, loue, and chastity." But "prize" itself has several possibilities: etymologically, it relates to the Old French *prise*, which refers to "taking" and suggests the conquest was the taking of, or by, peerless beauty. "Prize" also can refer to trophy, in which case the trophy *is* the prize, just as the poem (as trophy and important monument) will be the adornment of the "victor."

The third quatrain and couplet resolve the poet's question:

> Euen this verse vowd to eternity,
> shall be thereof immortall moniment:
> and tell her prayse to all posterity,
> that may admire such worlds rare wonderment.
> The happy purchase of my glorious spoile,
> gotten at last with labour and long toyle.

The first quatrain concerned the past, the second the present, and in this third quatrain he moves to the future. "Trophees" become a trophy, which becomes "this verse"—this particular sonnet, this sequence of sonnets, and even this poet, all of which will be an "immortall moniment." Similarly, "records" yield to "record," which, by extension, becomes the memory (L. *memoria*, "mindful") of this "moniment" (L. *monere*, "to remind"). The poet's poetry will recount, in the sense of recording the history, and will count, "tell," her praise. By its echo, "praise" picks up "prise" (the two being closer in sound in Elizabethan pronunciation than in today's); a part of the prize is the victor's praise. ("All posterity," while suggesting all people of all future times, actually is somewhat more limited than the line suggests. Given that the "immortall moniment" is this poem, it is only the reading posterity "that may admire such worlds rare wonderment"— suggesting both the lady and "this verse.")[1]

The couplet reiterates lines used in *Amor.* 27: "this verse, that neuer shall expyre, / shall to you purchase . . ." immortality. The "purchase" is now seen as part of his "glorious spoile." Or, playing upon the ambiguity of who actually "won" the victory, it is the happy "purchase" of me, the poet, as the glorious spoil. It is of no import to him that he had written in 67 of the lady having given herself "of her own will," and yet he here plays with the motif of victory, his own labor and long toil. It is a ludic element of the poet's game and the lover's joke. Its being a "happy purchase" recalls the analogic level of the previous sonnet, of the "buying" motif in which Christ, at great cost, bought our victory.

Of the last line's "toyle" much has already been heard in the poet's complaints ("restlesse toile" in *Amor.* 11, "weary toile" in 15, and "taedious toyle" in 49). The word is part of the "net" imagery used throughout the sequence to describe both his entrapping of the lady and her weaving to ensnare him. In addition to meaning "work," it has military connections by way of Middle English "toile" (dispute, warfare), rhetorical associations by way of Old French *toeillier* (to disturb, to dispute), and sartorial implications through Middle French *toile* (a cloth, particularly a net).[2]

This refreshing sense of the poet's freedom to take old themes and recast them in light of his post-Easter liberation makes *Amor.* 69 a fine example of the *Amoretti's* serious nonseriousness, a freedom transposed in 70 into gentleness. The joy of love, proclaimed in 68, is displayed in the joy of life; throughout the chain of being a surge of vitality is felt. Immortal life, brought about by the victory in 68 and discussed in terms of its poetical analogy in 69, is mirrored in the natural life of 70, in which nature rejoices in its own participation in and celebration of love. The rebirth of Christ, coincident with the rebirth of spring, rejuvenates humankind and nature as well. As Christ visited the apostles two days after the resurrection (though, of course, not by summons), so now, two sonnets after Easter, fresh spring responds to the call:

> Fresh spring the herald of loues mighty king,
>   In whose cote armour richly are displayed
>   all sorts of flowers the which on earth do spring
>   in goodly colours gloriously arrayd:
> Goe to my loue, where she is carelesse layd,
>   yet in her winters bowre not well awake:
>   tell her the ioyous time wil not be staid
>   vnlesse she doe him by the forelock take.
> Bid her therefore her selfe soone ready make,
>   to wayt on loue amongst his louely crew:

where euery one that misseth then her make,
shall be by him amearst with penance dew.
Make hast therefore sweet loue, whilest it is prime,
for none can call againe the passed time.

The sonnet repeats the spring theme of *Amor.* 4 (in which spring was called forth) and 19 (in which spring was coming forth). Here spring is summoned to attend upon the lady as love's messenger. In the earlier two spring sonnets, the poet was anxious because he was in the midst of the courtship difficulties; but now the lady is his. Spring is fresher than before and is gloriously arrayed. The carpe diem motif reappears but has been transformed: in 4 and 19 "lusty spring" was coming forth and the lady was called to prepare to entertain new love. In 19 the potentially rebellious lady was called to turn to love. In 70 the call is moderated by the unmistakable reference to the Song of Songs and its associations with marriage:

> My welbeloued spake & said vnto me, Arise, my loue, my faire one, & come thy way. For beholde, winter is past: the raine is changed, and is gone away. The flowers appear in ye earth: the time of the singing of birdes is come, & the voice of the turtle is heard in our land.
>
> Song of Songs 2:10–13

Spenser will echo the lines from the sonnet and the Song in the marriage hymn (22–33):

> Doe ye awake, and with fresh lusty hed,
> Goe to the bowre of my beloued loue,
> My truest turtle doue
> Bid her awake; for Hymen is awake,
> And long since ready forth his maske to moue,
> With his bright Tead that flames with many a flake, . . .
> Bid her awake therefore and soone her dight,
> For lo the wished day is come at last,
> That shall for al the paynes and sorrowes past,
> Pay to her vsury of long delight. . . .

The sonnet also has connections with 62, a "new year" sonnet of another sort. *Amor.* 4 showed the new year "looking out of Ianus gate," calling fresh love out of "sad Winters night," and warning the earth to prepare herself with good weather, fresh joys, and a mantle of fresh flowers. Fifteen sonnets later the cuckoo announced spring's readiness; time was in motion. Forty-seven sonnets later, in 62, the "weary year" had run its course, and again the poet hoped for a change of weather, both natural and metaphorical.

There are significant developments in the narrator, from 4 through 70, which might be noted. DeNeef finds that in 4 and 19 "King Cupid and the carpe diem injunction pronounced in his name are both interpreted literally by the poet-lover. His sense of the poetic and ethical dimensions of his words is limited by the equally literal seasons in which the poems are situated. Sonnets 62 and 70 transform both the literal seasons and their literal terms into metaphors. The threshold of New Year's Day becomes a metaphor for personal reformation and renewed commitments of all kinds, and the promise of spring becomes a metaphor for the spiritual uniting of all existence. The repetition of the seasonal site thus discloses the error of the poet-lover's initial perceptions, for we now see that even Sonnets 4 and 19 are metaphoric adumbrations of the broader perspectives in 62 and 70."[3] In short, the lover has learned to speak metaphorically with language that opens, expands, and dilates.

In 19 the cuckoo was the "messenger of Spring." Now spring itself is but the "herald of loves mighty king." Now that the King arrived triumphantly on Easter, the proper order is asserted. In 4 "Fresh Love" slept long in his cheerless bower; in 70 it is "my loue . . . carelesse layd, / yet in her winters bowre not well awake." Love appears in 19 "with a girland crouned." In 70 this simple phrase expands to three full lines, constituting most of the first quatrain; in 19 the preparations for love were used as a contrast to the lady's contrariness; in 70 they serve as part of the lover's revelling in the beauties of spring and the joys of love.

It is necessary to look at this sonnet in its post-Easter position in order to understand its exuberance. After the sacrifice comes triumph; after triumph, joy. The "ioyous day" of 68 becomes the "ioyous time" of 70, as all creation reacts to and participates in the rebirth. Easter puts all time in a new perspective. In 69 the poet used the past to reshape the present; in 70 he uses the present to anticipate the future. For the newly baptized Christian (67), Christ's resurrection is not merely a historical event; it affects the Christian personally and in community. The lady is called out of her "winters bowre" to "wait on loue amongst his louely crew"—to be part of the new community in which love's lesson is to be enacted. The penitent buried with Jesus of Nazareth on Good Friday rises with the new Christ on Easter. That resurrection becomes a paradigm for all transforming or "actualizing" experiences. It calls creation out of death ("winters bowre") to life. For Spenser it is important that the life is not one postponed in happiness until the future. Red Cross can neither go directly to the holy city nor remain on the Mount of Contemplation. Life is lived under hope, and therefore joyfully, because of Easter, but it is lived in the present in a paradoxical condition: it is necessary to be in the world without belonging to it (1 Cor. 7:31), to suffer even though already risen (2 Cor. 4:10–11), and to live by the resurrection while waiting to "appear with him in glory" (Col. 3:4).

The poet has learned a "new poetry," the lover a new song, and the lady is called to join in it with him. As "the flowers appear in ye earth," the lady is also called to "flourish" (the Geneva gloss for Song of Songs 2:11–12 relates the passage to the resurrection by interpreting the spring as meaning "sinne and error is driuen backe by the comming of Christ which is here described by the spring time, when all things florish"). The lady's flourishing will be particularly evident in the forthcoming marriage, the earthly "ioyous time" to which the lover in 70 now calls her. Far from being a move up a neo-Platonic ladder, as some earlier commentators interpreted this sonnet, it is a celebration of earthly love, of anticipation (through analogy with the Song of Songs) of sexual love, which will itself provide an analogue to divine love (the divine love celebrated in 68 and that "dilates" backward and forward from that point through the sonnets and into all time).

Love, like the spring flowers "displayd" on the "cote armour," displays itself with its own flowers. The once fairly cautious, fairly humorless poet-lover takes the opportunity (seizes time, occasion, by the forelock) for a return to the already used conceit of the spider capturing a foe. However, the "capture" of the lady has already been made (67), and Christ has brought away "captiuity thence captiue vs to win" (68); now the old metaphor can be used entirely playfully in its new context. Amor. 71, coming so soon after Easter, shows the difference between things before and things now.

Initially introduced in 23 when the poet expressed frustrations in terms of the Penelope myth, the web motif developed into a "net of gold" used by the cruel lady to entangle men (37), and then throughout the sequence into various expressions of entanglement, eventually leading to the tying of the two lovers in 67. Now, in Amor. 71 and in a witty reversal of the earlier complaints, the motif appears in the lady's "drawen work":

> I ioy to see how in your drawen work,
>   Your selfe vnto the Bee ye doe compare;

and mee vnto the Spyder that doth lurke,
in close awayt to catch her vnaware.

In 23 both the lady and the lover were depicted as the spider, weaving webs to capture. Such weaving and such a purpose were described as "fruitlesse worke . . . broken with least wynd." But here the lady is a bee, the poet a spider, and this delightful lady's drawing (sewing) of herself as the bee suggests her own playful rejoinder to his somewhat repetitious insistence on how he won her in the game of love. Her image is a reminder that the lady actually did participate in the game, that she was more than a passive observer in a *theatrum amori* in which she, as well as he, played parts. And it is a reminder of the lady as poet and creator (previously depicted in 23, but pulled together here as she pulls together threads of her "drawen work"). In the second stanza the witty lover amplifies what he noted in the first, agreeing with her comparison but exaggerating it:

> Right so your selfe were caught in cunning snare
>   of a deare foe, and thralled to his loue:
>   in whose streight bands ye now captiued are
>   so firmely, that ye neuer may remoue.

Not only has the spider caught her, he asserts, but she is "thralled to his loue," a charming play both on the (now) old warfare motif and on "enthralled." She had been assured in 65 of love's sweet bands and then had been "fyrmely tyde" in 67, images lovingly interwoven here in the "streight bands"—the betrothal and, perhaps, the banns to be published straightaway. In short, she may have captured him in her "drawen work," but he has captured her in a cunning poetic snare.

The third quatrain and couplet take us back to the "drawen work," drawing in strands of the glorious array of flowers in 70 and the paradoxical sweet constraint of 65:

> But as your worke is wouen all aboue,
>   with woodbynd flowers and flagrant Eglantine:
>   so sweet your prison you in time shall proue,
>   with many deare delights bedecked fyne.
> And all thensforth eternall peace shall see,
>   betweene the Spyder and the gentle Bee.

The fruitless work of *Amor.* 23 becomes a garden of earthly delights in 71, in which both spider and bee may prosper through "mutuall good will" (65). The lady's work is "wouen all aboue," perhaps a suggestion of its divine origin, perhaps a spatial referent to where the flowers are placed on the tapestry, perhaps meaning "all about." The flowers chosen are "clinging vines" noted particularly for their olfactory sweetness. The "eternal" reading-posterity referred to in 69 becomes here an eternal viewing-posterity of all who will see the "drawen work," artwork that, like the "immortall moniment" of 69, will eternally show the peace between the lover and the lady, the spider and the gentle bee.

The "drawen work" of 71 literally (by verbal repetition) draws the reader into 72, as does the sweetness of the lady's earthly delights. In this clearest statement of the position toward which the poet-lover has moved throughout the sequence, 72 removes any doubts about the lover's view of his relationship with his beloved:

> Oft when my spirit doth spred her bolder winges,
>   In mind to mount vp to the purest sky:
>   it down is weighd with thoght of earthly things
>   and clogd with burden of mortality,
> Where when that souerayne beauty it doth spy,
>   resembling heauens glory in her light:
>   *drawne* with *sweet* pleasures bayt, it back doth fly,
>   and vnto heauen forgets her former flight.
> There my fraile fancy fed with full delight,
>   doth bath in blisse and mantleth most at ease:
>   ne thinks of other heauen, but how it might
>   her harts desire with most contentment please.
> Hart need not wish none other happinesse,
>   but here on earth to haue such heuens blisse.

                                                    (italics mine)

The poem illustrates the poet's highest praise for the lady. In her he finds his greatest joy and greatest happiness; she is his heaven's bliss on earth. That location of his bliss is most significant in interpreting the sonnet and in seeing it as an important restatement of the *Amoretti* "lesson."

The sonnet's neo-Platonic and Petrarchan elements are obvious; they have been heard, seen, and read about before, both in this sequence and in numerous Renaissance literary and philosophical works. Spenser keeps very close to Tasso's well-known "L'alma vaga di luce e di bellezza / ardite spiega al ciel l' ale amorose" (The soul, lovely with light and beauty / boldly unfolds its loving wings to the heavens) in the first part of the sonnet; Spenser's readers would have known the Italian poem's use of the opposition of heaven and earth, with the lady placed on the earthly, mortal side. But by her mundane locus, Tasso's lady is associated with a lower form of love. Spenser subtly and smoothly reinterprets his source, making of this Petrarchan sonnet an un-Petrarchan assertion.

The poet begins with the image of his soul as a bird, a common symbol for the spirit ascending and descending at will and one that Tasso employs in his sonnet's "augellin." The typical neo-Platonic polarization of body and spirit, of earth and heaven, finds the lover frustrated. His airy spirit has "in mind" the mounting up, but is weighed down by mortality. His "winges" are pulled back by "thinges," just as the "sky" is debased by "mortality." Thus far his spirit has soared (first two lines) and descended (second two lines). Earlier in the sequence the lady herself had the same double motion: in *Amor.* 13 her "faire face . . . reares up to the skie," but shortly thereafter she looks to the earth "whence she was borne, / [and] her mind remembreth her mortalitie." But there is a difference between the two viewers (lover and lady); with the lady in 13 it was her own mortality she saw and nothing else. With the lover it is not only his mortality but the "thoght of earthly things." Yet in *Amor.* 13 the lover also noted how the lady, with her "lofty countenance seemes to scorn / base thing, and thinke how she to heauen may clime." By *Amor.* 72 the poet, too, in his own way, has learned to scorn base things and aspire to his own heaven.

The second quatrain begins the poet's diversion from the Petrarchan mode. The poet's spirit moved in line 3 to the thought of earthly things and to being clogged with mortality. Even the words of that fourth line—clogged (emburdened), burden, mortality—suggest heaviness. But the earthly things the spirit spies are far from being mortally heavy. The lady is "that souerayne beauty" (as she was also called in *Amor.* 3) and she resembles (and re-assembles) "heauens glory in her light." To that lady as his heaven the poet's spirit flies, forgetting both the former flight to and from heaven.

In *Amor.* 3 the poet had been "rauisht . . . with fancies wonderment"; now that earlier stasis turns to productive living when his fancy is "fed with full delight" and where it bathes "in blisse and mantleth most at ease." Lines 11–12 are key ones. Spenser, unlike the Petrarchans, can have his heaven while on earth. The lady is not a vehicle for transcending the world and leading the lover to God. Heaven being wherever God is, the lady is heaven itself, and the lover, in having one heaven, can have both. Significantly, there is no talk here of conquest, of winning her to him, of victors and victory. His delight is in pleasing the lady, something about which he wrote as far back as *Amor.* 1, but which had entirely different meaning at that point.

The couplet reiterates the sentiment of the last quatrain. In 46 he had differentiated between the heavens that sent rain and his "lower heaven," which sought to send him away. Now the image is even more important: earthly love is seen as completely compatible with divine love. This is the acting out "in-deed" of the great lesson of the Easter sonnet. His bliss becomes his pleasing of the lady in and through selfless acts that bring happiness to both of them.

This sonnet reintroduces the sequence's underlying motif of art-as-love and love-as-art. In 7.7.1, Spenser writes about his poetic muse in lines similar to the first ones here:

> Ah! whither doost thou now thou greater Muse
> Me from these woods and pleasing forrest bring?
> And my fraile spirit (that dooth oft refuse
> This too high flight, vnfit for her weake wing)
> Lift vp aloft. . . .

The image of poetry on wings also appears in the Dedicatory Sonnets ("but when my Muse . . . [does] lowly learne to fly / with bolder wing") and as early as the October eclogue: "There may thy Muse display her fluttryng wing." In *Amor.* 33 the poet complained to Lodowick of the conflict resulting from his not finishing *The Faerie Queene* for his "most sacred Empresse," and of enduring the "troublous fit / of a proud loue, that doth my spirite spoyle." In that sonnet's lines, in addition to his wonderful compliment to the lady, there are the poet's hints of the same dual directions his poetry presumably takes—the epic's lofty rhymes and the sonnet's more earthly lines. That being the case the poet may be said, on the one hand, to have made the choice—love for the lady, as depicted in the various *amoretti*, taking precedent over the bolder display in his epic. On the other hand, Spenser has it both ways; historically and literally he woos and wins the lady *and* completes six books of his major work.

The wings/poem image continues further into *Amor.* 72 than the first quatrain. The poet has associated pleasure with writing as early as *Amor.* 17 ("For though he colours could deuize at will, / and eke his learned hand at pleasure guide"). He is drawn back to that pleasure several times in the sequence; as a poet it is part of that "bait" that makes his artistry worth the effort. Having chosen his lower heaven (writing the sonnets), the poet, "drawne with sweet pleasures bayt," flies to that project where his fancy, far from being "rauisht," and his spirit, far from being "spoyle[d]," are productive. "Mantling" most at ease and "mantling" most when at ease suggest an image of the spirit-bird spreading its wings and of the poet freely flying with his images and coasting on thoughts. It also suggests "mantle" in the sense of the rich display of the "cote armour" of 70, denoting that his now-fed fancy can display itself like all the colorful flowers of spring, in the colorful flowers of his language.

Both as a poet and as a lover the narrator thus has his "heauens blisse" on earth. The extremes (only heaven, only earth) are mediated, reasserting the special significance of the Easter season—not only Christ's divinity but his intrinsic humanity—and humankind's participation in both.

The bird imagery of 72 continues in 73. But whereas in 72 the bird represented the lover's soul, it now represents his heart. And whereas the previous poem was *about* the lady, this one is *to* her. Like 72, it also concerns the poet's craft, in which the art/hart pun provides the pivot. Were this sonnet earlier in the sequence, its Petrarchan imagery and artificiality would have been worth harsh criticism; here it becomes an amusing palinode to, and continuation of, the previous poem, 72 being about freedom of flight and choice and 73 about a delightful captivity. Its "captivity" imagery cannot be taken seriously because (1) of where it appears in the sequence and because (2) "captivity" has a transformed meaning as a result of Easter.

> Being my selfe captyued here in care,
>> My hart, whom none with seruile bands can tye,
>> but the fayre tresses of your golden hayre,
>> breaking his prison forth to you doth fly.
> Lyke as a byrd that in ones hand doth spy
>> desired food, to it doth make his flight:
>> euen so my hart, that wont on your fayre eye
>> to feed his fill, flyes backe vnto your sight.
> Doe you him take, and in your bosome bright,
>> gently encage, that he may be your thrall:
>> perhaps he there may learne with rare delight,
>> to sing your name and prayses ouer all.
> That it hereafter may you not repent,
>> him lodging in your bosome to haue lent.

Here Spenser provides the poet's example of the lover's "bathing in bliss and mantling most at ease." Drawn with sweet pleasure's bait, the poet provides this witty praise of his captivity. In 37 the only "seruile bands" that could tie him were those "fayre tresses" which threaten to entangle, catch, enfold, and entrap. But his heart, analogous to his "selfe," broke out of its prison to fly to the lady. In 65 the lover then explained love's captivity as sweet bands, using the example of the "gentle bird [who] feeles no captiuity / within her cage, but singes and feedes her fill." In 73 the poet expands and personalizes the image by having his own heart fly to the lady to "feed his fill."

The third quatrain begins with the lover petitioning the lady to take the bird-poet into her bosom and gently encage it so it might be her thrall. There is then a return to the sequence's educative motif, whereby the lovers have instructed one another at various times. As the poet took the lady into his love-pined heart (*Amor.* 2), so she is requested to take him into hers. In her heart he will learn to sing ("singing" being one of his ongoing images for the creative process). Singing her praises is what he has wanted to do, and what he has done, since the start of the sequence. But the singing as poetry recalls that it is the poet's heart making this metaphoric flight, and he frequently compares his heart with his art. Both his art and his heart have been "captured" (that is, captivated by the lady's hair); it is his art that, as in 72, has flown high and low in its fancy, seeking to feed its fill on "your fayre eye." In *Amor.* 1 the poet wrote of his "rymes bath'd in the sacred brooke, / of Helicon" (perhaps "bath[ing] in blisse"), being happy "when ye behold that Angels blessed looke, / my soules long lacked foode, my heauens blis." And in the second sonnet he urged his "vnquiet thought" to "breake forth at length out of the inner part . . . and sustayne thy selfe with food." His rhymes and his thoughts have been associated with his poetry from the start; his feeding on the lady's sight is his inspiration. Her support, by being his inspiration, mutually benefits each of them.

The sonnet concludes with yet another example of the mutual benefits of their alliance. It also ends with another example of the poet's witty, yet restrained, sexual innuendos concerning the poet's heart, whereby his art—and the poet—lodge in the lady's bosom.

Mantling most at ease, the poet expanded his fancy into the heart-bird-art imagery of 73; but digression often leads to digression, and seeds sown in one field often ripen in another. Like the lady's light, like the Easter message, Spenser's words "dilate" into ever-increasing circles of meaning and metaphor. "Singing the lady's name and praises over all" takes the poet directly into the next sonnet, 74, where he withholds the lady's name, the poem's presumed subject, until the end.

> Most happy letters fram'd by skilfull trade,
> with which that happy name was first desynd:
> the which three times thrise happy hath me made,
> with guifts of body, fortune and of mind.

Having just echoed in *Amor.* 73 the food image from *Amor.* 1, the poet echoes now the first lines of that same first sonnet: "Happy ye leaues." For most of the sequence the poet used the leaves, lines, and rhymes to praise his beloved. Now, in his ultimate reduction, he will focus on the nine letters ("three times thrise") themselves.

The poem's post-Easter position in the sequence, and its appearance in a cluster of tender and playful sonnets on various subjects, suggests the vacation mood still enjoyed after the peak experience of 68. Throughout this sonnet "week" he has exulted, reflected, and shown awareness of the great love he bears the lady. In 74 he turns to a consideration of his gifted life, of how well "graced" he has been. Calidore does the same when his love for Pastorella leads him to the pastoral digression of Mount Acidale; there he finds Colin, himself digressing from praising the queen, piping to his country lass. In just such pastoral holidays as these the graces appear, partly as a response to Colin's piping and partly to inspire the piping. (The graces are themselves the daughters of a leisurely diversion, as Jove dallied in the shade on Venus's mount with Euronyme. And all those associations—Calidore and Pastorella, Colin and his lady, Jove and Euronyme, art and love—are part of the sonnet poet's dalliance in 74.) The letters of his graces' shared name provide a focus as he, like Colin, pipes their praises.

The sonnet's first quatrain provides the provocative setup of "three times thrise happy" followed by three gifts "of body, fortune and of mind." One need not read long in Spenser to know that the sonnet will unfold by, in, and with order, and that "nine" will somehow be important.

The remaining lines of the sonnet detail the gifts:

> The first my being to me gaue by kind,
> from mothers womb deriu'd by dew descent,
> the second is my souereigne Queene most kind,
> that honour and large richesse to me lent.
> The third my loue, my liues last ornament,

by whom my spirit out of dust was raysed:
to speake her prayse and glory excellent,
of all aliue most worthy to be praysed.
Ye three Elisabeths for euer liue,
that three such graces did vnto me giue.

In an unusual use of a repeated single word as the rhyme for two lines, "kind" serves both as a link to the poet's mother's gift of natural being and to the queen's (wished) generosity. The respective rhymes with which these two uses of "kind" alternate define the particular use of "kind." In line 6 "descent" qualifies the "kind" of line 5; in line 8 "lent," with its monetary connotations, provides the condition of "kind" in line 7. The third quatrain, given entirely to "my loue," keeps the promise of 73 to "sing . . . your prayses," and, in giving four lines to his love and only two each to the other women, the poet does praise her "ouer all." Not only is the lady saved until last (that is, highest) on his list, but hers is the gift of "mind," hierarchically highest among the body, fortune, and mind trio. Interestingly, the gifts of body and fortune are physical, that of "mind," metaphorical. On the other hand, the first two Elizabeths (his mother and his queen) are "graces" metaphorically, while the lady, whose real gift is herself, really is a grace. And it is through the third Elizabeth, his lady, that "grace" on the analogic level comes to the poet, the gift of grace being most worthy to be praised.

The couplet addresses the three women who bestowed the three gifts. The lady's name is noted for the first and only time in the sequence, and in all of Spenser's poetry, his mother's name is mentioned only here. Both women, like the queen, are Elizabeth, the nine letters of which provide the link with "three times thrise" in line 3. And the last line includes the ambiguous "graces," a word that refers to the three gifts as well as to the three women.

The situation of the graces presents links with Spenser's other works. Spenser carefully saves the word "graces" until the last line, just as he keeps the name Elizabeth until line 13. This is typical of Spenser's method of forming the picture before giving the title. That being the case, though, it forces a return to the sonnet to see who the Elizabeths and the graces are. Readers will recall the graces on Mount Acidale, those Boticellian sprites joyfully dancing a cosmic dance within a sacred circle. Twenty years earlier that ring of maidens had appeared to Colin; it was April then, too (the sonnet represents the sixth of April, Dante's special day, in which he sees Beatrice and begins his own encomium of 9):[4]

> Lo how finely the Graces can it foote
>   to the Instrument:
> They dauncen deftly, and singen soote,
>   in their meriment.
> Wants not a fourth grace, to make the daunce euen?
> Let that rowme to my Lady be yeuen:
>   She shalbe a grace,
>   To fyll the fourth place,
> And reigne with the rest in heauen.
>
> Aprill Eclogue, 109–17

The image of the fourth grace is complicated. Spenser uses it again in depicting her on Mount Acidale (6.10.27):

> Another Grace she well deserues to be,
>   In whom so many Graces gathered are,
>   Excelling much the meane of her degree;
>   Diuine resemblaunce, beauty soueraine rare,
>   Firme Chastity, that spight ne blemish dare;
>   All which she with such courtesie doth grace,
>   That all her peres cannot with her compare,
>   But quite are dimmed, when she is in place.

Others have treated this passage at some length,[5] and some have seen here a reference to Elizabeth Boyle (Spenser's autobiographical fiction in the *Amoretti* has it that he is completing the first half of *The Faerie Queene* at the same time he completes this part of the sequence). And certainly the lady's divine resemblance has been seen, her sovereign beauty heard of, and her "firme Chastity" and courtesie learned of throughout the sequence. The lady has been associated with "grace" of various kinds (*Amor.* 20, 21, 25, 31, 40, 57, 64), and those associations with grace are part of an extended network Spenser develops both in and out of the *Amoretti*.

That *Amor.* 74 contains three graces and Mount Acidale depicts a fourth in the center of the three should not be a problem. The sonnet is primarily an elaborate play on the nine letters of the lady's name. But it is also about Grace as a gift of body, fortune, mind, and, theologically, salvation. Grace is the means by which one's spirit is raised from dust (line 10); in, by, and through grace, God is perceived. In Colin's first April vision of the three graces circling within circles is an initially unnamed fourth grace. On Mount Acidale it is Gloriana herself who appears in the center of the circle; by analogy she is Venus, Elizabeth Boyle, Queen Elizabeth, and the divine incomprehensible unity at the sacred center of one's being, giving gifts of life for the purpose of life. But the theological connotations of "grace," unmistakable in this sequence, are reminders both of God's grace and of his grace being reflected in and through the *Amoretti* lady. Even more than the first two Elizabeths, his lady Elizabeth is herself a grace (gift) from God; in and through her, God's grace dilates into the lover's world just as that grace will radiate into the outer world through the poet's poetry.

Having praised the letters of the lady's name and the name itself, the poet picks up the "name" thread of 73 and 74 and weaves it into 75. The simplicity of the poem's language, the clarity of the poet's thought, the very realistic discourse between the two lovers, the motion suggested both by the sea as well as by the lines, and the tender assurance of the lover's affection for his beloved make this a fine expression of love and one of the finest poems in the sequence:

> One day I wrote her name vpon the strand,
>> but came the waues and washed it away:
>> agayne I wrote it with a second hand,
>> but came the tyde, and made my paynes his pray.
> Vayne man, sayd she, that doest in vaine assay,
>> a mortall thing so to immortalize,
>> for I my selue shall lyke to this decay,
>> and eek my name bee wyped out lykewize.
> Not so, (quod I) let baser things deuize
>> to dy in dust, but you shall liue by fame:
>> my verse your vertues rare shall eternize,
>> and in the heuens wryte your glorious name.
> Where whenas death shall all the world subdew,
>> our loue shall liue, and later life renew.

The poet notes the lady's name here three times, in lines 1, 8, and 12. Used at first literally, it gradually extends by metaphor to an attribute or extension of the lady herself and finally to a stellified, eternal inscription in "the heuens." The poet moves from a statement about "her name" to her comment about "my name," and concludes by addressing the lady concerning "your name." The poem's theme, poetic immortality, was noted several times earlier, but here the lady herself comments on the poet's "vaine assay" to immortalize her name. The third quatrain contains the lover's gentle rejoinder. He noted in the previous sonnet that the lady raised his spirit out of the dust; from that raised position he can now relegate to dying in dust things "baser" than the lady, who will live by fame. "Dust to dust" may apply to man's body, but the promise of resurrection allows for transcendence. The poet's words, thus reflecting the divine Logos, provide assurance that the lady will indeed endure because of the word/Word typology.

The third quatrain contains the lover's two claims: he will "eternize" her virtues through his verse and he will write her glorious name. The first assertion is one of the most well known of Renaissance poetic topoi, but here there is also one of Spenser's clever floating referents. He either will eternize her virtue through his verse, or her rare virtue will eternize his verse. In time, both have happened. The second claim, writing her name in the heavens, contains his third, and final, attempt at "writing" (lines 1, 3, 12); this is ultimately the only writing that will endure. Given the conquest and victory of *Amor.* 68, the poet sees the opportunity for his own conquest over death as he and his lady not only will live on through their poeticized love but as the two of them will be renewed in heaven. In an earthly sense the cycles of time will preserve the lady's name for eons; but the enshrining of the name in the heavens will preserve it even after such earthly time ceases to exist.

The position of this sonnet in its relation to the *BCP* calendar is revealing. *Amor.* 75 marks 7 April, the Sunday after Easter, called Low Sunday. "Low" in comparison with the great celebration of Easter, the tone of this sonnet clearly reflects that contrast. In addition, Christ's resurrection (and hence immortality) may be compared with the poet's attempts to immortalize the lady. The epistle for this day (1 John 5) provides an analogue between the scriptural lesson and the poem: "Al that is borne of GOD ouercommeth the world. And this is the victory that ouercommeth the world, euen our faith. Who is it that ouercommeth the worlde, but he whiche beleueth that Jesus is the sonne of God? This Jesus Christ is he that came by water and bloud; not by water onely, but by water and bloud. And it is the spirite that beareth witnes, because the spirite is truth. And there are three whiche beare recorde in heauen, the father, the woorde and the holy Ghoste, and these three are one." Later in the same passage is an admonition against false gods—and a statement of confidence that we have eternal life: "He that hath the sonne, hath lyfe." Overcoming the world, then, is the epistle's main theme, as it is, in one sense, of the sonnet. Furthermore, in the noting of waters and the sea's waves, in the witnessing (thus memorializing), in the bearing record and in the "word" (God's Word and the poet's), and in the confidence of the "later life" appear further analogues and echoes tying this sonnet to its propers.

Abruptly the sequence changes. The "vertues rare" and "heuens" of 75 are transformed in 76 and 77 to virtues and heavens of quite a different sort. Both poems celebrate the lady's breasts; the rich, sensuous imagery used to describe the lady's "fayre bosome," the exotic symbolism of the "goodly table of pure yvory" on which are laid "twoo golden apples of vnualewd price," combine to make this intimate encomium a fine expression of the sensuality present in the relationship. Having lifted the reader in 75 from the strand to the heavens, Spenser gives a reminder in these next two poems that the physical side of love is not to be ignored, and that the sexual love embodied in "lower heuen" consists, in part, of the bliss one finds in heaven itself.

> Fayre bosome fraught with vertues richest tresure,
>   The neast of loue, the lodging of delight:
>   the bowre of bliss, the paradice of pleasure,
>   the sacred harbour of that heuenly spright:
> How was I rauisht with your louely sight,
>   and my frayle thoughts too rashly led astray?
>   whiles diuing deepe through amorous insight,
>   on the sweet spoyle of beautie they did pray.
> And twixt her paps like early fruit in May,
>   whose haruest seemd to hasten now apace:
>   they loosely did theyr wanton winges display,
>   and there to rest themselues did boldly place.
> Sweet thoughts I enuy your so happy rest,
>   which oft I wisht, yet neuer was so blest.

Amor. 76

> Was it a dreame, or did I see it playne,
>   a goodly table of pure yvory:
>   all spred with iuncats, fit to entertayne
>   the greatest Prince with pompous roialty?
> Mongst which there in a siluer dish did ly
>   twoo golden apples of vnualewd price:
>   far passing those which Hercules came by,
>   or those which Atalanta did entice.
> Exceeding sweet, yet voyd of sinfull vice,
>   that many sought yet none could euer taste,

> sweet fruit of pleasure brought from paradice
> by Loue himselfe and in his garden plaste.
> Her brest that table was so richly spredd,
> my thoughts the guests, which would thereon haue fedd.
>
> *Amor.* 77

The two sonnets contain the poet's rhapsodic mental dalliance on the lady's breasts; the rich imagery, heavily drawn in 76 from sonnet literature and the courtly tradition and in 77 from the Song of Songs, actually leads the poet away from the literal breasts into the metaphors and analogies of erotic literature. *Amor.* 76 becomes not so much an encomium of the breasts but a contemplation of the lover's own thoughts about those breasts. *Amor.* 77 becomes not so much a sensuous or even sensual examination of the visual delights of the lady's breasts as it is a mental exploration of lush orient images used to depict breasts.

Amor. 76 begins with a catalogue of parallel adjectival phrases depicting the treasury of virtues contained in the lady's breasts—virtues such as love, delight, bliss, pleasure, the heavenly spirit. Each of these, in turn, is reposited in its own locus: a nest, lodging, bower, paradise, and sacred harbor. When looked at this way, separated into their units, the virtues and the places of their residence are hardly erotic; in fact, the poet has used for the respective loci places of security, comfort, and rest.

The second quatrain interjects a juxtaposition: "rauisht," "rashly," "led astray," "amorous insight," "sweet spoyle," and "prey" activate the quiet contemplation and wonder of the first quatrain. But again his real focus is on his thoughts, "fraile thoughts too rashly led astray," attending to what the poet has seen. The lovely "sight" (line 5) becomes amorous "insight" (line 7) as he internalizes the object; his thoughts take wings (as in 73), which play loosely between those breasts, now transformed to harvest-hastened May fruit.

The meditation does not end; it merely fades into gently amusing reverie—sweet thoughts about his own "sweet thoughts" on the "sweet spoyle" and sweet early fruit, as well as his confession that he "oft wisht" being able to "rest" where the thoughts now stay. He concludes even more wittily, ambiguously noting that he envies the happy rest "yet neuer was so blest." The rhyme words are informative; the importance in Spenser's poetry of "rest" has been noted,and here its explicit connection with the state of being "blest" is enforced by the words' position in the couplet. Given the nature of the topic, there is also the implicit connection of "blessed rest" as not only a heavenly aspiration but as something mirrored by, and achievable in, earthly consummation of sexual desire.

Yet for all its seeming eroticism *Amor.* 76 (which, with its companion piece, 77, is derived from a single sonnet by Tasso, "Non son si belli") remains more playful than passionate, more tender than teasing. The poet continues this image-making in 77 when the breasts, the lady, and the poet dissolve into abstract speculation. In 73 the poet compared his heart to a bird seeking its desired food; in 76 the bird was transformed into wings fluttering around May fruit; in 77 the fruit is first depicted as an abstract artifact and then transposed into the sensuously luscious fruit of the lady's breasts.

The delights of the banquet table are spread before the reader in colorful, tasteful, and qualitative array. The images are lushly olfactory, visual, and saporific. Clearly, they are symbolic and not realistic; the lady's breasts may be like apples but hardly could be golden! "Here is the intimate description of the body through symbols which deprive the image of erogenic qualities; the focus of the picture is the banquet-table, not the girl's body."[6] As the lady had been described in *Amor.* 15 as a treasure house of jewels and in 64 as a garden of flowers, so in this sonnet, in the manner of the Song of Songs, her breasts have become a banquet table.

The poem moves from the poet's questioning of his vision of a table to the silver dish with its two golden apples. The movement is an interesting one, starting as it does with a questionable reality, moving to a table that, whether it was real or not, is real to the vision, and then moving on to a digression on the "iuncats" and their worth. From there the poet draws his readers further into the vision, laying out his (possible) dream first by focusing on the dish, then on the apples, and then by providing the rich allusion to those even earlier apples of Hercules and Atalanta. From there Spenser moves into the apples themselves and to their sweet taste; then, having once touched on that (possible) reality, he leads readers to a digression on the apples' origin. The couplet returns to the wider view of the table with its guests and the feast, on which the poet "would thereon haue fedd" (this being said as he actually does feed his thoughts on the image).

The allusion to Atalanta and her apples is one Spenser makes elsewhere. In 2.7.54, for example, he also links her name with that of Hercules who, in Comes's depiction, stole the apples Venus gave to Hippomenes, apples used as well to entice Atalanta. *The Faerie Queene* reference is to the Garden of Proserpina, where the effect is a focus on the tempting properties of the apples. And the sonnet reference is also to temptation, but this time (given the prenuptual setting and the Christian analogues in the sonnets) to the positive temptation of acceptable sexuality in marriage.

But Spenser also uses the table image in a startlingly different way when depicting Serena on the altar among the "saluages" (6.8.42):

> Her yuorie necke, her alablaster brest,
>> Her paps, which like white silken pillowes were,
>> For loue in soft delight thereon to rest;
>> Her tender sides, her bellie white and clere,
>> Which like an Altar did it selfe vprere,
>> To offer sacrifice diuine thereon. . . .

Spenser emphasizes the contrast between the savages literally preparing to feed upon Serena and the poet metaphorically feeding his thoughts upon her. With the savages the feeding is sinful, and the woman's physical beauty has incited them to a morally repugnant decline into literal devouring. With the poet the feeding is "voyd of sinfull vice"; the same act of feeding becomes, in its metaphoric sense, positive and productive, a feeding that nourishes life instead of destroying it. The lady herself becomes identified with paradise, the same one noted in 63 ("After long stormes . . .") but one even more specifically sought in this sonnet.

The references to the table, the dish, the guests, and the desire to be fed have their analogue in the Communion service as well. In the references to the table "fit to entertayne / the greatest Prince," to the apples of "vnualewd price," and by the heavenly identification with the fruit "brought from paradice / by Loue himselfe,"[7] the sonnet alludes to the Christian's desire for the type of union possible with Christ after the resurrection and now on earth—Communion. Spenser, significantly, views the "Supper of the Lorde" not as a sacrifice but as communion, in which his "thoughts [as] guests" are entertained at a table. Among the foods ("iuncats") are the apples, the fruit associated not only with sinfulness and disobedience but, through an equally long and strong tradition, with Christ, who hung upon a tree. The natural garden in which Serena is the table as well as the sacrifice identifies that scene with temptation and destruction; the sonnet setting supports the lady as an analogue of Christ and, thus, with redemption and new life.

Amor. 78 introduces another abrupt break in the sequence. The elevated experiences in this post-Easter betrothal section cannot be sustained; life's realities impose demands on daily living, both for the lover (whose infatuation is tempered by the exigencies of practical living) and the Christian (whose faith is strengthened by life's tribulations). Thus this period is one of expectation and hope, yet one both demanding and trying, as well. The fantasies of 76 and 77 dissolve in the harsh reality of the lovers' separation in 78. While Elizabethan sonnet sequences typically end with the lady's rejection of her lover and the separation of the two, no rejection is implied here; the lovers are merely apart, and the absence produces a melancholic longing:

> Lackyng my loue I go from place to place,
>   lyke a young fawne that late hath lost the hynd:
>   and seeke each where, where last I sawe her face,
>   whose ymage yet I carry fresh in mynd.

No witty or elevated style marks the language, no clever plays distinguish the structure. The repetitions (place to place, where/where) suggest the lover's unimaginative state. The deer, won (found) in 68, now appears lost. The repetitions continue, reflecting the kinds of searching in which he engages:

> I seeke the fields with her late footing synd,
>   I seeke her bowre with her late presence deckt,
>   yet nor in field nor bowre I her can fynd:
>   yet field and bowre are full of her aspect.

Though he does not find her, visiting the places she has been ("late footing synd . . . late presence deckt") at least keeps fresh the image, the picture, of his beloved. Like the lover in the Song of Songs 3:1–4 who seeks the beloved in the streets and the broad ways, asking everywhere for "him whom my soule loued," the longing sonnet lover is almost desperate. The modulations of the third quatrain, with their outward movement retracted to inward reflection, repeat the sense of hopelessness. The nourishing feeding of 77 here gives way to unproductive feeding, just as the imaginatively productive "louely sight" of 77 is replaced in 78 by eyes idly seeking:

> But when myne eyes I thereunto direct,
>   they ydly back returne to me agayne,
>   and when I hope to see theyr trew obiect,
>   I fynd my selfe but fed with fancies vayne.

The couplet reveals his resolution as he turns an unproductive situation into a productive one, a negative into a positive. If sight will not work, insight will:

> Ceasse then myne eyes, to seeke her selfe to see,
>   and let my thoughts behold her selfe in mee.

The effectiveness of his resolution is depicted in *Amor.* 79. Echoing the Song of Songs 4:1 ("Beholde, thou art faire, my loue: beholde, thou art faire"), which verse comes after the lover in the *Canticles* has found the beloved and has returned home, this sonnet suggests a similar situation with the *Amoretti* lovers. A tender love song, it reflects on both the surface and analogic levels the lover's spiritual maturity in a way the earlier sonnets did not:

> Men call you fayre, and you doe credit it,
>   For that your selfe ye dayly such doe see:
>   but the trew fayre, that is the gentle wit,
>   and vertuous mind, is much more praysd of me.
> For all the rest, how euer fayre it be,
>   shall turne to nought and loose that glorious hew:
>   but onely that is permanent and free
>   from frayle corruption, that doth flesh ensew.
> That is true beautie: that doth argue you
>   to be diuine and borne of heauenly seed:
>   deriu'd from that fayre Spirit, from whom al true
>   and perfect beauty did at first proceed.
> He onely fayre, and what he fayre hath made,
>   all other fayre lyke flowres vntymely fade.

As with the previous sonnet, there is now a definite seriousness marked by a notable lack of verbal wit and humor. Turning into himself at the end of 78, his thoughts (which roamed so freely and exuberantly in 76 and 77) are drawn to her "ymage," an image depicted numerous times earlier as being "fair." *Amor.* 76 presents a reconsideration of "fairness," which in this post-Easter position assumes new meaning.

The poet begins with two contrasts: the difference between what men say and what he says, and the difference between "fayre" and "trew fayre." The sonnet repeats "fayre" seven times, with meanings ranging from "physically attractive" to "perfect beauty" (in a neo-Platonic sense). The first "fayre" (line 1) is physical, the second (line 3), mental and ethical, based on her gentle wit and virtuous mind. The third (line 5) takes in the entire range of all other "earthly" and "bodily" possibilities. The fourth (line 11) is spiritual; the fifth (line 13), divine (God); the sixth (line 13), God's creation (like the lady); and the last (line 14), everything not reflecting or mirroring God's own fairness.

The poet is contrasted with other men, suggested in part by what he appreciates. Other men see the lady as physically attractive; the lover, raised from base affections and out of the dust, sees more than physical appearance and even more than the "presence" and "aspect" noted in 78. Spenser was to note again in the *Hymne in Honour of Beautie* 90–91, "that Beautie is not, as fond men misdeeme, / An outward shew of things, that onely seeme." But it is precisely because he has changed that the poet appreciates the physical self as well as the gentle wit and virtuous mind other men only observe.

Repeating the immortality theme of 75, the poet brings the lady's argument from that poem into his own argument here; but he no longer claims to be able to immortalize her, such ability being something out of his power. The lady's true fairness already has its links with immortal being and is linked (and in the poem, becomes) "true beautie." In his *Hymne in Honour of Beautie,* Spenser deals at length with the nature of that beauty, preferring there the association of beauty with light. Here the association is with "heauenly seed," with divine engendering and spiritual proceeding (with a Spenserian play on pro-seeding). The heavenly seed, as a Petrarchan image, links sacred and secular love; in terms of Christian neo-Platonism it suggests a harmony of sexual and divine energies, procreative and resurrective powers, which transform the flesh into spirit.[8] The poet will use the same image soon in the "timely seed" of *Epith.* 386, producing "timely fruit (line 404), leading to an increase in the number of "blessed Saints" (line 423). (The timely seed and fruit perhaps echo by contrast this sonnet's "vntymely flowres.") Human seed, in short, is not just potentially divine, containing as it does divine elements; it *is* divine, being a part of God's creation. Similarly, the lady's "true beautie" (line 9) is true beauty because it contains seeds (line 12) of "perfect beauty" ("you" and "true" providing the informative rhyme links, as do "seed" and "proceed").

The couplet indicates the source of all beauty (and fairness), both in heaven and on earth. The "vntymely" of line 14 links the garden image of the flowers (line 14) with the seed of line 10, but while the latter seed grows, the former, being untimely, fades. These untimely flowers not only represent an improper "fayre," but they "faire" accordingly by fading, thus losing their original "glorious hew."

But the lover's contemplation is not on the lady as one whose fairness has lost its glorious hue; instead it is on her heavenly hue and her particular blending of the sacred and secular, heavenly and earthly. *Amor.* 80 takes him from lofty speculation and untimely flowers to more practical matters and timely rest. In the second Sunday sonnet (33) the poet addressed his friend Lodowick concerning the progress on *The Faerie Queene*. Now in 80, though with a change in approach, the character "Spenser" once again breaks the sequence framework by direct allusion to the poet Spenser's work on the epic. Once again this is a reminder of Spenser inside and outside his work, of the creator identified with his creation, and a reminder once more of being in the midst of an elaborate play of fiction and nonfiction in which author and character, character and reader, engage in the "entertaynement" presented on and in the *Amoretti* stage.

In *Amor.* 33 the complaints stemmed from the poet's inability to work on *The Faerie Queene* because the "troublous fit, / of a proud loue" spoiled his spirits and permitted no work save that of the courtship and the sonnets. In 80 the poet makes a startling confession; he had resumed his interrupted epic work sometime after 33 and actually has been working on the poem all along. And he has now completed half of it:

> After so long a race as I haue run
> Through Faery land, which those six books compile,
> giue leaue to rest me being halfe fordonne,
> and gather to my selfe new breath while.

The accomplishment is a major one for Spenser and (by extension) for the character "Spenser." The empirical poet has noted the greatness of this labor all along: in 1.12.1, after completing one book, the enormity of the task must have taken effect. There he depicts the work as "my wearie course" from which he hopes to "stay" his "feeble barke" a while. In 1.12.42 he contemplates the "long voyage" on which he is bent. By 2.10.2 the work is a "labour huge, exceeding farr my might," and by 6, Proem 1–2, the exhausted poet guides his "weary steps" along his "tedious trauell."

But in *Amor.* 80 the accomplishment of his epic task, far from having drained all his energies and abilities (as he feared in 33 it would), now encourages him.

> Then as a steed refreshed after toyle,
>   out of my prison I will breake anew:
>   and stoutly will that second worke assoyle,
>   with strong endeuour and attention dew.

The equestrian image is vigorous and strong; he will "break" forth and "stoutly" discharge the work with "strong" endeavor. Love has hardly dispirited him! In 33 he rhymed "toyle" with "spoyle," suggesting the effect of the work on his spirit; here in 80 "toyle" rhymes with "assoyle," his hearty and vigorous attacking of the work still at hand. The zesty words vivify the first quatrain's weary lines, exuberantly stating his excuse for not picking up "that second worke" immediately and also displaying his plan for continued work. Unlike Calidore, ready to abandon his quest in order to dally with love, the sonnet poet testifies to his ability to pursue both his poetic career and his private love. What was said of Calidore—"another quest, another game in vew he hath"—applies quite differently to the sonnets, where the "game" has already been won and the other quest becomes a poetic holiday.

The fatigue of the first quatrain and the fresh-spiritedness of the second give way to a third mood in the third quatrain, a pleasant, playful attitude concerning his lady and his writing about her:

> Till then giue leaue to me in pleasant mew,
>   to sport my muse and sing my loues sweet praise:
>   the contemplation of whose heauenly hew,
>   my spirit to an higher pitch will rayse.

Instead of the "prison" referred to in line 6 he refers in line 9 to the pleasant mew, the sweet confinement of his betrothed status. And instead of the work he will "assoyle," he asks leave to (1) sport his muse and (2) sing his love's sweet praise. Actually there may be a bit of his sporting right here; "sport" refers to "race" (line 1) and the "steed" of line 5. But "sport" also refers to play, to disport, and to exercise. The poet implies he playfully will exercise his poetic activity in order to produce those "leaves, lines, rhymes" for his lady-muse, who in turn will inspire him to further productivity, all the time praising his love as well as his lady-love. His "loues sweet praise" is either (or both) the sweet praise of his lady or the sweet praise of (within) his loves—his *amoretti*. The "glorious hew" of 79 becomes the "heauenly hew" of 80 when it refers specifically to the lady, the contemplation of whom will raise (instead of "spoyle," as in 33) his spirit to the higher pitch in which he will sing. Raising his spirit certifies the connection between lady and muse, as do the aural connections among "mew," "muse," and "hew."

The couplet extends the sporting with comments about the lady, his praise of her, and his poetry:

> But let her prayses yet be low and meane,
> fit for the handmayd of the Faery Queene.

Concerning the lady and her respective relationship with the queen, the poet may raise his pitch to sing her praises, but those praises still must be moderated both by her social status as well as by the poet's obligatory duty to his monarch. Saint George must yet fulfill his duty to Gloriana, Scudamour must still win Amoret, and Artegall must turn to completing his task. The Elizabethan poet's task is praising the queen; all else is presumably a diversion, and all praise, other than of the queen, must be moderate (low) and temperate (mean).[9]

But the poet has already spoken of his poems as "loves" and as "praises." Poetically speaking, sonnets are of a much lower pitch than the lofty sounds of epics; it would be a breach of decorum to write the "praises," the sonnets, in the high style of *The Faerie Queene*. His request at the end, then, and in fact in the whole sestet of the sonnet, is that the poet be allowed the diversion of sporting, given that he clearly has found a way both for the serious task of the epic and the pleasant play of the sonnets.

Appropriately, the following two sonnets (81 and 82) "sport his muse" and sing sweet praises to his lady. *Amor.* 81 is a beautifully symmetrical encomium, in praises low and mean, of the "fayre" lady. It praises her not for any supernatural qualities, not for her divinity or angelic characteristics, but for the human elements that make her so fair to her loving fiancé. The poem is distinguished from the earlier catalogues by the sheer exotic, lush physicality of its descriptions, many drawn from the orient richness of the Song of Songs. Each "fayre" listed is accompanied by an action that qualifies and, in some ways, accounts for the praise.

> Fayre is my loue, when her fayre golden heares,
> with the loose wynd ye wauing chance to marke:
> fayre when the rose in her red cheekes appeares,
> or in her eyes the fyre of loue does sparke.
> Fayre when her brest lyke a rich laden barke,

with pretious merchandize she forth doth lay:
fayre when that cloud of pryde, which oft doth dark
her goodly light with smiles she driues away.

In earlier sonnets the poet frequently praised the lady's fair-
ness; her hair, cheeks, and breasts have all been given note. But
earlier praises were metaphoric, and the lady herself was hardly
involved unless by hyperbolically depicted action. In 64, for
example, "her ruddy cheekes" were "lyke vnto Roses red." In 37
her golden tresses entangled in golden snares. In 64 her breasts,
"lyke lilyes," inspired him, and in 76 "her paps like early fruit in
May" aroused the lover's appetites. Now each "fayre" is preceded
and accompanied by an action, because it is "in action" (accord-
ing to Spenser) that things, including qualities, find their identi-
ties. The first quatrain praises three actions resulting in the lady's
fairness; the second quatrain praises two in more detail. The
third praises one:

> But fayrest she, when so she doth display
>   the gate with pearles and rubyes richly dight:
>   throgh which her words so wise do make their way
>   to beare the message of her gentle spright.
> The rest be works of natures wonderment,
>   but this the worke of harts astonishment.

In the third quatrain the octave's sensual delights transform
into a combination of sensual and spiritual joys. Her smile cap-
tures the lover's heart, but it is through her mouth that her wise
words pass, bearing her gentle spirit's message. This is the se-
quence's only reference to the lady's wise words, although her
comments, both directly and through the narrator, appear several
times. Again Spenser conjoins the physical and the spiritual, the
latter of which is certainly significant and which necessarily is
embodied in the flesh. Even more important than the words are
their message, a comment, perhaps, not just on Spenser's craft
and the relative importance he places on "delighting and teach-
ing," but on the whole ontological process. In that process logos
reveals Logos, in which (contrary to much current deconstruc-
tionist thinking) behind, beneath, and within the play of appear-
ances there is a discoverable reality, a message and Truth, and in
which a poem "means" as well as "is."

The argument for meaning distinct from words continues into
the next sonnet, Amor. 82, as does the praise of the lady. Amor. 80
played on the praises being "low and meane." The simple (low)

structure of 81 and its soft (low) tones exhibit the poet's treatment of the first half of that description; 82 develops the "meane" motif in a beautiful and clever interplay of relative "degrees":

> Ioy of my life, full oft for louing you
>   I blesse my lot, that was so lucky placed:
>   but then the more your owne mishap I rew,
>   that are so much by so meane loue embased.
> For had the equall heuens so much you graced
>   in this as in the rest, ye mote inuent
>   some heuenly wit, whose verse could haue enchased
>   your glorious name in golden moniment.
> But since ye deignd so goodly to relent
>   to me your thrall, in whom is little worth,
>   that little that I am, shall all be spent,
>   in setting your immortall prayses forth.
> Whose lofty argument vplifting me,
>   shall lift you vp vnto an high degree.

Mixed with a sense of his own unworthiness is his gentle, playful boasting of his poetry's power to elevate. His address commences with a comment on his good luck (with a play on blessing, lot, and lucky) in being "placed" so that he could love the lady; this contrasts with her own "mishap" in being "embased" by being loved by so mean a love as his. In earlier sonnets his thoughts focused almost entirely on his own condition; now he sees his situation in relation to hers and is free to sympathize in a way not possible before the "Easter" events.

His being "placed" suggests several possibilities, one of which is that he is socially and physically in a position to love her. But the phrase "that was so lucky placed" also refers to his "lot," suggesting that chance had a part in this arrangement and that chance arranged the love all along. (In the *Hymne in Honour of Beautie* Spenser states: "Then wrong it were that any other twaine / should in loues gentle band combynded bee, / but those whom heaven did at first ordaine," 204–6.) For the lover, it was good "placing"; for the lady, it was a "mishap" that lowered ("embased") her by so "meane" a love (referring to his own social status, or to "meane" as moderate, even less highly "pitched" than the songs sung to the Faery Queen in *Amor.* 80).

The second quatrain expands upon the first; it comments on the "equall heuens" gracing the lady. Presumably the heavens have graced (blessed) him with good chance, and they are equal (impartial) in their apportionment of such matters. But had they been equal (just) there might have been a different poet praising her. The poet plays here on a number of things, including (1) the connections between heaven's gracing the lady (both as they have graced the poet and as she has graced the lover), (2) the poetry motif (in which "inuent," "wit," "verse," and "enchased" have a part), and (3) a play on "inuent" in the sense of discovering a heavenly wit (poet)—not a real one—to effect the poetic immortalization. That heavenly wit, not our poet, could have "enchased" the lady's glorious name (that same "glorious name" the poet claims in *Amor.* 75 he will "eternize" in his verse and "in the heuens wryte"). But there is a catch to all this: "enchasing" is Spenser's word for portraying and displaying, but it also means to capture, to enclose, to confine. The lady's name may be captured in a golden monument, but it will also be captive there. That "heavenly wit" may inscribe her in a golden monument— but the poet, in *Amor.* 69, already has directed that "euen this verse vowd to eternity, / shall be thereof immortall moniment."

Given that he already has loaded the dice in his favor, he proceeds in the third quatrain to assert what he earlier insinuated—that his praises, "low and meane" though they may be, are better than those of some heavenly wit. "Little" as he is, he will spend all in setting ("enchasing") the lady's praises. He has moved from praises low and mean to immortal praises, which are encomia as well as poems themselves. What the poet presents here is his recommitment to poetry as well as his witty restatement of poetry's immortalizing power.

In *Amor.* 80 the poet prepared to "sport my muse and sing my loues sweet praise: / the contemplation of whose heauenly hew, / my spirit to an higher pitch will rayse." In the couplet of 82 the "lofty argument" of those praises both uplifts the poet as well as lifts up the lady "vnto an high degree." The poet's "argument" is important; it picks up the idea of setting forth reasons (as with the delineations of and reasons for the lady's fairness in *Amor.* 81). "Argument" also suggests outward signs or evidence (as with the physical poems arguing for his ability as a poet). It is also used as a form of rhetorical expression and, significantly, as an indicator of the work's matrix, or central idea. As in the previous sonnet, the poet alludes to the meaning of the words, the reality behind the signs. Here a "lofty argument" uplifts the poet, both in the sense of raising his spirits as well as elevating him in fame as a poet. It also "uplifts" in the analogical sense of his eventually attaining heaven.

The sonnet is situated in the position of 14 April 1594, the second Sunday after Easter. The epistle is from 1 Peter 2, the gospel from John 10. Both passages concern Christ the Good Shepherd, a theme extending beyond both pericopes and providing a complex of allusions. The theme of Peter's preaching never varies, always centering on Christ, first crucified and then raised up. The executors must turn from their ways, listen to the shepherd's voice, and, by Christ's example, find the green pastures. John relates that the good shepherd "giueth his life for his shepe," with the emphasis on the giving. It is done willingly, which is the only way one can enter into the proper relationship with God. While the *BCP* lesson ends with John 10:16, the chapter continues with the same theme building to a key point in verse 28: Christ gives his sheep eternal life. But that gift of life demands a response from the receivers—following the shepherd's path. Accompanying that response is the same sense of Easter joy and Easter hope that follows through the Easter season, a joy in the gift and a hopeful longing for the mystical marriage to come. Such joy and hope bring a sense of assurance, not merely in dealing with the present and the future, but in reinterpreting the past.

Amor. 83 provides the lover's example of such reinterpretation. Throughout the *Amoretti's* post-Easter section, in order to show the contrast between their previous use and the new meaning all things have assumed since the "old yeares annoy" turned to "new delight," the poet has reiterated previously used themes, motifs, and images. Webs of deceit are now bands of love; storm-tossed ships have found their way safely to port; concern solely with his infatuated self has turned to a loving regard and concern for his lady.

Yet Spenser's use of almost the same sonnet in two different positions in the sequence represents the most ingenious employment of his method of altered repetition. It marks one of his cleverest author-reader games. *Amor.* 83 is the notorious "repetition" of *Amor.* 35, and on these two poems rest many charges for the sequence's haphazard organization. Many earlier critics merely passed *Amor.* 83 off as a mistaken reprint of 35, and only a few early editions bothered to print it (thus misnumbering *Amor.* 83 and every sonnet following it).

However, in examining the sequence as it has unfolded in this study, and on the basis of (1) Spenser's elaborate horizontal and vertical structuring through the calendar year, (2) the church year, (3) the *BCP* pericopes, (4) the alternating moods of the lover and the poet's developing self, as well as (5) the importance of the pre- and then post-Easter views, there is no reason to doubt that the sonnet *should* appear in both places and that it should function importantly in both places. The one word difference between the two poems ("seeing" in line 6 of *Amor.* 83 and "hauing" in line 6 of 35) is crucial:

> My hungry eyes, through greedy couetize,
>> Still to behold the obiect of theyr payne:
>> with no contentment can themselues suffize,
>> but hauing pine, and hauing not complayne.
> For lacking it, they cannot lyfe sustayne,
>> and seeing it, they gaze on it the more:
>> in theyr amazement lyke Narcissus vayne
>> whose eyes him staru'd: so plenty makes me pore.
> Yet are myne eyes so filled with the store
>> of that fayre sight, that nothing else they brooke:
>> but loath the things which they did like before,
>> and can no more endure on them to looke.
> All this worlds glory seemeth vayne to me,
>> and all theyr shewes but shadowes sauing she.

In *Amor.* 34, having just complained of clouds covering the lady's eyes and the absence of her guidance, the poet wandered in "darknesse and dismay," his own eyes hungry for her guiding light and, metaphorically, for the lady herself. What he lacked, and what he felt he must have, constituted both the antecedent of "it" and of his "paine"—the "obiect," which is the lady herself. Not being with her caused his pain; ironically, being with her increased the pain because he could not have her.

But by 83 the lover does have the lady, and the word "hauing," with its latent suggestions of physical possession, loses its earlier significance. Now the focus is on seeing her. His eyes so filled with the "store of that fayre sight," he no longer even compares his lady to other women or to other things, confining his praises totally to descriptions of his beloved. This is the way he praised her in 81. Now his assessment of the lady's real value appears in the substance of these *remembered* motifs, feelings, and approaches.

Spenser treated a similar theme in the house of Alma, where he divided the mind into three faculties: fancy, reason, and memory. It might be considered that the *Amoretti* poet represents Phantastes, the imaginative faculty, while simultaneously representing reason, through which his calculated approach to wooing and winning has been gauged. Now, in this last section of the sequence, memory (which holds "things foregone through many ages") is called upon. Just as the cyclic return of the new year and of spring bring with them the memory of all past new years and springs, so do these last sonnet days give significance to their present. Likewise, because the feelings expressed here were expressed earlier, this poem assumes special significance in its position as 83. Now, as in *The Faerie Queene*, Spenser restates motifs and themes in a variety of emotional and metaphoric contexts; this allows him to espouse with greater resonance and clarity the complexity of all experience, as well as to explore and assert the importance of the contextual meaning of experience. In the scope of the sequence as a mirror of life, moving from birth images in the early poems to those of death in the last ones, the "repeated" poems, 35 and 83, suggest that the young man and the mature man (respectively) remain constant in their love but change in tastes with the cycles of mutable life.[10]

Because of what has intervened between the poem's first and second appearances, the difference in the poet's approach and desire, expressed in these two sonnets first as "hauing" and now as "seeing," ultimately becomes relevant. Just as 35 is paired with 34, which notes the unrequited stage of the lover's progress, so 83 pairs with 84 as the explanation, as Kaske suggests, for what the poet's eyes at this part of the engagement now hunger. In 35 he wanted to see her more; now (in 83 and then in 84) he wants to see more of her. His hungry eyes are part of a body "which is and will be 'starv'd' . . . until the 'greedy pleasure' of the wedding-night (*Epith.* 1. 365). Thus the proverb 'Inopem me copia fecit' is wittily apt for the frustration of the betrothed who sees but cannot see, possesses yet cannot possess his intended. The promise exacerbates the desire; to dramatize how anticlimatic this is [Spenser] actually repeats a prebetrothal sonnet."[11]

While Kaske is correct about the wittiness of the new situation and thus the new meaning (the new context yielding a new text and vice versa), the serious part of this nonseriousness must also be considered. The change from "having" to "seeing" also denotes the movement from Petrarchan unenlightenment to spiritual enlightenment.[12] Enlightened by the Christ-lady's beauty, the poet no longer is susceptible to this world's "shewes."

The lover's assessment of the real value of his experiences surfaces through the substance of reverie or memory, and in 83 the poet provides a virtual microcosm of the entire sequence. The poem maintains the Petrarchan idiom (now transformed), the autobiographical elements, the vanity theme, shadowy neo-Platonism, and the contrasts between sterile and nourishing love. But in 83 the lover is no longer the *voyeur* but the *voyant;* what he sees is the experience of the past through new eyes, allowing him to see the present face to face. As in the raising of visors and veils in *The Faerie Queene,* with their accompanying revelations, the "seeing" of 83 allows the poet a glimpse at the inner core of experience. Spenser sees that core as luminous and illuminating; it contains that fair sight that puts all else in shadows. In 35 the "fayre sight" was the lady alone. In 83 the lady, as she reflects the Easter Christ, provides the vision.

The "enlightened" vision may be noted on both the surface and the analogic levels. Earlier, in the discussion of *Amor.* 75, the Collect and epistle for Low Sunday were noted. The *BCP* gospel lesson for the day described Christ's appearance to his disciples; but this did not afford correspondences with the sonnet. The reason for the nonconnection of the *BCP* and *Amor.* 75 is that the reading comprised verses 19–23 of John 20. However, the remainder of that chapter, verses 24–29, provides significant material not just for Low Sunday but also for *Amor.* 83:

> But Thomas one of the twelue, called Didymus, was not with them when Iesus came. The other disciples therefore said vnto him, We haue *sene* the Lord: but he [Thomas] said vnto them, Except I se in his hand the print of the nailes, and put my finger into the print of the nailes, and put mine hand into his side, I wil not beleue it. And eight daies after againe his disciples were within, and Thomas with them. Then came Iesus, when the dores were shut, and stode in the middes, and said, Peace be vnto you. After, said he to Thomas, Put thy finger here, and *see* mine hands, and put forthe thine hand, and put it into my side, and be not faithles, but faithful . . . Iesus said vnto him, Thomas, because thou hast *sene* me, thou beleuest: blessed are they that haue not *sene,* and haue beleued.

This passage (italics mine) provides various links. Eight sonnet days after *Amor.* 75 brings the arrival of 83, where the key images are sight and seeing. While the sonnet poet is in no sense a doubting Thomas, the sonnet, because of its structural position and, by extension, because of its *BCP* parallel, metaphorically alludes to the Christian who, like Thomas, still feels the need to see Christ in order to believe and "sustayne" his life. The Christian's hope of seeing Christ and the frustration of living in this world in ongoing anticipation provide an analogous reading of the sonnet lover's hope and frustration in these latter days of the betrothal.

The ocular imagery of 83, which began with the double image of the poet's hunger and greed (especially as displayed in his hungry eyes), continues in 84, where the poet chastises himself for feelings he believes are reflected in glances of sensual desire. This is a return to another consideration of vision and sight. Virtually all the sequence's "eye" sonnets concern or address the lady's, not the lover's, eyes; *Amor.* 35 and 83 are exceptions, having to do with the poet's eyes and, by extension, with his vision. *Amor.* 84 holds his vision, literally and figuratively, up to his own scrutiny. Apparently the "greedy couetize" of 83 led the poet's eyes astray; he now attempts to reason away the passion that increases as the marriage approaches. The sonnet's language is strong, the poem firm in its (presumed) rejection of lustful passion. It is also amusing in its overall statement concerning the lover's situation two months before his wedding:

> Let not one sparke of filthy lustfull fyre
> > breake out, that may her sacred peace molest:
> > ne one light glance of sensuall desyre
> > Attempt to work her gentle mindes vnrest.
> But pure affections bred in spotlesse brest,
> > and modest thoughts breathd from wel tempred sprites,
> > goe visit her in her chast bowre of rest,
> > accompanyde with angelick delightes.
> There fill your selfe with those most ioyous sights,
> > the which my selfe could neuer yet attayne:
> > but speake no word to her of these sad plights,
> > which her too constant stiffenesse doth constrayn.
> Onely behold her rare perfection,
> > and bless your fortunes fayre election.

The first quatrain's rhyme words, fire/desire, molest/unrest, combined with spark, filthy lust, light, sensual, and attempt, testify to the intensity with which the poet makes his assertion. They overwhelm the "sacred peace" and "gentle mind." The double entendre on "sacred peace" adds to the erotic emphasis, an emphasis boldly declared even as it is being rejected. The words make the contrast that much greater between the first and second quatrains, where lustful fires breaking out yield to modest thoughts breathing, and where pure affections replace sensual desires. The forceful initial rhymes give way to breast/rest and sprites/delights. As passion's fires subside the poet resumes a flexibility in structuring his language; the first line's emphatic "let not" is paralleled by and syntactically suspended until the "goe visit" of the third line, second quatrain. Even "accompanyde with angelick delights" floats among "her," "her chaste bowre," "rest," and those affections and thoughts he sends.

But the lover's conflict is not over. The lustful fire of the first quatrain was almost extinguished by the purity of the second—almost, but not entirely. Mention of breasts, bowers, and delights revives the passion, and the third quatrain once again leads him to amorous dilemmas. "Delights" lead to thoughts of "sights"; the conflict in seeing and not having yields "plights." Similarly, "attayne" and "constrayn" rhyme as well as inform concerning the hope and the thwarting of it. The command of line 7 to "goe visit" becomes "fill your selfe" in line 9, echoing the Narcissus-like poet whose eyes are "filled with the store of that fayre sight."

The pure affections and modest thoughts are to visit and fill, and the sonnet's humor comes forth. The affections and thoughts are to fill themselves on those joyous sights the poet himself has not yet attained, but has thoughts of soon attaining. In so writing, the poet returns to the start of 83, where these immediate problems with seeing first began; even the rhymes "attain"/"constrain" of 84 connect with the "payne"/"complain" of 83. What are the affections and thoughts to do? Fill themselves. What not to do? "Speake no word to her of these sad plights." He is precisely in the situation noted in line 4 of Amor. 83 in "hauing[,] pine, and hauing not[,] complayne." The "plights" are, of course, the passions, the lustful fires and light glances, brought on by her too-constant firmness of attitude, presumably in reserving sexual consummation for the marriage bed. (One can hardly overlook the lover's implied complaint in describing the lady's being too constant in restraint.)

Nor can one overlook that thus far this entire sonnet has been one of the most suggestive ones in the entire sequence, an amusing situation for a poem whose declared purpose is the rejection of "filthy lustfull fyre." Denied of the lady's charms, the lover sends his "pure affections" and "modest thoughts" to visit her, but the visit is hardly a mere polite social call. It is only his sight, not his vividly amorous imagination, that is denied the sensual pleasures of which he protests too much.

The couplet addresses the "your" of line 9, either the affections and thoughts or the poet himself. In either (or both) case(s), "seeing" turns to beholding, the sensual to the abstract, and the poet returns to the same thoughts expressed in 82: "I blesse my lot, that was so lucky placed." The lady is both rare and perfect, just as such perfection is itself rare. But it is that lady as "perfec-

tion" whose "election" of the poet has resulted in his good lot
and fortune. As in 82, the poet ends on an uplifting note and the
lady's rare perfection leads the poet into the last segment of the
Amoretti.

Five sonnets from the beginning of the sequence the poet, in a
defense of the lady's pride, addressed the outside world:

> Rudely thou wrongest my deare harts desire,
>   In finding fault with her too portly pride:
>   the thing which I doo most in her admire,
>   is of the world unworthy most enuide.

Five sonnets from the end of the sequence, *Amor.* 85, the poet
again addresses an external world about the lady's worth:

> The world that cannot deeme of worthy things,
>   when I doe praise her, say I doe but flatter:
>   so does the Cuckow, when the Mauis sings,
>   begin his witlesse note apace to clatter.
> But they that skill not of so heauenly matter,
>   all that they know not, enuy or admyre,
>   rather then enuy let them wonder at her,
>   but not to deeme of her desert aspyre.

The poem threads together various themes: the poet's defense
of his poetry against the world's criticism, praise of the lady, and
the poet's confidence in himself and in the power of his poetry to
immortalize her. A notable difference in attitude between *Amor.*
5 and 85 is evident; in the former the poet felt obligated to defend
and define, whereas in this latter one he counterattacks and, in
the process, reintroduces the theme of the lady as inspiration.
Furthermore, in *Amor.* 6 the poet wrote that "deepe is the wound,
that dints the parts entire / with chast affects, that naught but
death can seuer." Here, having spoken of his "pure affections
bred in spotlesse breast" in the previous sonnet, he picks up the
theme of the lady's rare perfection and its interiorization in
himself, with an echo of *Amor.* 6:

> Deepe in the closet of my parts entyre,
>   her worth is written with a golden quill:
>   that me with heauenly fury doth inspire,
>   and my glad mouth with her sweet prayses fill.
> Which when as fame in her shrill trump shal thunder,
>   let the world chose to enuy or to wonder.

Like Astrophil, the poet looks into his heart. Inspired with "heauenly fury" he fills his voice (as he was "filled" with sights in 83 and 84) with her praises.

The poet begins ambiguously: the world cannot judge worthy things (which suggests that the world does not recognize the lady's, or the poet's worth). The praises he all along claimed he would write are now being called flattery, an attack he counters by comparing the world's sounds to those of the cacophonous cuckoo, whose clatter interrupts the song thrush.

Another attack begins the second quatrain, where the world is said (1) to lack the skill in understanding or appreciating such heavenly matter as the poetry (or the lady as heavenly matter) and (2) in its ignorance to envy or admire such matter without understanding it. The world should wonder, he asserts, rather than envy but should not attempt to judge the lady's worth (incapable as it is of doing so).

Quatrain three finds the poet once again moving into the center, drawing himself into the matrix of his being, where truth is both kept and revealed. Whereas earlier his "parts entyre" contained a deep wound, here those parts serve as a closet, a *musaeum clausum* wherein the lady's worth is written with a golden quill. The "heuenly wit" of *Amor.* 82 could "enchase" the lady's name in a golden monument; here the monument is the human heart, but the name is written by the golden quill of the poet who knows "heauenly matter."

The lady's worth inspires the poet with heavenly fury, the inspiration that fills his glad mouth with sweet praise. He has come a long, long way from being pained with unquiet thoughts breeding in the love-pined inner parts of *Amor.* 2, and from the dazed amazement that stopped his tongue with "thoughts astonishment" and ravished his pen with "fancies wonderment," as it did in *Amor.* 3. Now in 85 his mouth is "glad" and filled with praise.

That which results from the condition related in the third quatrain is (figuratively and literally) his coup de grace. With all the pride of a poet assured that his poetry will live and will therefore grant immortality to its subject, as well as with the assurance of the Christian whose acceptance of the Easter lesson assures him of his own immortality, the poet defames fame that, like the Cuckow and the Mavis, has its own sound—a shrill, thundering trumpet. But the "world's fame" is not really the poet's object; it plays a "shrill trump[et]," but it is also a "trompe," an illusion and a sham that deceives ("all this worlds glory seemeth vayne to me, / and all theyr shewes but shadowes saving she," *Amor.* 83).

Now that he is skilled in heavenly matter, the poet's concern is eternal fame, which will triumph (trump) over wordly fame. The world, which did not know if it should envy or wonder at the poetry, called it flattery. But when it hears the thunder of eternal fame, which the poet's praise brings the lady, then the world will be in a position to choose to envy the lady or be in wonder of her. Whatever the world's choice, the poet, his poetry, and his praise will have trumped and triumphed.

Unfortunately, the world chooses to envy (which is so often the case), and the poet's reverie collapses. At the beginning of the sequence, four poems "elapsed" before any narrative action began; here at the end, the four final poems provide the movement to end the first act of a three-part drama (*Amoretti*, anacreontics, and *Epithalamion*) that ends in the comedic and unitive wedding. On the analogic level the narrator is learning an important lesson: living in the world, but not of it, is no easy matter. The "world" cannot rightly judge worthy things and, because of envy, it attempts to attack those worthy things in its attempt at universal mediocrity. Although living with post-Easter hope, the betrothed individual must believe without having the satisfaction or consolation of seeing (as in the "doubting Thomas" story and *Amor.* 83). Although having experienced with Christ the agon, Passion, crucifixion and resurrection during the Lenten-Easter section, the lover must yet live a life filled with tribulation (and joy), of persecution (and hope), of suffering (and endurance). The lover encounters in these last sonnets the negative side of his passage from post-Easter joy to eternal bliss. In that encounter he comes head-on with one of Spenser's recurring motifs: although heaven may be seen on earth, no one is permitted to live in *this* heaven forever.

The separation from any touch of heaven is always a painful one, never brought on willingly. Dante would observe the Rose eternally; Red Cross would always habitate the Mount of Contemplation; Calidore would live in pastoral seclusion forever. But the separation comes and is part of the epic, pastoral, and sonnet tradition in which ladies and lovers must part. Between the resurrection and Christ's Second Coming the world goes through a biregnum; Satan and the elemental spirits have been deposed and defeated, but they still exercise power. Christ has been enthroned as king and lord in heaven but has not yet taken possession of his earthly domain. The Christian, strengthened by the

Easter experience, must still fight against Satan's "venemous toung," although the fight separates him both from the peace he had and the comfortable situation of "heaven on earth."

In Spenser the separation frequently is brought on by one or another of the Blatant Beast's relatives or by the beast itself. Envy, Sclaunder, Occasion, Detraction, Malfont—all are involved with disharmony and separation. The causes and effects are clear yet multiple. Even those not bitten by the beast are affected by it, and many of the good knights and ladies of Faery either run from their blatant adversary or are attacked by it. Calidore, the "beautiful gift" of courtesy, cannot keep the beast chained; it breaks out of the iron bonds and threatens even the epic poet, breaks the narrative frame of the concomitantly written sonnet sequence, jumps from the epic to the sonnets, and infects the poet and his lady. Six sonnets after relating he has finished the halfway mark in writing *The Faerie Queene* (where, at the end of Book 6, the narrator notes the beast's escape), the sonnet poet finds that public or private slander has forced him and his lady apart.

In the *Amoretti* the lovers have been caught unawares; in the midst of their happiness, the world's envy turns to the world's attack. Had the sonnet poet heeded his own writings (having just completed book 6 of the epic) he would have recalled that immediately after winning Pastorella, in fact, in the same stanza (6.10.38), Calidore

> . . . of his loue . . . reapt the timely frute,
> And ioyed long in close felicity:
> Till fortune fraught with malice, blinde, and brute,
> That enuies louers long prosperity,
> Blew vp a bitter storme of foule aduersity.

Pastorella, too, is carried off by brigands, as Serena had been by cannibals, and as, in 86, the sonnet lady is by vicious lies:

> Venemous toung tipt with vile adders sting,
> Of that selfe kynd with which the Furies fell
> theyr snaky heads doe combe, from which a spring
> of poysoned words and spitefull speeches well.
> Let all the plagues and horried paines of hell,
> vpon thee fall for thine accursed hyre:
> that with false forged lyes, which thou didst tel,
> in my true loue did stirre vp coles of yre,
> The sparkes whereof let kindle thine own fyre,

and catching hold on thine owne wicked hed
consume thee quite, that didst with guile conspire
in my sweet peace such breaches to haue bred.
   Shame be thy meed, and mischiefe thy reward,
    dew to thy selfe that it for me prepard.

The very structure of *Amor.* 86 reflects the poet's heated passion against the unnamed person(s). With the final couplet a separate sentence (a curse on the detractor), the rest of the poem, for all practical purposes, is composed of one continuous stream of heated words instead of one sentence per quatrain (as is the usual pattern in the *Amoretti* sonnets). Packed with terms expressing the lover's opprobrium, the sonnet-curse draws on exactly the same devices as those his foe prepared for him. Every image, every term, is carefully and passionately employed to portray the wickedness and vileness of that "venemous toung" and to express the poet's disgust, anger, and intensely retributive frame of mind.

The sonnet provides a reminder at its start that the cause of discontent, the cause of separation, is words. The snakelike, metonymic "toung" bifurcates words by the same process that results in a Duessa being mistaken for an Una. The beast with its venemous tongue "tells"; he is the antipoet, whose telling reviles, not reveals. Instead of truth (the poet's goal), Slander's and the beast's goal is falsehood. The words "poysoned," the speeches "spitefull,"[13] the intent is to divide and separate people from one another, people from themselves, and poets from their own meed. The world claimed the poet was a flatterer (85) and here, as in *The Faerie Queene*, the beast, with his words, attacks the poet's words: "Ne may this homely verse, of many meanest, / hope to escape his venemous despite" (6.12.41).

In the sonnet, the poet vents his anger. The "coles of yre" stirred up in the "false forged lyes" are to spark the flaming destruction of the "venemous toung" and "wicked hed." The string of rhymes links sounds and related thoughts: adders' "sting" and a "spring" of words inflict wounds; the "fell" furies connect by association with the "well" of spiteful speeches. Both are tied to "hell" for what they "tell." The accursed "hire" is the stirring up of coals of "ire," producing a "fire" because of "conspiring" to produce the breach. ("Conspire" pulls together, etymologically, the blowing on the coals, the guileful blowing together to stir fires.)

The poet's "reward" for good poetry is fame (as in 85). For the antipoet, the "venemous toung," the curse is "shame" and mischief ("calamity" and, even more so, "misfortune").

Some of the sonnet's imagery appeared earlier, although certainly without the strength of attack observable here. In *Amor.* 2 the poet commanded his own "vnquiet thoughts" to "breake forth at length out of the inner part, / in which thou lurkest lyke to vipers brood." The tangled nest of snakes at length bred the subsequent sonnets. The breeding occurred again in 84, where the poet referred to "pure affections bred in spotlessee brest" But in 86 the "sacred peace" of 84 and the "sweet peace" of 86 have been conspired against for "such breaches to haue bred." Persons of spotless breasts yield good progeny (pure affections); the mother of lies produces breached births.

Some critics classify *Amor.* 86 with the concluding three sonnets because it appears to describe the cause of the lovers' separation, yet there is actually no indication in 86 of a physical separation at all, whereas 87–89 all mention the lady's absence from her lover. In 86 all that is known is that the "world" has guilefully conspired to create a breach and that the world has sought shame and mischief for the poet.[14] The tone shift between 86 and 87 clearly suggests that if there had been an "estrangement" it ceased before the subsequent physical separation, the cause of which separation is not revealed.

Again, the time schemes are important. The separation, as such, is presumably part of the historical time that is operant in the sequence. It parallels in ritual time the period after Christ's ascension. While Ascension Day is celebrated as the fortieth day after Easter, thus placing it at 10 May and out of the calendar section represented by the *Amoretti* (which ends on 21 April), there is no reason not to see in the narrator's extension and contraction of psychological time an extension into the "sacred time" of the Christ-lady's absence. In fact, the absence has so distorted the lover's sense of time that time itself is a motif uniting the last three sonnets. With the narrator now so integrally associated with his lady, her absence (in a way) causes the temporary discontinuance of his time-awareness. For all practical purposes he is in a limbotic state. Not becoming, he suspends active being.

The violence of emotion expressed in 86 apparently subsided, some reconciliation has occurred and, for an unexplained reason, the lady and lover are parted for a period of time. In *Astrophil and Stella* the final sonnets lament a lost love; in Petrarch's last sonnets there is the unattainable (because of death) separation. Such is not the case with Spenser's last three sonnets. For him, real love does not end in ashes but moves toward temporal transcendence. In *The Faerie Queene* the betrothals are celebrated but the knights leave to finish quests before their weddings. Yet they leave with the promise of a joyful return. Likewise in the *Amoretti* the lovers, although apart, remain betrothed; the poet, "lyke as the Culuer on the bared bough," waits expectantly for the reunion.

Sonnets 87 and 88 begin with parallel constructions: "Since I did leaue the presence of my loue" (87) and "Since I haue lackt the comfort of that light" (88). Both proceed with discussions of the disorder the poet experiences because of his lady's absence. *Amor.* 87 describes his disrupted sense of time:

> Since I did leaue the presence of my loue,
>   Many long weary dayes I haue outworne:
>   and many nights, that slowly seemd to moue
>   theyr sad protract from euening vntill morne.
> For when as day the heauen doth adorne,
>   I wish that night the noyous day would end:
>   and when as night hath vs of light forlorne,
>   I wish that day would shortly reascend.

The doleful lover does not lament a love now lost but merely a love now absent; in fact, the sonnet suggests that it is he, not she, who has left the presence of his love. The rush of anxiety felt in 86 yields to the languor of longing in 87, when weary days and slowly moving nights lengthen the time until they are together again. The long nights "protract" both space and time—spatially in moving from west to east and temporally in moving from "euening untill morne." The move is full circle in the first quatrain as the days become nights and as the evenings fade into mornings, a repetition suggestive of the weariness (weary days) that outwears ("weary" and "outworn") him.

The poet's sadness and weariness linger into the second quatrain; his own discomfiture extends to distraction with the natural world. In spite of day adorning the heavens, day is now viewed as "noyous." Similarly, when night arrives he wishes it were day. Night, the poet writes, "hath vs of light forlorne," in which "forlorne" not only suggests the state in which he finds himself but echoes the sense of weariness and sadness already stated in the first quatrain. The lady, metaphorically his light, is gone and he longs for her/its reappearance. That reappearance would bring another protraction of time and space as the sun spatially reascends the sky, thus temporally lengthening the morning into day. The "long . . . dayes" of line 2 bring about a desire for day's "short" reascension in line 8, just as the slowly moving nights of line 3 are to yield a short (quick) return of day. The distortions of time and space are paralleled by the second quatrain's rhymes. "Adorne" moves to the height of day and "forlorne" to its antithesis in the complete absence of light; the longed-for "end" of day (when the sun descends) is contrasted with hopes of a "reascend"ing new day.

This temporal and celestial roller coaster leads in the third quatrain to another reason why the days seem weary and the nights slow. He began the octave with the situation that caused all this: he has left the presence of his love. In the sestet he adds that these changes he experiences are in part because of his great expectations for the reunion. He is "beguiling" (whiling away) his "griefe with chaunges." The lines are complex:

> Thus I the time with expectation spend,
>   and faine my griefe with chaunges to beguile,
>   that further seemes his terme still to extend,
>   and maketh euery minute seem a myle.
> So sorrow still doth seeme too long to last,
>   but ioyous houres doo fly away too fast.

In suggesting he "faine[s] . . . to beguile" his grief he relates that he is obligated or compelled, under the circumstances, to give preference to the matter (that is, he fain would beguile his grief). Not only does he "fain," but he "feigns." By the very fact that he can objectively write about the distortions he has made between day and night and among the various time awarenesses, he admits to knowing the difference between objective time and psychological time. He is "faining his grief"—deceiving it, dissembling it, as well as "feigning" his grief (fashioning it) in verse. More important, though, are the "chaunges," a word Spenser uses to suggest such things as alteration, transformation (and "turning"), different positions (here and in the heavens), and reversals. The "changes" now are made to beguile (negative), but the effect of beguiling is to help him overcome (at least feign) his grief (positive).

Nonetheless, his grief has overcome him, instead of vice versa, and his own little game, clever as it may be, only "extends" the grief (just as he had experienced the "sad protract" of the nights). Grief's "term" in line 11 refers to its conditions (the necessity of weary days and long nights) as well as its duration. Thus in attempting to beguile his grief with changes, he has done precisely what grief would have one do—extend the term of grief and make "euery minute seeme a myle." This second "term" of grief is interesting. It combines the temporal (minute) and the spatial (mile) as well as gives an example of the extended time, representing the protraction of a minute to that length of time it takes to walk a mile. There is yet another meaning for "myle" that, in Spenser's pronunciation, would have made it closer to "moyle" than to today's "mile"; Spenser uses "moyle" only once (*HHL*, 220), referring to drudgery. If this is Spenser's punning intention in *Amor.* 87 then, in addition to the other meanings for the line, he might also be suggesting that, because of the poet's sorrow, his every minute becomes a drudgery—an interpretation clearly supported by the rest of the poem.

In the rather anticlimatic couplet the poet points out the obvious. The "long" elements of the earlier parts of the poem are associated with sorrow, the "quick" ones with joy. "Noyous day" (line 6) yields to "ioyous houres" in line 14, and "slow" (line 3) to "fast" in the same line. Days and nights, contracted to minutes (line 12), are at least on their way back to being hours (line 14) as the sonnet ends. Three times in the sonnet the poet refers not to what things are but to what things "seem" to be; time no longer is a day or night or hours or minutes. For the anxious lover these units seem (lines 3, 11, 13) to relate only to what they formerly were.

The subjective nature of time, in which common units contract and protract (as in 87), or even as the metaphoric and calendric years interplay with one another (as in 60), continues into *Amor.* 88. The absence theme of 87, in which the poet, like night, is "of light forlorne," and in which days and nights become metaphoric extensions of the poet's moods, extends as part of his grief:

> Since I haue lackt the comfort of that light,
>> The which was wont to lead my thoughts astray:
>> I wander as in darknesse of the night,
>> affrayd of euery dangers least dismay.
> Ne ought I see, though in the clearest day,
>> when others gaze vpon theyr shadowes vayne:
>> but th'onely image of that heauenly ray,
>> whereof some glance doth in mine eie remayne.
> Of which beholding the Idaea playne,
>> through contemplation of my purest part:

with light thereof I doe my selfe sustayne,
and thereon feed my loue-affamisht hart.
But with such brightnesse whylest I fill my mind,
I starue my body and mine eyes doe blynd.

The reality adjustments of 87 give way to reality assessments in 88. The poet plays not only on the previous sonnet but especially on 83 ("My hungry eyes. . . ."). He begins with the obvious parallel to 87, but whereas the "since I did leaue" of 87 referred to time, the "since I haue lackt" implies "because." The echo of the first use of "since" (87) still sounds in its second use (88), tying the two words together, as they surely are meant to be. "Since the time I left I have lacked. . . .," the poet suggests. Furthermore, the "presence of my loue" phrase (87) is grammatically paralleled by and thematically linked to the "comfort of that light." Her presence is the comfort. His (lady) love is that light.

But in 88 he reveals that the comfort/lady (or the love/light) "was wont to lead my thoughts astray," an experience already observed in the beguiling of his grief through the psychologically complex "changes" in 87. His thoughts may be led astray in line 2, but he himself wanders in line 3; his enlightenment is clouded by the benighted condition resulting in being "affrayd of euery dangers least dismay." There are, he suggests, real dangers, but without the light to steer him even the "least" dismays cause alarm.

The metaphoric condition of the first quatrain, in which he wanders "as in darknesse," is literalized in the second quatrain when contrasting what he sees (even in the clearest day) with what others see. He obliquely paraphrases himself from Amor. 83, where he observed that "all this worlds glory seemeth vayne to me, / and all theyr shewes but shadowes sauing she," compressing the lines to "when others gaze vpon theyr shadowes vayne." The repetition redirects us to the earlier sonnet (83), where his eyes (at that time) were so "filled with the store of that fayre sight" they could tolerate nothing else. The same condition remains, in addition to which he cannot even see the clearest day.

Contrary to what early commentators thought about this sonnet's presumed neo-Platonic implications, there is nothing to suggest the poet's seeing through and behind the image of the lady for intellectual or heavenly Beauty. The lover holds the lady's image in his mind's eye and, in the tenebrous world, he is sustained by the very thought of her. By (be)holding her he sustains (L. *sustinere*, "to hold") himself, and does so by "contemplation of my purest part." In *Amor.* 2 his "inner part" contained unquiet thoughts; by 85 this came to be the "closet" of his "parts entyre." But between those two poems he had built a "temple fayre" within his mind, in which to place her "glorious ymage" (*Amor.* 22). In 88 the reformed and transformed lover's parts become "purest"—and then move back into the temple of the mind through contemplation (L. *con-templum*), where the "ymage" of 22 has now become the "Idaea playne." The idea, like the lady herself, lightens his way; holding her in his heart (if not in his arms) he is reassured, strengthened, reilluminated. Others may "gaze" but he "contemplates." What they see are shadows; what he sees is light.

Sustaining himself not only plays etymologically upon beholding but draws upon the "nourishment" motif associated with the lady. In *Amor.* 2 the poet sought to "sustayne [him] selfe with food"; in *Amor.* 1 he called the lady his soul's "long lacked foode." Now at the other end of the sequence the very thought of the lady feeds his "loue-affamisht hart." The food metaphor is also present in 35/83, where the poet's "hungry" eyes displayed "greedy couetize" through the analogy with Narcissus, whose "eyes him staru'd." But by 88 the eyes have been fed and the mind filled, recalling how in 84 he sent his affections and thoughts to "fill your selfe with those most ioyous sights." The following line in the same sonnet contained the ambiguous phrase, "the which my selfe could neuer yet attayne." In 88 he still has not attained her, but he is closer in time to doing so than he was in 84.

The echo both of filling his thoughts and of the sly "yet" of 84, the ironic *Amor.* 83 story of Narcissus, whose "eyes him staru'd" and who through plenty was left poor, reassemble in the couplet of 88, as do the light and food motifs. Any neo-Platonic reverberations are stilled by the frank return to the physical world and its contrast with the spiritual. "But with such brightnesse whylest I fill my mind, / I starue my body and mine eyes doe blynd." That is, the lady's "light" may lighten his mind, but her absence does nothing for his body. Here his plenty may not make him poor, but it does nothing to feed him. His eyes are no help; despite all the focused seeing and beholding, they blind him by not revealing the real lady's presence whose comfortable (L. *comforte*, "strong") light is not physically there to guide and enlighten.

While expressed subtly and wittily, the lover's frustration—

expressed by food/starving images—is part of the premarital ten-
sion brought on by waiting for the proper time of consummation,
the wedding night. Amoret, in the House of Busyrane, experi-
ences this same anxiety (in fact, kept captive by Busyrane for
seven months she "was like to sterue"); Florimell in the cave of
Proteus does likewise. (Amusingly, both Busyrane and Proteus
are older men and the respective women are young and lovely;
the sonnets portray the older narrator "Spenser" experiencing
the same frustration felt by the ladies.) And in the *Hymne in
Honour of Loue* the "faire blossomes of youths wanton breed" are
chastised for feeding their lovers' feeble eyes but "sterv[ing] their
harts, that needeth nourture most" (38–39).

Nor does the situation get any better in *Amor.* 89, the last in the
sequence. It is 21 April 1594, but to the lover the scene is one of
winter emptiness and desolate quietness. In tone among the
quietest poems in the series, the final sonnet reiterates and ex-
presses the lover's loneliness during his absence from the lady:

> Lyke as the Culuer on the bared bough,
>   Sits mourning for the absence of her mate:
>   and in her songs sends many a wishfull vow,
>   for his returne that seemes to linger late.
> So I alone now left disconsolate,
>   mourne to my selfe the absence of my loue:
>   and wandring here and there all desolate,
>   seek with my playnts to match that mournful doue:
> Ne ioy of ought that vnder heauen doth houe,
>   can comfort me, but her own ioyous sight:
>   whose sweet aspect both God and man can moue,
>   in her vnspotted pleasauns to delight.
> Dark is my day, whyles her fayre light I mis,
>   and dead my life that wants such liuely blis.

Reflected in the first quatrain's description of the culver
mourning for its mate, in the employment of such words as
"bared" and "mourning," and in terms such as "wishfull vow"
and "lingring late," the sonnet's solitary and melancholy mood
makes possible the transition between the image of the longing
bird and the lonely lover. Earlier, Spenser joined images of bird,
lover, and mourning poet in "The Teares of the Muses," where
Euterpe compares herself to Philomele and then observes that we
(the muses) "All comfortlesse vpon the bared bow, / Like wofull
Culuers doo sit wayling now."

The comparison of the poet-lover to the mourning bird is

fitting; the bird's songs, in which she sends "many a wishfull vow," clearly are to be compared with those of the poet. It is important to recognize here not (as some have seen) the lamenting of final separation, but the sorrow of a temporary absence. The bird's, and the poet's, songs are filled with wishful vows for the return of him (she/Him) "that seemes to linger late." The temporal disjunctions of *Amor.* 87, in which time seemed longer or shorter because of the beloved's absence, continue here, although the "late lingering" eventually will lead to the "returne." "Turning" has been a meaningful motif in the entire sequence; the poet played on turnings, returnings, and reflexes in numerous important instances. It becomes part of the poet's poetic process as things unfold and then fold back on themselves, as the poems expand and then infold upon themselves. It also suggests Spenser's ontological concerns in which ontology constantly repeats, albeit with variations, previous developments. Here, as the larger *Amoretti* "poem" is about to fade away, the poet catches up its threads and pulls them back into itself. The reference to the lover's return is not at all the same as lovers being parted forever; while things in Spenser tend not to reach closure, they also do tend to return—and begin again. The "wishful vows" sung by the bird-poet are only another form of a song such as that sung in the first sonnet, where "leaues, lines, and rymes" were sent to "seeke her to please alone." The melody may differ but the singing continues.

While the culver-poet comparison is explicit, there is a difference between the activities of the two figures. The culver "sits mourning" and "sends" the songs; the poet "mourne[s]," "wandring here and there," and seeks with his "playnts" to match the dove. Twice earlier in the sequence the poet used wandering in reference to his separation from the lady: in 34 he roamed erratically like an unguided ship, and in 88 he wandered "as in darknesse of the night." *Amor.* 89 conjoins both kinds of wandering as he moves disconsolately, "here and there," in days darkened by absence of the lady's light (line 13).

The "ioyous houres" recalled in 87 become in 89 "ne ioy of ought" except the return of "her owne ioyous sight," a motif carried over from 83 and 88. That there is "ought that vnder heauen doth houe" that can comfort him provides, in the word "houe," both a description of the life of anxious expectation (as he depicted it in 87) as well as another link with the bird imagery of the first quatrain. The hovering bird "hovers" between absence and return, as does the lover. "Houe" also means "to rise"; there are no joys under heaven that rise, or lift the spirits, like the joy of seeing her.

The last quatrain contains the rather surprising declaration that her "owne ioyous sight" is such that "both God and man" are moved by her "sweet aspect." This marks the only time in the sequence that God is noted by this name; he has been called the Maker, and his attributes have been listed or likened, but he has not been named. To suggest that the lady can "moue" him might seem outrageously blasphemous until it is considered why he, like the smaller maker, the poet, is moved: "in her vnspotted pleasauns to delight." In the Christ-lady's "vnspotted" nature God delights; his delight is reflected (re-bent, re-turned) back into the world, where it provides the light, in the Christ/lady, that lightens and enlightens the poet. While Dante concludes the *Commedia* with "l'amour che move il sole e l'altre stelle," the love that moves here in the *Amoretti* is both God's movement as well as the lady's "lume reflesso."

That there is nothing under heaven "but her owne ioyous sight" that can comfort him, here suggests, as it did earlier in the sequence, the lady's heavenly qualities. Those qualities have been expressed primarily in terms of light, and the emphasis on the light-darkness contrast in 88, and its chiaroscuro effect again in 89, also reminds us of Dante, where light, with no shadow and little or no color, is the single most exploited image in the *Paradiso*. It is by gazing on the "somma luce," the supreme light, that more light is given, light from light in eternal succession. *Luce* and *lume*, light as source and light defused, are the means of human sustenance (*Amor.* 88); without them not only are days dark (*Amor.* 89) but lives are dead (89). The Christ-lady is revealed as the Christ-Lady, the light of the world, whose followers are to walk in the light as children of light.

The sequence narrative actually began in the fifth sonnet (the first four poems being preparatory), which marked a Sunday. This last sonnet also corresponds to a Sunday—the third Sunday after Easter (which links it with *Amor.* 5, the third Sunday before Lent). The *BCP* subject of the gospel lesson for this Sunday is constancy. John 16 contains Christ's assurance to his disciples that although going to heaven, he would still be present:

A litle while, and ye shal not se me: and againe a litle while, and ye shal se me: for I go to my father. . . . Verely, verely I say vnto you, that ye shal wepe and lament, and the worlde shal reioyce: and ye shal sorowe, but your sorowe shalbe turned to ioye. . . . And ye now therfore are in sorowe: but I wil se you againe, and your hearts shal reioyce, and your ioye shal no man take from you.

The return of Christ, whose "sweet aspect both God and man can moue," is thus promised. He, whose "vnspotted pleasauns" delights all creation, gives promise for a return, as does, by correspondence, the lady. The metaphoric place of human love within the divine pattern and of divine love within the human drama are mutually reinforced by the surface and analogic levels; the vertical reading of the sonnets yields those "comfortable" words (as the *BCP* refers to them, and as the poet himself seeks "comfort" in 89) which provide the hope to sustain and the faith to live.

In just this way Spenser chooses *Amor.* 89's culver, or dove, in part because of the traditional association of that bird with gentleness and constancy. But the dove also symbolizes the Holy Spirit, who, as part of the Godhead, is "with you always, until the end of the world." While the lover "mournes" the absence of his love, he also, by analogy, is sustained by the constancy of his own association with the dove and, by further analogy, is sustained by the Holy Spirit, promising the beloved's return.

At the very start of the sequence the poet glorified the bright "starry light" of "that Angels blessed looke, / my soules long lacked foode, my heauens blis" (*Amor.* 1). Dante's vision had begun in darkness but ended with the unity of light ("il sole e l'altre stelle"); Spenser's began with "stelle" (the "starry light" of *Amor.* 1) and moved toward separation and darkness. The promised return to light will come, but not until the great wedding. The "heauens blis" of *Amor.* 1 echoes quietly through the sequence to the very last part of the last sonnet, where "blis" is mentioned for the final time in the *Amoretti's* very last word:

> Dark is my day, whyles her fayre light I mis,
> and dead my life that wants such liuely blis.

Commencing with joy and ending with quiet melancholy, suffused with light at the start and filled with absence and darkness in the end, the cycle quietly passes. In a sense it does not end. The poet's fiction generates the start and the ending, but such a "beginning" and an "ending" can be expressed spatially only in the way it is here. The image of the dove singing its "wishfull vows" remains; there is hope of its mate's return, just as the poet continues spending his time "with expectation" and anticipation of the lady's return. Likewise, Una, on the threshold of her marriage, is left "to mourne" for Red Cross until his promised return (1.12.41); Una, the ascetic virgin of the early cantos, like Britomart, becomes the promising and fruitful bride of Christ awaiting her bridegroom. So, too, the Christian awaits the return of Christ, waiting with love and expectation for the future consummation. The paradoxical measure of foreshortened and protracted time coincides with the sonnet lover's paradoxical situation in which the end (the marriage), although near, appears painfully far.

The sequence narrative does not "end," partly because the exploration of language, of love, and of life is an ongoing process. Every change in life calls for a new examination of life; each stage of development provides opportunities for further exploration in light of new roles one plays. Language, too, is consistent only within a context, and the preresurrection context is radically different from the postresurrection life. Spenser's "stories," including the *Amoretti*, do not conclude; the old year leads to a new one, one quest's ending marks another's beginning, and the Sabbath rest is always ahead.

There are many turnings and returnings in the *Amoretti* other than the allusion in the last sonnet to "returne": the recurrence of seasons, actions, poetic motifs, and images and the reassurance of Love's continuance by means of and through the annual celebration of Christ's Passion and resurrection all underlie the notion of cyclical return. Even the sequence's ending on a Sunday suggests forward movement; in the postapostolic interest in the typology of numbers, Sunday is part of the octave, the eighth day, which begins a new week and opens the endless day of the life to come. And Sunday is also the first day of the week, the day of the resurrection, the day foreshadowing the final re-creation at the end of the world.

It is but a short time until the endless monument of the *Epithalamion* shows the lady conforming to the universal pattern of return. In that wedding poem the various *amoretti* of the sonnets combine in a magnificient paean to the perfect consummation of earthly love in a chaste marriage. Yet it is here in the *Amoretti*, where Christian love is the basis for the whole sonnet sequence, that Spenser prepares his narrator, his lady, and his readers, for a Love "vowd to eternity" (*Amor.* 69).

NOTES

Introduction

1. Rosalie L. Colie, *The Resources of Kind* (Berkeley: University of California Press, 1973), 103.

2. Laura Kendrick, *The Game of Love: Troubadour Wordplay* (Berkeley: University of California Press, 1988), 2–7.

3. James Nohrnberg, *The Analogy of The Faerie Queene* (Princeton: Princeton University Press, 1976), xi.

4. T. R. Wright, *Theology and Literature* (Oxford: Basil Blackwell, 1988), 92–93.

5. Timothy Gorringe, *Redeeming Time* (London: Darton, Longman and Todd, 1986), 7.

6. Simone Weil, *Waiting on God* (London: Collins/Fontana, 1959), 71.

Chapter 1. Amor and the Calendar: Love in a Timely Romance

1. J. W. Lever, *The Elizabethan Love Sonnet* (London: Methuen and Company, 1956), 97.

2. Peter Hutchinson, *Games Authors Play* (London and New York: Methuen, 1983), 14, provides a useful distinction between play and game. He views "play" as culturally the precursor of "game" and, in a superficial sense, less structured, less of a challenge, and often less intellectual than "game." By contrast, game "implies a more developed structure, [and] is often not as obvious or as fleeting as the playful indulgence."

3. The application of play theory to literary criticism is relatively new, yet the bibliography has expanded quickly. On ludic literary criticism in general see, e.g., the following articles from *Yale French Studies* 41 (1968): Jacques Ehrmann, "Homo Ludens Revisited," 31–57; Michel Beaujour, "The Game of Poetics," 58–67; A. J. Greimas and Francois Rastier, "The Interaction of Semiotic Constraints," 86–105. Peter Hutchinson, *Games*, contains a helpful, select bibliography. See also: Z. Ben-Porat, "The Poetics of Literary Allusion," *PTL: A Journal for Descriptive Poetics and Theory* 1 (1976): 105–28; N. D. Berman, *Playful Fiction and Fictional Players. Games, Sport, and Survival in Contemporary American Fiction* (Port Washington, N.Y.: Kennikat Press, 1981); E. Bruss, "The Game of Literature and Some Literary Games," *New Literary History* 9 (1977): 153–72.

4. From Appendix 7 of *The Works of Edmund Spenser: A Variorum Edition* (Baltimore: The Johns Hopkins Press, 1932–49), 629–30. Hereafter cited as

Spenser: Works. All citations to Spenser's texts, unless otherwise noted, are from the variorum edition.

5. A. Kent Hieatt, *Short Time's Endless Monument* (New York: Columbia University Press, 1960), 51.

6. Carole V. Kaske, "Spenser's *Amoretti* and *Epithalamion* of 1595: Structure, Genre, and Numerology," *English Literary Renaissance* 3 (Autumn 1978): 271–95; Anne Lake Prescott, "The Thirsty Deer and the Lord of Life: Some Contexts for *Amoretti* 67–70," *Spenser Studies* 6 (1985): 33–76; Charlotte Thompson, "Love in an Orderly Universe: A Unification of Spenser's *Amoretti*, 'Anacreontics,' and *Epithalamion*," *Viator* 16 (1985): 277–336.

7. See Alexander Dunlop, "The Unity of Spenser's *Amoretti*, in *Silent Poetry*, ed. Alastair Fowler (New York: Barnes and Noble, 1970), 153–69; O. B. Hardison, Jr., "*Amoretti* and the Dolce stil Novo," *English Literary Renaissance* 2 (Spring 1972): 208–16; William C. Johnson, "Spenser's *Amoretti* and the Art of the Liturgy," *Studies in English Literature* 14 (Winter 1974): 47–62; Alexander Dunlop, "The Drama of the *Amoretti*," *Spenser Studies* 1 (1980): 107–20; Thompson, "Love."

8. Thompson, "Love," 278–79.

9. All biblical citations are from *The Geneva Bible: a Facsimile of the 1560 Edition*, intro. Lloyd E. Berry (Madison: University of Wisconsin Press, 1969).

10. See William C. Johnson, "Amor and Spenser's *Amoretti*," *English Studies* 54 (1973): 217–26.

11. Isabel MacCaffrey, *Spenser's Allegory: The Anatomy of Imagination* (Princeton: Princeton University Press, 1976), 40–41.

12. Judith Anderson, " 'Nor Man It Is': The Knight of Justice in Book V of Spenser's *Faerie Queene*," *PMLA* 85 (1970): 70.

13. Etymologically, Busyrane is also tied to the word "abusion" (deception). See Harry Berger, "Busyrane and the War Between the Sexes: An Interpretation of *The Faerie Queene* III xi–xii," *English Literary Renaissance* 1 (1971): 100. See also Thomas Hyde, *The Poetic Theology of Love* (Newark: University of Delaware Press, 1986), 169–75.

14. J. C. Gray, "Bondage and Deliverance in the *Faerie Queene*: Varieties of a Moral Imperative," *Modern Language Review* 70 (1975): 3.

15. Maurice Valency, *In Praise of Love* (New York: The Macmillan Company, 1961), 21.

16. Enid Welsford, *Spenser: Fowre Hymnes; Epithalamion: A Study of Spenser's Doctrine of Love* (Oxford: Basil Blackwell, 1967), 27.

17. John Erskine, *The Elizabethan Lyric* (New York: Columbia University Press, 1905). Also, Robert Kellogg, "Thought's Astonishment and the Dark Conceits of Spenser's *Amoretti*," in *The Prince of Poets*, ed. John R. Elliot, Jr. (New York: New York University Press, 1968), 139–51; also, Louis L. Martz, "The *Amoretti*: 'Most Goodly Temperature,' " in *Form and Convention in the Poetry of Edmund Spenser. Selected Papers from the English Institute* (New York: Columbia University Press, 1961), 146–68. Peter M. Cummings, "Spenser's *Amoretti* as an Allegory of Love," *Texas Studies in Literature and Language* 12 (1970): 167–79; A. Kent Hieatt, "A Numerical Key to Spenser's *Amoretti* and Guyon in the House of Mammon," *Yearbook of English Studies* 3 (1973): 14–27. Also, Thompson, "Love"; Dunlop, "Drama"; and Johnson, "Liturgy."

18. Lever, *Love Sonnet*, 101–3.

19. Edwin Casady, "The Neo-Platonic Ladder in Spenser's *Amoretti*," in *Renaissance Studies in Honor of Hardin Craig*, ed. Baldwin Maxwell. (Stan-

ford, Calif.: Stanford University Press, 1941), 92–103; Lilian Winstanley, ed., *Faerie Queene, Book I* (Cambridge: Cambridge University Press, 1920); Mohinimohan Bhattacherje, *Platonic Ideas in Spenser* (London: Longmans, Green, 1935); and Bhattacherje, *Studies in Spenser* (Calcutta: University of Calcutta Press, 1929).

20. Hardison, "Dolce Stil Novo," 208–16; also, Robert Ellrodt, *Neoplatonism in the Poetry of Spenser* (Geneva: Librarie E. Droz, 1960); Welsford, *Fowre Hymnes, passim*; Nobuyuki Yuasa, "A Study of Metaphor in Spenser's *Amoretti*," *Studies in English Literature* 37 (1961): 165–86. Also, Nohrnberg, *Analogy*.

21. See Thompson, "Love," 282–83, for her fine review and critique of various positions on the *Amoretti* calendars.

22. Kaske, "Structure," ignoring the references in *Amor.* 22 to the "day" (and focusing only on the "season"), chooses to focus on Spenser's temporal references in *Amor.* 60 when that poem itself concerns an "open" interpretation of the meaning of "years."

23. In Guy le Fevre de la Boderie's introduction to Giorgio's *L'Harmonia du Monde* (1579), the numerical structure of the world he depicts contains the number 60 in the exact center of the world system, corresponding to the planet Mars.

24. Thompson, "Love" (286–335), provides an elaborate and expansive argument for Spenser's having included two superimposed calendars, the first extending from 22 January to 21 April 1594, and another beginning 13 February and extending to 30 April. She further argues for the second calendar's connections with the year 1553, which is significant as the probable year of Spenser's birth and as the year of Mary Tudor's ascending the throne.

25. See Reginald L. Poole, "The Beginnings of the Year in the Middle Ages," in the *Proceedings of the British Academy* 10 (1921): 113–37.

26. Josephine Waters Bennett, "Spenser's *Amoretti* LXII and the Date of the New Year," *Renaissance Quarterly* 26 (Winter 1973): 433–36.

27. There were several editions of the *BCP* with which Spenser would have been familiar. The first would have been the *First Prayer Book of Edward VI*, which in 1549 was incorporated into the Act of Uniformity. The second would have been the *Second Prayer Book of Edward VI*, first published in 1552. Elizabeth's *Prayer Book* (1559) was only slightly different from the 1549 edition on which it was based. In 1561 a revision of the calendar in the *BCP* was instituted, although the changes were small. Spenser apparently did not confine himself to any one of these as a source, drawing upon them freely for his poetic purposes. I have used Edward's *First Prayer Book* for quotations and for the psalms that, in that *BCP*, are listed as propers for various significant days.

28. Naseeb Shaheen, *Biblical References in The Faerie Queene* (Memphis, Tenn.: Memphis State University Press, 1976), 21–35. The Sarum rite, the missal of which went through sixty-seven editions between 1487 and 1557, was widely available in Protestant England. See Grace Landrum, "Spenser's Use of the Bible and his Alleged Puritanism," *PMLA* 41 (1926): 517–44, on the various Bibles Spenser used; see also Prescott, "Thirsty Deer," for possible borrowings from *Sarum*.

29. Spenser, with only a few exceptions, does not follow the "Table and Calendar for Psalms and Lessons" as they pertain to the "weekdays" of the segment of time encompassed by the *Amoretti* (23 January–21 April). Most notable of the exceptions are *Amor.* 3 (Friday, 25 January) and the weekdays of Holy Week.

30. Helen Flanders Dunbar, *Symbolism in Medieval Thought* (1929; reprint, New York: Russell and Russell, 1961), 1.

31. Edwin Honig, *Dark Conceit: The Making of Allegory* (New York: Oxford University Press, 1966), 63: "In Book One of *The Faerie Queene* the relationship between characters continually shifts, although they preserve their parallel identities in fixed opposition to one another. The figure of Una is a good example. She is generally related to the Red Cross Knight, who serves her, as Truth to Holiness; but by the same virtue, she is progressively set against Duessa, Archimago, Sansloy, Sansfoy and Sansjoy—the figures of deception and faithlessness actively opposing her. She also appears in various guises, as the embodiment of the Virgin, Elizabeth the Queen, Chaste Love, and the True (Protestant) Church. These identities become clear as the action successively focuses on her happy juxtaposition or her perilous opposition with other figures."

32. Rhodes Dunlap, "The Allegorical Interpretation of Renaissance Literature," *PMLA* 82 (1967): 42.

33. Petrarch makes some of these same connections when writing that his love for Laura began on the sixth day of April 1327—Good Friday (which actually fell on 10 April that year, not the sixth):

> Il 6 d'aprile 1327 fu un lunedi; ma perche al poeta conveniva di contrapporre le pene dellamour suo a quelle di Cristo morto in croce, e, secondo il calendario cristiano, Cristo spiro di venerdi, il poeta si riporto al giorno storico del gran supplizio secondo il rito giudaico.

Like Spenser, Petrarch thus forces a contrast as well as a parallel between his two passions, one empirical and one fictional, one physical and one spiritual, by showing them together during the end of Holy Week. See Carlo Calcaterra, *Nella Selva Del Petrarca* (Bologna: Licinio Cappelli, 1942), 212.

34. Peter Dronke, *Medieval Latin and the Rise of European Love-Lyric* (Oxford: Clarendon Press, 1965), 1:71.

35. Dronke, *Medieval Latin*, 14, indicates another instance ("Song of the Hundred Words") in which "the lover's sacrifice of himself to love and his redemption by the beloved are metaphorically identified with the events of Holy Week." Dronke, "The Conclusion of Troilus and Criseyde," *Medium Ævum* 33 (1964): 50, also indicates that "the metaphor of the Easter-night as the night of redemption in human love is unfolded on the grand scale in the imagery underlying Chaucer's portrayal of the union of Troilus and Criseyde."

36. Myron Turner, "The Imagery of Spenser's *Amoretti*," *Neophilologus* 72 (1988): 284.

37. *Spenser: Works, Minor Poems* 2:422.

38. Dunlop, "Spenser's *Amoretti*," 159.

Chapter 2. *Amoretti* 1–21

1. Dunlop, "Unity," 160.

2. Edgar Wind, *Pagan Mysteries in the Renaissance*, rev. ed. (New York: W. W. Norton & Company, 1968), 230.

3. Lever, *Love Sonnet*, 2.

4. A. Leigh DeNeef, *Spenser and the Motives of Metaphor* (Durham, N.C.: Duke University Press, 1982), 67.

5. Stevie Davis, *The Idea of Woman in Renaissance Literature: The Feminine Reclaimed* (Brighton, Sussex: The Harvester Press, 1986), 43.

6. Martz, "Most Goodly Temperature," 129.

7. See Reed Way Dasenbrock, "The Petrarchan Context of Spenser's *Amoretti*," *PMLA*, 100, no. 1 (January 1985): 38–49 for a brief analysis of *Amor.* 10, Wyatt's "Behold, love, how thy power she dispiseth" and Petrarch's "Or vedi, Amor."

8. Donald Cheney, *Spenser's Image of Nature* (New Haven and London: Yale University Press, 1966), 111–12.

9. Spenser also uses "garlond" as "glory" in "Colin Clout" (498–99): "She is the ornament of womankind, / and Courts chief garlond with all vertues dight."

10. Humphrey Tonkin, *Spenser's Courteous Pastoral* (Oxford: Clarendon Press, 1972), 208.

11. See Tonkin, *Courteous Pastoral*, 178–205 and Edward William Tayler, *Nature and Art in Renaissance Literature* (New York: Columbia University Press, 1964).

12. C. S. Lewis, *The Allegory of Love: A Study in Medieval Tradition* (London: Oxford University Press, 1936), 327–28.

Chapter 3. *Amoretti* 22–68

1. Hardison, "Dolce stil Novo," 211.

2. See Adrian Nocent, *The Liturgical Year*, vol. 2, trans. Matthew J. O'Connell (Collegeville, Minn.: The Liturgical Press, 1977); Reginald H. Fuller, *Lent with the Liturgy* (London: S.P.C.K., 1968); Marion J. Hatchett, *Commentary on the American Prayer Book* (New York: Seabury Press, 1981); Edward T. Horn III, *The Christian Year: Days and Seasons of the Church* (Philadelphia, Penn.: Muhlenberg Press, 1957); Dom Gregory Dix, *The Shape of the Liturgy* (London: Dacre Press, 1945); and W. K. Lowther Clarke, ed., *Liturgy and Worship: A Companion to the Prayer Books of the Anglican Communion* (London: S.P.C.K., 1932).

3. Lisle Cecil John, *The Elizabethan Sonnet Sequences* (New York: Columbia University Press, 1938), 102. Also see the very good explication of *Amor.* 22 (which is based on Desportes's *Diane* 1.43) in Lever, *Love Sonnet*, 105–7.

4. Angus Fletcher, *The Prophetic Moment* (Chicago: University of Chicago Press, 1971), 12–53.

5. See Jacqueline T. Miller, "'Love Doth Hold My Hand,' Writing and Wooing in the Sonnets of Sidney and Spenser," *ELH* 46 (1979): 549–51.

6. Miller, "Writing and Wooing," 551.

7. Judith Dundas, *The Spider and the Bee: The Artistry of Spenser's Faerie Queene* (Urbana and Chicago: University of Illinois Press, 1985), 1–8.

8. Miller, "Writing and Wooing," 552–56, provides an excellent analysis of these two poems.

9. Martz, "Most Goodly Temperature," 154.

10. Miller, "Writing and Wooing," 556.

11. Cheney, *Image of Nature*, 116.

12. Edmund Spenser, *The Faerie Queene*, ed. A. C. Hamilton (London and New York: Longman, 1977), 365.

13. See: Louise Vigne, *The Narcissus Theme in Western European Literature* (Lund, Sweden: Gleerups, 1967), 169–70; William Elford Rogers, "Narcissus in

Amoretti 35," *American Notes & Queries* 15, no. 2 (October 1976): 18–20; and Calvin R. Edwards, "The Narcissus Myth in Spenser's Poetry," *Studies in Philology* 74, no. 1 (January 1977): 63–88.

14. See Tonkin, *Courteous Pastoral*, 213, and E. N. Tigerstedt, "The Poet as Creator: Origins of a Metaphor," *Comparative Literature Studies* 5 (1968): 455–88.

15. F. Edward Hulme, *The History, Principles and Practice of Symbolism in Christian Art* (London: Swan Sonnenschein and Company, 1891), 42. Also, Jean Seznec, *The Survival of the Pagan Gods* (New York: Harper and Row, 1953), 213. For a much earlier account, see Augustin Chesneau, *Orpheus Eucharisticus* (Paris: F. Lambert, 1657).

16. See Sister Ritamary Bradley, "Speculum Backgrounds in Medieval Literature," *Speculum* 29 (1954): 100–115; Gordon Worth O'Brien, *Renaissance Poetics and the Problem of Power* (Chicago: Institute of Elizabethan Studies, 1956), 2–40; and the summary and enumeration of various speculum items related to Spenser in *Spenser: Works*, vol. 1, 509–70.

17. DeNeef, *Motives*, 160–61.

18. Martz, "Most Goodly Temperature," 163. Also, S. K. Heninger, Jr. ed., *Selections from the Poetical Works of Edmund Spenser*, (Boston: Houghton Mifflin, 1970), 208–21, especially 214n. See, too, Judith Kalil, " 'Mask in Myrth Lyke to a Comedy': Spenser's Persona in the *Amoretti*," *Thoth* 13, no. 2 (Spring 1973): 25.

19. Martz, "Most Goodly Temperature," 163.

20. Frederick Bateson, *English Poetry and the English Language* (1934; reprint, Oxford: Oxford University Press, 1973), 29–30.

21. Michael Leslie, *Spenser's 'Fierce Warres and Faithfull Loves'* (Cambridge: D. S. Brewer, 1983), 89.

22. See Kathleen Williams, "Spenser: the Sea and Storm-tossed Ship," *Research Opportunities in Renaissance Drama* 13–14 (1970–71): 138–40.

23. Martz, "Most Goodly Temperature," 164.

24. Analogically there also exists a connection between Mars and Christ; in Dante's *Paradiso* 14. 100–102, it is in the sphere of Mars (moved by the Virtues, the second order of the middle hierarchy of intelligences, who contemplate the Son as he is in himself) where the central attention of the poem is first directed toward Christ in his earthly human life. This is effected by focusing on his cross. Like the Milky Way, dotted with its various points of light, "si costellati facean nel profondo Marte quei raggi il venerabil segno che fan giunture di quandranti in tondo" (so did these beams, so constellated, make in the depth of Mars the venerable sign that the crossing of quadrants makes in a circle).

25. DeNeef, *Motives*, 64.

26. Israel Baroway, "The Imagery of the *Song of Songs*," *Journal of English and Germanic Philology* 33 (1934): 39.

27. John D. Bernard, "Spenserian Pastoral and the *Amoretti*, *ELH* 47, no. 3 (Fall 1980): 427.

28. William Bowman Piper, "Spenser's 'Lyke as a Huntsman,' " *College English* 22 (1961): 405.

29. Dasenbrock, "Petrarchan Context," 45.

30. See Prescott's "The Thirsty Deer," 67–70, unquestionably the most thorough and best study of source materials on the deer image.

31. Sallie TeSelle, *Literature and the Christian Life* (New Haven: Yale University Press, 1966), 11.

32. Gray, "Bondage and Deliverance," 4–5.

33. Joseph H. Summers, *George Herbert: His Religion and Art* (London: Chatto and Windus, 1954), 61.

34. *Patrologiae Latinae* 26.949: "He desires to come unto Christ in whom is the fountain of light, so that, washed in baptism, we receive the gift of remission."

35. Prescott, "The Thirsty Deer," 47. See also Harold L. Weatherby, "What Spenser Meant by Holinesse: Baptism in Book One of *The Faerie Queene*, *Studies in Philology* 84 (1987): 286–307.

36. Hieatt feels that the number 68 signifies the total of seasons, months, and weeks in a year. Whether Spenser had this in mind there is no way of knowing, although it certainly would provide a significant addition to the various aspects of calendric importance in this poem if it were so. See Hieatt, *Short Time*, 67.

37. G. K. Hunter, "Spenser's *Amoretti* and the English Sonnet Tradition," in *A Theatre for Spenserians*, ed. Judith M. Kennedy and James A. Reither (Toronto: University of Toronto Press, 1973), 136.

38. DeNeef, *Motives*, 73. Also see Peter J. Strachan, "The Linguistic Contexts of the Elizabethan Love Sonnet" (D.Phil. diss. Oxford University, 1987), 243–45.

39. James Ashcroft Noble, "The Sonnet in England," *Contemporary Review* 38 (1880): 454.

40. Carole V. Kaske, "Another Liturgical Dimension of 'Amoretti' 68," *Notes and Queries* 24, no. 6 (December 1977): 518–19.

41. Prescott, "Thirsty Deer," 56.

42. In 5.5.10 Radigund "gan to triumph with great boast," perhaps another example of the military victor's use of "triumph" not just as a victorious celebration but of an actual shout.

43. Turner, "Imagery," 290.

44. Kaske, "Another Liturgical Dimension," 518.

Chapter 4. *Amoretti* 69–89

1. See A. Kent Hieatt's observations on Shakespeare's "Not marble nor the gilded monuments" in "The Genesis of Shakespeare's *Sonnets*: Spenser's *Ruines of Rome: by Bellay*," *PMLA* 98, no. 5 (October 1983): 807.

2. Shakespeare uses the word to mean a "snare" when Cleopatra would catch another Antony "in her strong toil of grace."

3. DeNeef, *Motives*, 66.

4. Compare to Dante's three ladies: Mary, Saint Lucia, and Beatrice.

5. Nohrnberg, *Analogy*, 461–70; Gerald Snare, "Spenser's Fourth Grace," *Journal of the Warburg and Courtauld Institutes* 34 (1971): 350–55; Tonkin, *Courteous Pastoral*, 227–37.

6. Baroway, "Song of Songs," 42.

7. See Song of Songs 4:12, 13, 16. Also see Diethild Bludau, "Humanismus und Allegorie in Spenser's Sonetten," *Anglia* 74 (1956): 325–27.

8. See Jack F. Stewart, "Spenser's *Amoretti*, LXXIX, 10," *Explicator* 27, no. 9 (May 1969), item 74.

9. See Joanne Craig, "The Queen, Her Handmaid, and Spenser's Career," *English Studies in Canada* 12, no. 3 (1986): 255–68.

10. Thompson, "Love," 291–97.

11. Kaske, "Structure," 275–76.

12. Don M. Ricks, "Convention and Structure in Edmund Spenser's Amoretti," *Proceedings of the Utah Academy of Sciences, Arts and Letters* 44, no. 2 (1967): 449, sees this as Platonic enlightenment, although the Christian focus in the sequence suggests that while there may be elements of neo-Platonism, these are secondary to Spenser's purified Christian approach.

13. See Leslie Hotson, "The Blatant Beast," in *Studies in Honor of T. W. Baldwin*, ed. Don Cameron Allen (Urbana: University of Illinois Press, 1958), 34–37; Arnold Williams, *Flower on a Lowly Stalk* (East Lansing: Michigan State University Press, 1967), 8–13; Nohrnberg, *Analogy*, 688–96.

14. See Millar Maclure, "Spenser's Images of Society," *Dalhousie Review* 63 (1983): 22–23.

BIBLIOGRAPHY

Anderson, Judith H. " 'Nor Man It Is': The Knight of Justice in Book V of Spenser's *Faerie Queene*." *PMLA* 85 (1970): 65–77.

Baroway, Israel. "The Imagery of the *Song of Songs*." *Journal of English and Germanic Philology* 33 (1934): 23–45.

Bateson, Frederick. *English Poetry and the English Language*. 1934. Reprint. Oxford: Oxford University Press, 1973.

Beaujour, Michel. "The Game of Poetics." *Yale French Studies* 41 (1968): 58–67.

Bennett, Josephine Waters. "Spenser's *Amoretti* LXII and the Date of the New Year." *Renaissance Quarterly* 26 (1973): 433–36.

Ben-Porat, Z. "The Poetics of Literary Allusion." *PTL: A Journal for Descriptive Poetics and Theory* 1 (1976): 105–28.

Berger, Harry. "Busyrane and the War Between the Sexes: An Interpretation of *The Faerie Queene* III xi–xii." *English Literary Renaissance* 1 (1971): 99–121.

Berman, N. D. *Playful Fiction and Fictional Players. Games, Sport, and Survival in Contemporary American Fiction*. Port Washington, N.Y.: Kennikat Press, 1981.

Bernard, John D. "Spenserian Pastoral and the *Amoretti*." *ELH* 47 (Fall 1980): 419–32.

Bhattacherje, Mohinimohan. *Platonic Ideas in Spenser*. London: Longmans, Green, 1935.

———. *Studies in Spenser*. Calcutta: University of Calcutta Press, 1929.

Bible, The Geneva. Facsimile of the 1560 edition. Introduction by Lloyd E. Berry. Madison: University of Wisconsin Press, 1969.

Bludau, Diethild. "Humanismus und Allegorie in Spenser's Sonetten." *Anglia* 74 (1956): 292–332.

Bradley, Sister Ritamary. "Speculum Backgrounds in Medieval Literature." *Speculum* 29 (1954): 100–115.

Bruss, E. "The Game of Literature and Some Literary Games." *New Literary History* 9 (1977): 153–72.

Calcaterra, Carlo. *Nella Selva Del Petrarca*. Bologne: Licinio Cappelli, 1942.

Casady, Edwin. "The Neo-Platonic Ladder in Spenser's *Amoretti*." In *Renaissance Studies in Honor of Hardin Craig*, edited by Baldwin Maxwell. Stanford, Calif.: Stanford University Press, 1941.

Cheney, Donald. *Spenser's Image of Nature*. New Haven and London: Yale University Press, 1966.

Chesneau, Augustin. *Orpheus Eucharisticus*. Paris: F. Lambert, 1657.

263

Clarke, W. K. Lowther, ed. *Liturgy and Worship: A Companion to the Prayer Books of the Anglican Communion*. London: S.P.C.K., 1932.

Colie, Rosalie L. *The Resources of Kind: Genre-Theory in the Renaissance*. Berkeley: University of California Press, 1973.

Craig, Joanne. "The Queen, Her Handmaid, and Spenser's Career." *English Studies in Canada* 12, no. 3 (1986): 255–68.

Cummings, Peter M. "Spenser's Amoretti as an Allegory of Love." *Texas Studies in Literature and Language* 12 (1970): 163–79.

Dasenbrock, Reed Way. "The Petrarchan Context of Spenser's Amoretti." *PMLA* 100, no. 1 (1985): 38–49.

Davis, Stevie. *The Idea of Woman in Renaissance Literature: The Feminine Reclaimed*. Brighton and Sussex: The Harvester Press, 1986.

DeNeef, A. Leigh. *Spenser and the Motives of Metaphor*. Durham, N.C.: Duke University Press, 1982.

Dix, Dom Gregory. *The Shape of the Liturgy*. London: Dacre Press, 1945.

Dronke, Peter. "The Conclusion of Troilus and Criseyde." *Medium Ævum* 33 (1964): 47–52.

———, *Medieval Latin and the Rise of European Love-Lyric*. 2 vols. Oxford: Clarendon Press, 1965.

Dunbar, Helen Flanders. *Symbolism in Medieval Thought*. 1929. Reprint. New York: Russell and Russell, 1961.

Dundas, Judith. *The Spider and the Bee: The Artistry of Spenser's Faerie Queene*. Urbana and Chicago: University of Illinois Press, 1985.

Dunlap, Rhodes. "The Allegorical Interpretation of Renaissance Literature." *PMLA* 82 (1967): 39–43.

Dunlop, Alexander. "The Drama of the Amoretti." *Spenser Studies* 1 (1980): 107–20.

———. "The Unity of Spenser's Amoretti." In *Silent Poetry*, edited by Alastair Fowler, 153–69. New York: Barnes and Noble, 1970.

Edwards, Calvin R. "The Narcissus Myth in Spenser's Poetry." *Studies in Philology* 74, no. 1 (January 1977): 63–88.

Ehrmann, Jacques. "Homo Ludens Revisited." *Yale French Studies* 41 (1968): 31–57.

Ellrodt, Robert. *Neoplatonism in the Poetry of Spenser*. Geneva: Librairie E. Droz, 1960.

Erskine, John. *The Elizabethan Lyric*. New York: Columbia University Press, 1905.

The First and Second Prayer Books of King Edward VI. London: Dent, 1968.

Fletcher, Angus. *The Prophetic Moment*. Chicago: University of Chicago Press, 1971.

Fuller, Reginald H. *Lent with the Liturgy*. London: S.P.C.K., 1968.

Gorringe, Timothy. *Redeeming Time*. London: Darton, Longman and Todd, 1986.

Gray, J. C. "Bondage and Deliverance in the *Faerie Queene*: Varieties of a Moral Imperative." *Modern Language Review* 70 (1975): 1–12.

Greiman, A. J., and Francois Rastier. "The Interaction of Semiotic Constraints." *Yale French Studies* 41 (1968): 86–105.

Hardison, O. B., Jr., "Amoretti and the Dolce stil Novo." *English Literary Renaissance* 2 (Spring 1972): 208–16.

Hatchett, Marion J. *Commentary on the American Prayer Book.* New York: Seabury Press, 1981.

Hieatt, A. Kent. "The Genesis of Shakespeare's Sonnets: Spenser's *Ruines of Rome: by Bellay.*" *PMLA* 98, no. 5 (October 1984): 800–814.

———. "A Numerical Key to Spenser's *Amoretti* and Guyon in the House of Mammon." *Yearbook of English Studies* 3 (1973): 14–27.

———. *Short Time's Endless Monument.* New York: Columbia University Press, 1960.

Honig, Edwin. *Dark Conceit: The Making of Allegory.* New York: Oxford University Press, 1966.

Horn, Edward T. III. *The Christian Year: Days and Seasons of the Church.* Philadelphia, Penn.: Muhlenberg Press, 1957.

Hotson, Leslie. "The Blatant Beast." In *Studies in Honor of T. W. Baldwin,* edited by Don Cameron Allen, 34–37. Urbana: University of Illinois Press, 1958.

Hulme, F. Edward. *The History, Principles and Practice of Symbolism in Christian Art.* London: Swan Sonnenschein and Company, 1891.

Hunter, G. K. "Spenser's *Amoretti* and the English Sonnet Tradition." In *A Theatre for Spenserians,* edited by Judith M. Kennedy and James A. Reither, 124–44. Toronto: University of Toronto Press, 1973.

Hutchinson, Peter. *Games Authors Play.* London and New York: Methuen, 1983.

Hyde, Thomas. *The Poetic Theology of Love.* Newark: University of Delaware Press, 1986.

John, Lisle Cecil. *The Elizabethan Sonnet Sequences.* New York: Columbia University Press, 1938.

Johnson, William C. "Amor and Spenser's *Amoretti.*" *English Studies* 54 (1973): 217–26.

———. "Spenser's *Amoretti* and the Art of the Liturgy." *Studies in English Literature* 14 (Winter 1974): 47–62.

Kalil, Judith. " 'Mask in Myrth Lyke to a Comedy': Spenser's Persona in the *Amoretti.*" *Thoth* 13, no. 2 (Spring 1973): 19–26.

Kaske, Carole V. "Another Liturgical Dimension of 'Amoretti' 68." *Notes and Queries* 24, no. 6 (December 1977): 518–19.

———. "Spenser's *Amoretti* and *Epithalamion* of 1595: Structure, Genre, and Numerology." *English Literary Renaissance.* 3 (Autumn 1978): 271–95.

Kellogg, Robert. "Thought's Astonishment and the Dark Conceits of Spenser's *Amoretti.*" In *The Prince of Poets,* edited by John R. Elliot, Jr., 139–51. New York: New York University Press, 1968.

Kendrick, Laura. *The Game of Love: Troubadour Wordplay.* Berkeley: University of California Press, 1988.

Landrum, Grace. "Spenser's Use of the Bible and his Alleged Puritanism." *PMLA* 41 (1926): 517–44.

Leslie, Michael. *Spenser's 'Fierce Warres and Faithfull Loves'.* Cambridge, England: D. S. Brewer, 1983.

Lever, J. W. *The Elizabethan Love Sonnet*. London: Methuen and Company, 1956.

Lewis, C. S. *The Allegory of Love: A Study in Medieval Tradition*. London: Oxford University Press, 1936.

MacCaffrey, Isabel. *Spenser's Allegory: The Anatomy of Imagination*. Princeton: Princeton University Press, 1976.

Maclure, Millar. "Spenser's Images of Society." *Dalhousie Review* 63 (1983): 22–33.

Martz, Louis L. "The Amoretti: 'Most Goodly Temperature.'" In *Form and Convention in the Poetry of Edmund Spenser. Selected Papers from the English Institute*, edited by William Nelson, 146–68. New York: Columbia University Press, 1961.

Miller, Jacqueline T. "'Love Doth Hold My Hand,' Writing and Wooing in the Sonnets of Sidney and Spenser." *ELH* 46 (1979): 541–58.

Noble, James Ashcroft. "The Sonnet in England." *Contemporary Review* 38 (1880): 446–71.

Nocent, Adrian. *The Liturgical Year*. Vol. 2. Translated by Matthew J. O'Connell. Collegeville, Minn.: The Liturgical Press, 1977.

Nohrnberg, James. *The Analogy of* The Faerie Queene. Princeton: Princeton University Press, 1976.

O'Brien, Gordon Worth. *Renaissance Poetics and the Problem of Power*. Chicago: Institute of Elizabethan Studies, 1956.

Piper, William Bowman. "Spenser's 'Lyke as a Huntsman.'" *College English* 22 (1961): 405.

Poole, Reginald L. "The Beginnings of the Year in the Middle Ages." *Proceedings of the British Academy* 10 (1921): 113–37.

Prescott, Anne Lake. "The Thirsty Deer and the Lord of Life: Some Contexts for *Amoretti* 67–70." *Spenser Studies* 6 (1985): 33–76.

Ricks, Don M. "Convention and Structure in Edmund Spenser's *Amoretti*." *Proceedings of the Utah Academy of Sciences, Arts and Letters* 44, no. 2 (1967): 438–50.

Rogers, William Elford. "Narcissus in Amoretti 35." *American Notes & Queries* 15, no. 2 (October 1976): 18–20.

Seznec, Jean. *The Survival of the Pagan Gods*. New York: Harper and Row, 1953.

Shaheen, Naseeb. *Biblical References in* The Faerie Queene. Memphis, Tenn.: Memphis State University Press, 1976.

Snare, Gerald. "Spenser's Fourth Grace." *Journal of the Warburg and Courtauld Institutes* 34 (1971): 350–55.

Spenser, Edmund. *The Faerie Queene*. Edited by A. C. Hamilton. London and New York: Longman, 1977.

———. *Faerie Queene, Book I*. Edited by Lilian Winstanley. Cambridge: Cambridge University Press, 1920.

———. *Selections from the Poetical Works of Edmund Spenser*. Edited by S. K. Heninger, Jr. Boston: Houghton Mifflin, 1970.

———. *The Works of Edmund Spenser: A Variorum Edition*. Edited by E. A. Greenlaw, C. G. Osgood, F. M. Padelford, R. Heffner, H. G. Lotspeich. 10 vols. Baltimore: The Johns Hopkins Press, 1932–49.

Stewart, Jack F. "Spenser's *Amoretti*, LXXIX, 10." *Explicator* 27, no. 9 (1969): item 74.

Strachan, Peter J. "The Linguistic Contexts of the Elizabethan Love Sonnet." D.Phil. diss., Oxford University, 1987.

Summers, Joseph H. *George Herbert: His Religion and Art.* London: Chatto and Windus, 1954.

Tayler, Edward William. *Nature and Art in Renaissance Literature.* New York: Columbia University Press, 1964.

TeSelle, Sallie. *Literature and the Christian Life.* New Haven: Yale University Press, 1966.

Thompson, Charlotte. "Love in an Orderly Universe: A Unification of Spenser's *Amoretti*, 'Anacreontics,' and *Epithalamion*." *Viator* 16 (1985): 277–336.

Tigerstedt, E. N. "The Poet as Creator: Origins of a Metaphor." *Comparative Literature Studies* 5 (1968): 455–88.

Tonkin, Humphrey. *Spenser's Courteous Pastoral.* Oxford: Clarendon Press, 1972.

Turner, Myron. "The Imagery of Spenser's *Amoretti*." *Neophilologus* 72 (1988): 284–99.

Vigne, Louise. *The Narcissus Theme in Western European Literature.* Lund, Sweden: Gleerups, 1967.

Valency, Maurice. *In Praise of Love.* New York: The Macmillan Company, 1961.

Weatherby, Harold L. "What Spenser Meant by Holinesse: Baptism in Book One of *The Faerie Queene*." *Studies in Philology* 84 (1987): 286–307.

Weil, Simone. *Waiting on God.* London: Collins/Fontana, 1959.

Welsford, Enid. *Spenser: Fowre Hymnes; Epithalamion: A Study of Spenser's Doctrine of Love.* Oxford: Basil Blackwell, 1967.

Williams, Arnold. *Flower on a Lowly Stalk.* East Lansing: Michigan State University Press, 1967.

Williams, Kathleen. "Spenser: The Sea and Storm-tossed Ship." *Research Opportunities in Renaissance Drama* 13–14 (1970–71): 135–42.

Wind, Edgar. *Pagan Mysteries in the Renaissance.* Rev. ed. New York: W. W. Norton, 1968.

Winstanley, Lilian, ed. *Faerie Queene, Book 1.* Cambridge: Cambridge University Press, 1920.

Wright, T. R. *Theology and Literature.* Oxford: Basil Blackwell, 1988.

Yuasa, Nobuyuki. "A Study of Metaphor in Spenser's *Amoretti*." *Studies in English Literature* 37 (1961): 165–86.

INDEX

Individual *Amoretti* sonnets

Spenser: Characters, Places, and Works (Excluding *Amoretti*)

General